Cycles of Faith

Cycles of Faith

The Development of the World's Religions

Robert Ellwood

A Division of Rowman & Littlefield Publishers, Inc.
Walnut Creek • Lanham • New York • Toronto • Oxford

AltaMira Press
A Division of Rowman & Littlefield Publishers, Inc.
1630 North Main Street, #367
Walnut Creek, California 94596
www.altamirapress.com

Rowman & Littlefield Publishers, Inc.
A Member of the Rowman & Littlefield Publishing Group
4501 Forbes Boulevard, Suite 200
Lanham, Maryland 20706

PO Box 317
Oxford
OX2 9RU, UK

British Library Cataloguing in Publication Information Available

Library of Congress Cataloging-in-Publication Data

Ellwood, Robert S., 1933–
Cycles of faith : the development of the world's religions / Robert Ellwood.
p. cm.
Includes bibliographical references and index.
ISBN 0-7591-0461-1 (alk. paper)—ISBN 0-7591-0462-X (pbk. : alk. paper)
1. Religions—History. I. Title.
BL80.3.E435 2003
200—dc21

2003004888

Printed in the United States of America

∞™ The paper used in this publication meets the minimum requirements of American National Standard for Information Sciences—Permanence of Paper for Printed Library Materials, ANSI/NISO Z39.48-1992.

CONTENTS

PREFACE

This volume is a considerably revised version of a book that appeared in 1988 under the title *The History and Future of Faith*.[1] Since then, much has happened: in world history, in the religious life of the planet, and in my own thinking about the meaning of it all. Whereas the first study was a model for the development of world religions, the present study is far more focused and leaves extrapolation into the spiritual future largely to the reader's own imagination. The five stages hypothesized for the life of a world faith—Apostolic, Wisdom/Empire, Devotional, Reformation, and Folk Religion—were previously all contained in one long chapter; now, each stage has its own chapter. Every attempt has been made to connect the hypothesis to what has recently happened (and is currently happening, as of this writing) out there in the "real world." Since 1988 that real world has seen nothing less than the collapse of the secular communist "faith" and the intensification of world-threatening conflict based on religious fault lines, particularly between humanity's youngest great religion, Islam, now (according to the present hypothesis) in its dynamic Reformation phase, and its neighbors of older creeds.

I would like, however, to reproduce some lines from the preface to the earlier edition. The acknowledgments, thanks, and sentiments of these paragraphs remain as valid today as ever.

> *The History and Future of Faith* was many years in the making, and as I have tried to think through the tangled web of issues it has raised, it has gone through several changes of concept. Chapters 5 and 6 [10 and 11 in the present edition, title and contents modified] were originally presented as a paper at a conference on "Religion and Modernity," at the University of British Columbia in December 1981. This paper has recently appeared

under the title, "Modern Religion as Folk Religion," in *Modernity and Religion*, edited by William Nicholls.[2]

The writing was essentially completed in South Africa in the fall of 1986, while I was serving as visiting professor in the Department of Religious Studies at the University of Cape Town. I am deeply grateful to this faculty for the honor of their invitation, for affording me quiet time for writing, and above all for numerous helpful suggestions and critiques as I presented much of this material in graduate and faculty seminars. I am also grateful to the faculty of the Department of Religious Studies at the University of Natal, Pietermaritzburg, South Africa, for a most useful discussion of the same material during a briefer visit to that campus.

In thanks and tribute to these two fine departments of religious studies [then involved in work and struggle under apartheid], I would like to inscribe words cited by the late distinguished South African Christian and novelist Alan Paton in an unfinished essay penned only a few days before his death. They are from a tablet in an old English church:

> ". . . When throughout England all things sacred were either profaned or neglected, this church was built by Sir Robert Shirley, Bart., whose special praise it is to have done the best things in the worst times and to have hoped them in the most calamitous."[3]

It remains to add that some descriptive passages in this book are adapted from the author's writing in Robert S. Ellwood and Barbara A. McGraw, *Many Peoples, Many Faiths: Women and Men in the World Religions*, 6th ed. (Upper Saddle River, N.J.: Prentice Hall, 1999).

R. E.

CHAPTER ONE
RELIGION PAST AND PRESENT

What future, if any, has religion on planet Earth?

Whatever the answer, we can be sure that it is in no small part being shaped today. The religious life of Buck Rogers' twenty-fifth century is now being prepared by the thoughts, words, and deeds of countless personages great and small on Earth, even as the long shadows of Renaissance humanists and Protestant reformers of more than four centuries ago still fall over much of the spiritual world.

The religious future is shaped by the religious past. The thesis of this book is that the larger religions of the world have followed a broadly predictable pattern of development. Awareness of this pattern contributes to understanding of our religious world and to an intelligent apprehension of what may be coming next in the world of faith. Unassailable knowledge of the present state of world religion, and especially of religious history, is not easy to garner. Religion does not make itself easy to study dispassionately. Faith lives by its own stories and self-images, and religious study produces an observer effect as it tries to objectify what is by nature subjective. Religion, the redoubt of myth and belief, generates myths and nonempirical beliefs about its own past and present as avidly as it does about the supernatural.

So as to what is really happening in religion now, reports vary considerably, just as they do concerning what happened in the religious past. It is hard to assess the evidence concerning a matter ultimately so deeply rooted in the secret places of subjectivity, however much it may be outwardly expressed. In the eyes of critics and believers alike, a religion may be world-conquering, or it may be a voice from the past, but the truth is more likely to be a muddle in the middle.

There are those, both religionists and others, who contend that faith is obviously in decline. Ours, they insist, is no more than a mustard seed of belief compared with the fervor of our forefathers and foremothers. But the piety of the past has been a stock-in-trade of religion—from the Hebrew prophets to the ancient Buddhist notion of the decline of the Dharma to the Hindu of the Kali-yuga to the nineteenth-century idealization of medieval faith among Catholic romantics and, finally, to the twentieth-century American belief in the piety of the Founding Fathers. No doubt, more than half of the pious past is a religious myth produced because present religion needs it, perhaps as an extension of the myth of a golden age or an unfallen primal state. The evils of the present to which religion feels called to point are all the better showcased against a more godly past, and the divine origins of the faith are better legitimated when its first fruits are portrayed as unambiguously virtuous. Yet the actual data for the extent of past devotion and practice, scanty as it is, raise hard questions.

In odd alliance with the religious myth of the pious past is the social science idea of secularization, which is essentially the notion that religion is being replaced by worldly, especially scientific, views of reality and clues to appropriate human action. Secularization as an idea no doubt reflects some sort of truth. At the same time, as an account of reality that expresses in historical narrative form the paradigm by which its devotees themselves work and live, it can in a technical sense be called a myth. (In religious studies, the term *myth* does not imply a judgment of whether a narrative is true or not; it only judges its function within its culture—that is, a myth is not a casual fable or entertainment, but an embodiment in story form of certain basic values and ultimate reality perceptions.)

In other words, the truth may be that it is the secularization theorists themselves who were secularized and not necessarily anyone else—and their argument really is circular, since science and social science methodologically require the capacity to look at religion as a nonsupernatural social phenomenon. In the idiom of the postmodernist critics to whom we shall later turn, the story of the decline of religion and rise of science is a Grand Narrative, an epic whose overall sweep—in the eyes of its tellers—overshadows any contrary particulars . . . and which can take on the character of social myth.

As the twenty-first century begins, opinion on religion by those not firmly and believingly in the camp of one religion or another seems to be turning sour. Several events have shown up the dark side of religion all too clearly, and questioning whether religion of any kind is necessarily a good thing appears to be becoming more respectable even in a country as traditionally favorable to religion as the United States. The child-abuse scandals in the Roman Catholic Church; the actions of Islamic extremists, most egregiously on September 11, 2001; the intensifying, harsh, and anti-intellectual stance of traditionalists or "fundamentalists" in several faiths; even the dubious claims of the Raelian sect to successful cloning have begun to produce a backlash in less credulous quarters. Religious historian Bruce Lincoln, in *Holy Terror*, dissected the religious references in the instruction manual given to the September 11 hijackers, and he also compared the implicit religious rhetoric of President Bush's speech of October 11, 2001, which announced a military response in Afghanistan, with that of Islamic militants. Religion, one might conclude, is widely regarded by activists as the most powerful available instrument for rebellion against perceived injustice and aggression. But faith can then animate both sides in a conflict, fomenting holy terror and holy war all around.[1] That can lead one to appreciate the power of religion, but also to ask if there might not be a better way.

On the other hand, there are those for whom religion is advancing (or at least holding its own) about as well as ever, which is a good thing, at least as long as it is good religion. These are, first, the triumphalists of all faiths who, like the sundial, count only the sunny hours. Their notice registers only the "up" statistics, and they joyfully see the world turning their way; it is bound to fall before the next evangelistic crusade or with the maturation of the Aquarian generation.

In addition to the triumphalist, two other sanguine readings of the religious future are available, which may be termed *philosophical* and *empirical.* Philosophical religious optimism is generally based on a belief that the world is advancing toward an age of the spirit, as taught by philosophical visionaries from Joachim of Flora to Hegel and Teilhard de Chardin and many lesser lights of religious evolutionism for whom it is axiomatic that spiritual development must parallel biological evolution, and march along with "progress" in science, ethics, and political institutions. Thus, the religious, or at least the spiritual world, would have to be getting better and affecting more people for good over the millennia. Religion's progress from tribalism to universalism, and from blood sacrifice to "ethical monotheism," or the mountaintop vistas of the great mystics, are cited. This scenario may not necessarily bode well for institutional religion, though, for it may be an ascent toward the heavenly Jerusalem of the Book of Revelation, where no temple stands, "for the Lord God Almighty and the Lamb are the temple of it." But overall philosophical spiritual evolutionism suggests that, rather than flat-out secularizing, religion is taking higher and higher forms.

On the empirical front, one can point to spotty but significant evidence that the religiosity of the past was not on such a high level as the mythologies make it appear. Religion's present strength, in fact, may represent less a decline than just a perpetuation of what—shorn of glamor—the case has always been and so presage for religion as respectable a future as it has ever had.

All historians know, for example, that the American republic was not founded wholly by devout Christians but by a motley array of believers, skeptics, deists, and sheer worldlings. Most of the Founding Fathers were deeply affected, to say the least, by the Enlightenment's deism. Society as a whole, after the Great Awakening but prior to the popular evangelical revivals of the nineteenth century, was represented by far fewer than half of its numbers on church membership rolls at the time of the American Revolution. Among vast segments of the population—southern slaves, settlers on the frontier, people in urban slums—spiritual life was tenuous and chaotic, even if capable of being stirred up. Thomas Jefferson enjoined only the ethical teachings of Jesus, preparing his own abridged New Testament to this end, and expected that by the end of his life Unitarianism would be universally adopted because of its superior rationality. Benjamin Franklin, in 1790, the year he died, affirmed belief in one God, Creator of the universe, but added: "As to Jesus . . . I have . . . some doubts as to his divinity; though it is a question I do not dogmatize upon, having never studied it, and think it needless to busy myself with it now, when I expect soon an opportunity to knowing the truth with less trouble."[2] Needless to add, public opinions of this order would be political suicide for any American politician in recent decades, and leave us wondering which way secularization, or the disentanglement of religion from the state that Jefferson and Franklin so devoutly desired, has gone.

Or suppose we go back to the Middle Ages, the "Age of Faith." Meticulous work in social history is now beginning to paint a picture of popular religion up to the eve of the Reformation, and it is a picture that is rather different from the conventional vision of a sea of Catholic piety. We perceive a population only lightly Christianized, in which various disorganized but potent pagan carryovers were at least as trusted as the Church. Even in the best of times, sizable components of people—in mountainous or wooded backcountry, among an underclass of rural and urban poor—were hardly touched by the faith at all, save on the most casual and quasi-magical level. Very often, of course, it was not the best of times in medieval Europe, and infidel invasion, feudal war, famine, and plague would completely disrupt ecclesiastical life. At the same time, the appeal of spiritual enthusiasms, largely heretical, was never to be discounted among the hard-pressed masses.

Emmanuel Le Roy Ladurie, in his valuable study of late medieval life in the southern French community of Montaillou and its environs, indicates that although baptism was virtually universal and church festivals were popular, only about half the population attended church on an average Sunday—a figure comparable to the probably-too-high 40 percent pollsters got for the United States in the late twentieth century. Le Roy Ladurie comments: "There is nothing surprising about this lukewarm attitude. Specifically Christian piety was always the attribute of an elite in the Middle Ages and even when, in time of panic, this elite grew very numerous, it still remained urban rather than rural, and did not include the mountain dwellers."[3]

Among the elite, one might add, chivalry was no less potent a force than the faith, and one whose values were not seldom at odds with it. William Marshall, first earl of Pembroke and a powerful political figure under several English kings, was urged by a cleric upon his deathbed in 1219 to sell some eight fine robes and give the money to the poor for the salvation of his soul; the earl declined, saying he was obliged to give them to the knights who had served him. He also refused to return his tournament winnings for the assurance of heaven, saying, "If because of this the kingdom of God is closed to me, there is nothing I can do about it." But he added that the teachings of the priests on such matters must be false, "else no one would be saved."[4] Such attitudes were by no means atypical of the medieval lay aristocracy, who (with some exceptions, such as the frankly nonreligious William "Rufus" II of England) may have professed Christ but whose real moral culture was that of the tournament ground and the blood-stained field of honor.

Returning to Montaillou, Le Roy Ladurie cites examples of actual unbelievers as well as the indifferent among the common people of the thirteenth and fourteenth centuries. There were those who denied God, the soul, and the afterlife. One peasant said that the soul consisted merely of blood and therefore disappeared after death, heaven being when you were happy in this world and hell when you were miserable, and that was all there was to it.[5]

To be sure, Montaillou was in a part of France heavily affected by the Albigensian or Cathar heresy; the detailed information the modern author is able to present is derived for the most part from testimony presented at a bishop's court inquiring into this problem. But it corroborates other opinions that lead us to doubt whether any picture of religion on a terminal downslide since a medieval high point can be wholly credited. Keith Thomas, in his magisterial *Religion and the Decline of Magic*, concludes: "We do not know enough about the religious beliefs and practices of our remote ancestors to be certain of the extent to which religious faith and practice have actually declined."[6]

Likewise, it would be false to think matters were much different in premodern India, China, Japan, or in the Islamic world. Here, too, the lay upper classes generously mixed their Hindu, Buddhist, Confucian, or Muslim faith with knightly or other worldly values. For the vast lower classes, when the sheer struggle for survival did not shoulder out all other concerns, religion like bread itself was a haphazard thing, usually only an aspect of, and subordinate to, identity as a member of family and village.

Some were devout, some were superstitious, but many then as now were religious only in the sense that, in their illiteracy, they were not self-consciously unbelievers in the only spiritual culture they knew, and could be counted on to swell the crowds at great religious processions and festivals. What supernatural beliefs and rites impinged on their lives were at least from out of the same cultural world as the official religion, or were perhaps distorted, ill understood, or remnants of earlier eras.

Against this picture, optimists for religion can perceive ways in which religion may well be more deeply rooted now than then. Bishops and mandarins may not exercise the political influence of bygone days but, on the other hand, the spread of literacy means that far more believers than before have a fair idea of what they believe; understanding a faith enhances commitment as often as it disillusions. Vastly improved transportation makes the practice of religion accessible in its fullness as never before. The mountain and forest people, excluded in the Middle Ages, can now drive to church in a pickup if they wish. Many times the past numbers can now make pilgrimage to Mecca, Rome, Jerusalem, or Banaras by charter jet. One need only mention the religious impact of the electronic media. The vast technological revolutions that have changed the Middle Ages and the eighteenth century into the modern world have had, in other words, a complex and ambivalent impact on religion.

Take, for example, the evangelical and pentecostal revivals within Christianity. Needless to say, this development, with its emotion and biblical credulity and its seeming indifference to the scientific revolution, has surprised and appalled secularists. Martin E. Marty has demonstrated, however, how well Evangelical Christianity really competes in a modern, supposedly secularized world.[7] Indeed, the recent rise of Evangelicalism can be said to have virtually a symbiotic relationship with modernism and secularization.

As a largely subjective, intensely personal rather than societal religion, Evangelicalism fits effectively into the compartmentalization of modern life. Its institutions, based on congregationalism and charismatic preachers, flourish in the "free enterprise" religious life left after the withering away of state churches and cultural faith. Evangelicalism has been particularly successful in the use of modern communications technology—radio, television, videos, websites, and the like—despite its alleged antiscientific message. Of course, for Evangelicalism, technology and scientific theory are two quite different things. Its egalitarianism—the idea that anybody can have a saving experience or have as much insight into the scriptures as anyone else—fits the individualist, antiauthoritarian consciousness of many moderns. To be sure, most of life in a complex modern society is governed by "experts" and technocrats toward whom even the rebel must defer, but the very pervasiveness of the "rationalized" bureaucratic system makes for counterpressures in subjective areas of life like religion. People yearn to find some different and more exciting experience—conversion, the blessings of the Spirit—in the secret places of the heart.

The intellectual questions raised by the science behind this technology and the massive disruption of traditional patterns of life it has entailed have undoubtedly unsettled the faith of some. Yet science and technology have served on other fronts to buttress religion: the aforementioned charter jets for pilgrimage and the nonstop preaching by electronic media to audiences of a size the prophets and predicants of the past could scarcely imagine.

The jury is still out on the question of whether the conditions of the modern world are really advantageous or detrimental for religion—not religion as it was in the Stone Age or the twelfth century, but religion as it might be able to adapt itself to the twentieth century—and the twenty-first.

Of course, there is another way to look at the history of these religions of mass culture, and that is in terms of a pattern of development intrinsic to religions themselves. The thesis of this book is that the "great" or "world" religions display certain comparable stages in their history based on the internal needs within such a religion itself and based on their responding, as they certainly do, to changes in the external world. The religions to which this paradigm would apply are five, embracing hundreds of millions of followers, and which have been dominant religiously in the life of large continental cultures—Hinduism and the Chinese religions—or have been effectively transcultural on a large scale—Buddhism, Christianity, and Islam. The stages are here termed Apostolic; Wisdom and Imperial; Devotional; Reformation; and Folk Religion. Their nature, and reasons for this model, will be presented later.

For now let us remark that this pattern may lead to phenomena that give misleading impressions, when understood merely in relation to the "world" rather than fitted into long-term cycles in the evolution of a religion. For example, the medieval era worldwide, broadly construed, embraces the five hundred years or so of the Devotional era, the third stage according to the present schema in the development of world religions. Devotionalism gives an impression of fervor, but (as Chaucer's Canterbury pilgrims remind us) it may not necessarily indicate a subjective faith deeper than that of many moderns.

Likewise, the next stage, Reformation—usually corresponding with a rise in literacy, in intellectual independence, and of skepticism in some quarters—could be taken as an overall time of a receding tide of faith. But such a judgment would be quite misplaced if it overlooked the way in which the same qualities of intellectual ardor and serious learning led many others, whether Lutheran or Pure Land Buddhist, to a richer if more personalized and perhaps less demonstrative faith than that of the medieval enthusiast. In the present pattern, Christianity (and Hinduism) have been in the Reformation stage circa 1520–2020, and Islam is now entering it. This stage refers not only to the initial religious revolution, but to some five hundred years thereafter in which Reformation issues and institutions, or reactions to them, have broadly dominated the religion's life. It lies behind the missionary expansion of Christianity (and universalizing trends in Hinduism) from the sixteenth century to the present, and no less behind the intellectual intensity of its theological life, as it has attempted with Reformation seriousness to make itself the intellectual equal of all other realms of thought in the modern world. That energy and commitment on the part of millions help interpret why reformed religions have been quite successful in recent centuries, despite the acids of modernity and the many sectarian divisions of postreformation faiths.

Our view, so far as the history and future of religions is concerned, is that religious epochs with distinct "mentalities" do exist. Furthermore, they not only advance one after another in reaction to what is going on in the world, but are also impelled by dynamics internal to religious history. In this sense, one can speak of an autonomous history of spiritual consciousness.

At the same time, this history need not be seen as determinative of the consciousness of individuals, even of seriously religious individuals. Dynamics other than the prevailing religious mentality can affect the individual, and they do. Different persons may be affected differently by the hurricanes of history, by new symbols, and by dissonant experiences. More mentalities than one may be in the air, and crosswind pressures rise within the souls of men and women. Overall, though, the assumption here is that, by a sort of statistical average, the religious mentality of the majority will be that of the era in terms of this schema.

But before taking a further look at the weather vane atop the churches and temples of today, we need to look back to where religion came from and ahead to what it might become.

CHAPTER TWO

RELIGIOUS ORIGINS AND MEANINGS

How did human religion begin? The nineteenth century was much taken with the problem of origins. Not only the origin of religion, but the origin of speech, of species, and of life itself preoccupied modern savants as they struggled to reorient understanding of the world to conform to Enlightenment values, empirical methods, and Darwinian evolutionary models.

Ultimately, the scientific quest for beginnings was not as far removed as one might think from the romanticism that also tinted the Victorian century. For both scholar and poet, the quest for sunrise origins was a form of renewal of the ancient mythical quest for *meaning* in origins, founded on the assumption that if one knows where something came from, one knows what it really is, and therefore what it means.

Such is the premise behind creation myths around the world. Compare the Vedic account of Prajapati with the creation story according to Genesis. In the Hindu version, the primal being makes the world by dividing up his own body as a great sacrifice; in Genesis, God calls sky, sea, and land into existence as entities outside himself, as though pictures painted by an artist or cabinets made by a carpenter. The first narrative tells us that the world *is* God in disguise; to find God, we look around and, above all, within. The second reveals that God is *not* the creation—indeed, to confuse Creator and creature is the supreme blasphemy—but rather the world owes everything to the sovereign will by which it was made, and therefore it should reply with gratitude, love, and faithful service. Two paradigms of religious life, and two pictures of ultimate meaning, are contained in these narratives of origins.

Yet the nineteenth century, in its new empirical quest for origins and its new biological evolution narrative, could only be painfully ambivalent as to meaning. Darwinism presumed movement from the simpler to the more complex. Simple to complex seemed to be the way things worked, not only in biology, but also in cosmology, language, society, religion.

But is this progress? On many levels, from mystical virtue to "elegant" science informed by Occam's razor, simplicity is what is commended. Evolution from the primordial slime to the four-legged and finally the large-brained; the growth of language from grunts to Shakespeare—ordinarily one accounts this progress, just as the Darwinian age itself was marked by immense "progress" in both technology and democracy.

Yet it was possible to idealize instead evolutionary starting points in light of Enlightenment images of the noble savage and the romanticist's idealization of the distant and the past, making the time of origins a dawn of forgotten wonder and wisdom. That was the era perhaps of Thoreau's "Bhagvat-Geeta, since whose composition years of the gods have elapsed, and in comparison with which our modern world and its literature seem puny and trivial."[1] For in looking for wisdom, the sage of Walden said elsewhere, "I hear only the resounding of the ancient sea."[2]

But as the century advanced, the romantic patina more and more wore off to bare the hard metal of the social Darwinism of Herbert Spencer or Comtean evolutionary positivism. It seemed increasingly clear that the Darwinian meaning better suited those reductionists who wished to say that life was "nothing but" the primal muck decked out in pretentious array, or religion "nothing but" the crude sorcery from which it presumably derived.

Theories of the origin of religion, then, inevitably started with a rude and simple one-dimensional original, from which faith proceeded step by step to "higher" levels. The anthropologist John Lubbock (1834–1913), in *The Origin of Civilization and the Primitive Condition of Man*, proposed a pattern of religious evolution commencing with the absence of religion and proceeding through "fetishism," nature worship, totemism, shamanism, anthropomorphism, monotheism, and ethical monotheism. The great pioneer ethnologist Edward B. Tylor (1832–1917) hypothesized that religion started in animism, a belief in souls separable from the body first suggested by the experience of dreams, in which one apparently left one's body during sleep to travel to far places and even to meet the souls of the deceased. It was no great extrapolation then to find souls in other entities as well, in animals or the moving wind and sun, and to elaborate doctrines of ancestrism and afterlife. A further short step led to polytheism, and then a long one to monotheism, in which all these powers are brought under a single rule with ethical consequences.

However, Andrew Lang (1844–1912), the distinguished Scottish folklorist, was disturbed by ethnographical reports from the field that, contrary to animist theory, told of belief among some of the technologically most underdeveloped peoples in a quasi-monotheistic "high god." He proposed a primal monotheism, whose deity was Creator and often moral legislator. Critics, however, were quick to point out that this figure was frequently a *deus otiosus*, an inactive divine shadow resting in the background who did not really interfere with the prevailing evolutionary schema. Nonetheless, Wilhelm Schmidt (1868–1964), a German-Austrian priest and anthropologist, enthusiastically took up the cause of *Urmonotheismus* and published voluminously in its support.

R. R. Marett (1866–1943), an English anthropologist critical of both Tylor and Lang, traced religion back past animist to a "pre-animist" state of "animatism," the veneration of that which incites feelings of sheer impersonal supernatural power, the energy known by such names as *mana* or *wakan*. Sir James Frazer (1854–1941), in his much-cited *The Golden Bough*, put magic in first place, contending that primitives worked sorcery before they conceived of gods, turning to the propitiation of personal deities only when they found that magic did not consistently succeed. The great popularity of Frazer's writings, despite the lack of real empirical support for his hypothesis, is a tribute to his elegant, if often condescending, presentation of religious lore from around the world, and to the sovereign power of the simple-to-complex evolutionary model.

In the early twentieth century, the search for a primordial simplicity by which to interpret the origin of religion persisted, though with psychological perspectives tending to displace anthropological ones. Lucien Lévy-Bruhl spoke of "primitive mentality" as an associational way of thinking in which cause-and-effect relationships were overlooked in favor of magical and symbolic connections. Émile Durkheim emphasized the societal origins of religion in the "social effervescence" of a tribe or group in dance or festival; like many nineteenth-century scholars, he gave great importance to the totem as a sacrament of tribal unity.

The centrality of totemism was taken up by the father of psychoanalysis, Sigmund Freud, who viewed it as the relic of the unspeakable crime for which religion atones: the primal patricide. Jungian thinkers such as Erich Neumann put at the beginning an undifferentiated consciousness, the "ouroboros," which gradually divides itself up into various archetypes that are the stuff of gods and goddesses. Other thinkers, more strictly in the history of religions tradition, tended to attribute the beginning of religion to a single psychic capacity. For G. van der Leeuw it was the quest for "power"; for Rudolf Otto, a sense of the "numinous," that which is "Wholly Other" and a *mysterium tremendens et facinans.*

But it was becoming increasingly clear that explanations on the order of these, which strove to reduce religion to some single transparent source, would at best never be more than partial. They did not really deal with all the complexity that is religion. They continually gave one a feeling of trying to cover a jagged parcel with a wrapping that never quite fits; when one corner is well enveloped, it slips somewhere else, leaving a whole side exposed to the light.

It became clear that the question of the "origin of religion" cannot be answered in terms of any single definable experience. Unless one take the highly traditional view that humans were infused with an immortal soul at one single point, one can no more say when our religious "organs" emerged than tell exactly when human anatomy transcended the animal, or speech was first spoken, or symbolism appeared in hand or head: all have precursors far back in the prehuman world. Animals have rituals; they have territory that they can "mark" in symbolic ways, and Jane Goodall tells us that that the chimpanzees she studied in Africa display attitudes both of grief and of ecstasy (as at a certain "sacred" waterfall), which clearly anticipate the emotional roots of human religion.

So then it seemed that we needed to set aside the quest for origins and simply understand more deeply what religion is. That was the midcentury task of structuralism and its allies in the phenomenological study of religion. The fashionable labors of Claude Lévi-Strauss stressed the importance of polarities in thinking, thus providing tools for the understanding of ritual versus ordinary behavior, the meaning of culture, and the analysis of myth. The more religiously sensitive scholarship of Mircea Eliade emphasized the dialectic of the sacred and the profane, and the countless manifestations the sacred can take. His work served well to bridge the gulf between the romantic and the reductionist; in it, the sacred and profane may change expression as they move from the primordial to the modern, but the fundamental dialectic remains—even among contemporaries; hidden remnants of the holy linger.

A final stage, to date, seems to be the "deconstructionism" of Jacques Derrida and the related "postmodernism" of writers such as Jean-François Lyotard and Richard Rorty. Their work may be summarized under two agendas: they criticize the "modern" approach, which sees history as a "Grand Narrative" or "metanarrative" of progress from myth and mystification to enlightenment and rationality; and they try to show that any quest for language freed from metaphor, and therefore innocent of any incipient mythicization submerging particulars under a grand scheme, is destined to fail.

Lyotard has identified the two great reigning metanarratives (or myths, in religious language): first, the emancipation of humanity by progress, both political and scientific; second, the unity of knowledge in a way amenable to rational, "scientific" abstraction and technological implementation.[3] On these premises the modern university is built, and any "knowledge" not reducible to their categories is marginalized or excluded—for the most part not even seen. Lyotard writes that "modern" designates "any science that legitimates itself with reference to a metadiscourse of this kind [essentially the enlightenment and emancipation narratives by which science interprets its career] making an explicit appeal to some grand narrative, such as the dialectics of Spirit, the hermeneutics of meaning, the emancipation of the rational or working subject, or the creation of wealth."[4] We are, however, moving past this level of perception: "Simplifying to the extreme, I define *postmodern* as incredulity toward metanarratives. . . . This incredulity is undoubtedly a product of progress in the sciences; but that progress in turn presupposes it."[5] Science continually bursts fables, including—most painfully—its own. We have seen that religion also builds and breaks mythicizations of its own history, whether triumphalist or secularizationist.

Postmodernism proceeds to postulate that a purely rational language unifying all truth, mythless and metaphorless, has not been shown possible; the modern illusion that modern observers have a privileged line of vision that sets them apart from their medieval or earlier counterparts is an idolatry of the present we must get beyond. Historians of religion, for all their honest endeavors to recover empathetically the spiritual past, have not always been free, in the last analysis, of presuming to do so from the uniquely high ground of the "modern" age. Obviously, the "myth of modernity" was egregiously represented, not only by the likes of Comte,

Marx, or Spencer, but also by the origin-of-religion theorists we have noted, with their neat progressions from naïve beginnings through fetishism, polytheism, or magic to a modern high point, whether "ethical monotheism" or the transcendence of religion altogether.

The postmodern critique has not pleased everyone. Lyotard's great philosophical antagonist, Jürgen Habermas, has asked, "But where are the works which might fill the negative slogan of 'postmodernism' with a positive content?"[6] The point is well taken in that postmodernism, like deconstructionism, seems satisfied merely with dismantling the towering edifices of modernity in the mind, regardless of whether their wrecking ball leaves only a wasteland. To some extent, Habermas himself shares that project; he talks of the way historical or scientific narratives leave "subtexts," matters about which they are silent, under their flow of words—the lives of the past human multitudes who did not "make history" as the Grand Narratives understand it, the orphan truths that do not fit into the current scientific unified view. Yet, fundamentally, Habermas accepts the Enlightenment belief that knowledge, fully known and freely communicated, will emancipate. Failure to accept liberating knowledge even as an ideal, he believes, leaves the postmodern camp merely negative, liable to fall for either bleak pessimism or some neoconservative nostrum.

Others might feel it is precisely liberation from abstract goals and ideals that leaves one truly free and effective. One is now free to enjoy the art and wisdom of all times and places without chronological comparison, and one is free to do what needs to be done to meet human needs directly without mystification by politics or ideology. To be sure, several layers of self-deception can obtain in the quest for this kind of freedom before it is authentically actualized. For some, deconstruction and postmodernism have led to a Heideggerean, or Zen, kind of voiceless awareness of things as they appear and of action-needs as they are preformed, in all their concreteness, without myth or theory. If in the process one casts aside as discredited the modern rational outlook, including its liberal religious and social agendas, that rejection need not require the compensatory purchase of some conservative or other myth. Perhaps one could optimistically hold, with William LaFleur, that

> the problem is not that emancipation is unreal or not worth searching and fighting for—although some post-modernists may have gone to that

> conclusion. Rather it is that emancipation is real and recognizable enough to be able to do without the grand old metanarratives of modernity. It also is something that can be encouraged and forced by the concerned—without the need for some kind of belief in the possibility of getting a language 'freed' of metaphor.[7]

That conclusion would, more than coincidentally, be supported by much of the more sophisticated recent historiography, whether Herman Ooms's *Tokugawa Ideology* (from a review of which the above passage by LaFleur is taken) or the harvest of the Annales school of social history, such as Le Roy Ladurie's *Montaillou*, cited in the previous chapter. Scholars such as these have convincingly shown that the situations vis-à-vis myth and reason in times past were by no means as clear-cut as the metanarratives of modern "enlightenment" would have had it.

Either way, the implications of deconstruction and postmodernism for the history of religions are profound. They may succeed in demolishing that discipline altogether, showing it to be a project hopelessly bound to modernism. They may leave in its place only a nihilism and a conviction that the history of religions absurdly overabsolutized its own standpoint —at least on the level of a role as Eliade's "new humanism," able to achieve "phenomenological empathy" and "intuit essences" with faith across the ages. To the contrary, historical minimalists may urge, nothing can be known, especially of the religious past; if it can, it can only be intuited subjectively but not communicated in words, but if words are used, they can only point to the scattered outer husks of faith, not to any essence or splendid story.

Nonetheless, our position is that a history of religions founded on a concept of stages of spiritual mentalities is possible. Ideally, this history would not be one subject to any metanarrative; rather, it would be a history of reigning metanarratives themselves. It would thus take the demolishers of metanarratives at their word, allowing them to set the historiographical agenda; for if metanarratives are not more than mere bogeymen—or even if they are—they must themselves have a history and one not far distanced from the history of religion.

Therefore, one does not see five stages in the life of a world religion (like those here proposed) as "progress," as though medieval Devotionalism or even Reformation were *better* than Vedantic or patristic wisdom, nor does one see (with many reformers of all faiths) the five stages as a benign regression for the sake of the soul. The reformers may contend that a religion's first expression, in its founder and original scriptures, presents a kind of purity to which one can only wish to return, but this judgment is not the sort that a historian qua historian could render.

Rather, in the spirit of Wilhelm Dilthey's *verstehen,* or understanding based on imaginatively entering into the specific experience of another era, each age must be made its own center.

Its deepest and truest religious meaning is not what was imparted to it by its predecessors or successors; rather, it is evoked by the language, symbols, and sociology of its own time. Of course, these icons are not without a past. But their religious meaning is what that past meant to those for whom the period under study was the present. The Apostolic era of Christianity, for example, had significantly different meanings for the medieval devotionalist than it did for the Reformation Protestant. As Dilthey said:

> [I]f I now consider the period of the Middle Ages I find that its horizon is distinct from that of previous periods. Even where the results of these periods persist they are assimilated into the system of the medieval world. *It has a closed horizon.* Thus an epoch is *centered* on itself *in a new sense.* The common practices of an epoch become the norm for the activities of the individuals in it. The pattern of the systems of interaction of the society of an epoch has constant features. Within it the relations in the comprehension of objects show an inner affinity. The ways of feeling, the inner life and the impulses which arise from it, are similar to each other. The will, too, chooses similar goals, strives for related goods and finds itself committed in a similar way. It is the task of historical analysis to discover the climate which governs the concrete purposes, values and ways of thought of a period. Even the contrasts which prevail there are determined by this common background. Thus, every action, every thought, every common activity, in short, every part of this historical whole, has its significance through its relation to the whole of the epoch or age. . . .
>
> The historical world as a whole, this whole as system of interactions, this system of interactions as a source of values and purposes (that is, as creative), the understanding of this whole form within itself, and, finally the centering of values and purposes in ages, epochs, and in universal

history, these are the points of view from which the projected system of the human studies must be considered.[8]

The five stages in the development of a world religion under consideration must be regarded in this sense. The past, as well as the five-stage model (if it be accepted), helps to *explain* the religious phenomena of an age, but that external explanation is not to be conflated with intuiting its *meaning* for believers, for whom it was more or less a timeless present reality. As a major interpreter of Dilthey, H. A. Hodges, has put it:

> This widening of consciousness through historical knowledge has disconcerting results. Every age expresses its attitude to life and the world in certain principles of thought and conduct, which are regarded in that age as absolute and unconditionally valid, as constituting a "law of nature" which only frivolity or ill-will can question. The historian discovers these principles in every age which he studies, but he also discovers that they vary from age to age, and that, in spite of the claim to absoluteness which is always made, changed circumstances always result in changed principles, which are therefore historically relative. The historian who discovers this has of course principles of his own, and these will appear in the manner in which he writes history. He may slip into rating these as absolute.[9]

Insofar as this is the case, the appearances of every spiritual age are equally real and true. If there is "development" in the thought and practice of a religion—the emergence, say, of monasticism and devotion to Our Lady in Christianity, or of Pure Land or Vajrayana in Buddhism—let us view it in terms of John Henry Newman's concept of the development of doctrine. Writing of this process, of course, in the context of Christianity, Newman expressed the basic principles of the concept in terms of these points:

> [T]hat the increase and expansion of the Christian creed and ritual, and the variations which have attended the process in the case of individual writers and churches, are the necessary attendants on any philosophy or polity which takes possession of the intellect and heart and has had any wide or extended dominion; that, from the nature of the human mind, time is necessary for the full comprehension and perfection of great ideas; and that the highest and most wonderful truths, though communicated to the world once for all by inspired teachers could not be comprehended all

> at once by the recipients, but, as received and transmitted by minds not inspired and through media which were human, have required only the longer time and deeper thought for their full elucidation.[10]

The relevant Newmanian idea is that much may be implicit that is not outwardly expressed in the original formulae of a faith. That hidden content is capable of fuller expression in later times in a manner consistent with the original formulae. The later timely expression of what was first occulted keeps the religion alive as it produces treasures new and old; it also makes available the original deposit of faith continually enhanced by vividly new words and symbols.

One thinks of the Mahayana Buddhist teaching that the great sutras of this faith were originally delivered by the Buddha; however, they were hidden until the right moment, and then presented to the world after simpler Theravada texts had done their preparatory work. One may also think of Cardinal Newman's own time and in his own Roman Catholic Church, the papal definition of the doctrine of the Immaculate Conception in 1854, and the conciliar definition of papal infallibility itself in 1870. In each case, one can certainly find ways, if one is so inclined, to argue that the "new" teachings were implicit or hinted at in the original, but they required the intervening centuries to mature to the point where they could be expressed fully; and for historical reasons, they were particularly needed at the time they were so articulated.

The originally implicit (and later, explicit) formulation is, one may say, like a seed that time brings to flower or like a river flowing silently, not yet striking the rocks of history that will give it voice. Take, for example, Pure Land Buddhist experience of wonderful liberation through faith in Amida Buddha's Original Vow to save all beings who call upon his name in faith. Can one see the marvelous inner freedom granted by Amidist faith as congruent with the historical Buddha's experience of enlightenment under the bodhi tree, or as a valid bestowal of the grace engendered by Amida's own buddhic enlightenment? If so, one could see Pure Land teachings, though certainly not explicit in the original Dharma, as a legitimate development of doctrine; likewise may Roman Catholic Mariology or Islamic sainthood be interpreted.

Newman dealt forthrightly with the accusation that many so-called developments of doctrine actually represent the incorporation of items from other traditions into the faith, such as the adaptation of the ancient Mediterranean cult of the Great Goddess into the Christian cult of the Blessed Virgin Mary. He called it *assimilation,* and he lauded the way such wise accommodations help ordinary people adjust to a new faith. But he also argued that while the outward appearance of, say, the Catholic Virgin may seem not unlike that of Isis, the intent and meaning are quite different and not at all inconsistent with monotheism.[11]

Our assumption will be that as a descriptive device, such a universalization of Newman's development of doctrine concept is a valid way of looking at religious history, and it is one not inconsistent with Diltheyan *verstehen*. It helps give the experience of religion in all ages equal meaning and truth, for what of the fullness of each is not explicit is there latently, like the silence of a river.

As Dilthey would remind us, the principle of each age its own center demands introspection of the part of the contemporary historian surveying a past of discrete centers of meaning no less than it summons her to imaginative empathy toward various eras of antiquity. We ourselves see the past in light of our own presuppositions about the human experience and human life generally—different though these may be from those of our subjects. As we have dealt with progressivist modernism and the presumed liberations of postmodernism, we have had to come to terms generally with attitudes toward the human past. We now need to realize that any idea of historical stages, while by no means modern (compare the dispensationalism of the Bible or of Tiantai Buddhism), are always a way one age tries to bring other ages into its own center of meaning—ways that are valid for that age as "present" but not necessarily for the ages being subordinated to the schema. Nonetheless, our task is now to explore whatever light this model may shed, and to that endeavor we now proceed, starting with the earliest religion, proceeding to the "discovery of history" crisis out of which the "great" religions emerged, and continuing on to examine the stages of those religions' historical destinies.

This history is the story of the myths and metaphors, illusory or not, that have dominated the historical development of religions. Not all persons have had equal relations to those stories and symbols, but they have affected the great religious institutions and usually the political institutions as well. In order to remain independent of any "modern" tale or other tale, this history ought to take each religious era as its own center of meaning, emphasizing the internal dynamics of religious development rather than the role of religions as parts of a larger world process.

We may now return to the quest for origins, again bearing in mind that any spiritual age, including the putatively first, can only be understood in its own terms, as its own center of meaning, not in light of its meaning for later generations. It is in this perspective that the question of the "origin" of religion is the wrong question, for it assumes the evolutionary simple-to-complex story upon which the modernist stance was built. Indeed, when a question proves itself as intractable as this one has, we can be confident that it is somehow not being rightly put. We must recognize that, just as we cannot locate any "prereligious" human society past or present, at least since *Homo sapiens*, so we cannot pinpoint any particular experience as where it all began. On one level, religion is simply cultural behavior—that is, learned behavioral innovations that are spread by example and imitation among social groups and to succeeding generations. Recent research has shown that such culture, once thought to be exclusive to humans, can be found among chimpanzees, who evolved some seven million years ago, and it can be also found among orangutans, who go back fourteen million years and whose culture includes such learned and transmitted behavior as goodnight kisses.[12] The question is, When did such culture become religious culture? That is, when did it acquire connotations that linked it to ultimate sanctions on behavior and symbolic concepts of, shall we say, spirit in contrast to body (i.e., soul); and meta- or trans-species (i.e., divine) or ultimate reality?

The development of human religion is clearly coeval with the development of two profoundly interrelated *Homo sapiens* faculties—thought and language. How did this happen? We must note that religion simply runs in the channels of human thought itself, in that it provides bipolar categories by which to divide up the world into ours and theirs, right and wrong, dangerous and useful, good feelings and bad. Religion provides exemplars for the correct and incorrect way to do things, models for what communicates co-inherence with other humans and what does not, and categories for understanding what gives one power and what weakens one. The transmission of such distinctions is perhaps initially through dramatic, dancelike enactments and, soon, stories about ideal types—the great hunter or warrior or mother. But quickly and without fuss the models become ontological, for religion inevitably sets the truly real against the only apparently real, thus affirming that the latter cannot properly "work." Early religion required no metaphysical subtlety to assume tacitly that the ritual gestures that really work are aligned with the inner forces that keep the universe going, or that the archetypal hunter, whom other hunters sought to emulate in the field and to whom they even yearned to be mystically joined, had a sort of aseity and hunting omniscience.

These images in the mind are no more than parts of human verbalized thought, for they are what speech is all about. What is there to talk about except to make such contrasts as between right and wrong ways of hunting or socializing or between good and bad feelings? To establish one's identity in terms of these contrasts and the various situations life presents? It is a question, however, of *how* contrasts and personal identities are talked about and with what referential signposts. Here is where the inseparability of thought, language, and metaphor shows itself. For how can one talk about, say, right and wrong behavior without story and without example, in which the part stands for the whole and the concrete for the abstract? How can one talk about right and wrong behavior prior to the appearance of the generic language that can only come after stories and concrete examples, since it generalized from them? Two sources for such metaphor-making references present themselves.

One is the capacity for protolanguage and protoreligious behavior *already* embedded in the human psyche, having been carried over, as we have suggested, from the animal kingdom. Before the human dawn, our animal ancestors already bore a fairly complete set of potentially "religious" gestures, ready to have bestowed on them the gift of speech to make them vehicles for behavior testing ("ethics") and ontological reification (i.e., placed in the context of beliefs about the structure of reality). One thinks of the ritualized activity by which certain species define territory and inaugurate mating, or the responses—often highly symbolic—by which animals deal with danger, rivalry, and the presence of food or water. The playful running and scuffling of young animals' imitating adult behavior suggests not only the festive play of religious life, but it also suggests religion's ritual imitation of "real life" activities—the hunt or the communal meal—under controlled conditions to enact their ideal form and inner meaning. A more poignant note is offered by the obvious sorrow that primates can show for the death of a child or mate and for the altruism of members of primate bands who, in well-documented instances, have given their lives for the sake of the group.

All these examples clearly demonstrate feelings and actions that, given speech, would easily describe and enact themselves through story, itself half–acted out as it would be by any good storyteller. The story in turn perpetuates act and attitude, thus making it and its protagonists part of a timelessly available firmament of referents. The hunter, the bereaved one, or the self-sacrificer becomes a hero or god or the reflection of one here below; the ritual play time and places are, in the Australian term, the dreamtime of ultimate origin and power.

The second source of metaphor-making referents is the metaphorical material at hand. The fundamental religious images are cosmic: light and dark, high and low, center and periphery, cause and effect. They are always there, waiting to be internalized and then revalorized as virtue and sin, gods and demons. Thus, religion can provide a language, a vocabulary and grammar, for talking about contrasts and coordinating them with cosmic good and bad, right and wrong, positive and negative.

What kind of language would be religious? The definition of religion is a notoriously thorny problem, and the difficulty probably tells us that, as in the case of the origin of religion, the definitional question is the wrong, or at least a highly artificial, way to put the issue. Although we may be talking about where religion (as we call it) came from, to think of our early ancestors' gestures and acted stories as their "religion" is anachronistic by hundreds of thousands, perhaps millions, of years.

People were doing and saying things we might label religious long before any such term or separate territory existed. As William Cantwell Smith has shown, words and concepts for religion in the modern sense—as a clear, distinct, and detachable area of human life with its own institutions, having to do with faith in the supernatural—are modern creations in the major languages.[13] Traditional labels such as Dharma, Tao, or Islam embrace the social order, a proper way of life for an individual, and the sacred cosmos that is its ultimate context and legitimation; these constitute an inseparable, seamless whole. All the less, in that long-forgotten human daybreak when speech was being forged, would any distinction between religious and secular speech obtain.

To name someone a "god" or "hero" would be no different from assigning him or her a role; to hold to a kinship between a tribe and its "totem" animal, or its sacred tree or mountain, would be no different from naming the tribe and knowing its place in the universe. The kinship might be portrayed in art, cemented with offerings, or enacted in dance; to say that such behavior is in accord with the ways of the ancestors or the dreamtime is no different from saying it is right, though the right ways may be enforced through the sense of mysterious dread that talk of ancient ones and otherness can instill.

But the point is that to use such language, language labeled by us "religious," is no special thing, save in terms of our own "modern" metanarrative, which makes religion a separate, more or less optional, part of human experience and one at odds with "modern" enlightenment and rationality. At the dawn of speech, religious talk was neither peculiarly exalted nor was it Max Muller's "disease of language"; it was simply a way of speech that was at hand, inbred in already-present animal–human moods and rituals, waiting to be given names that both made important distinctions and enforced them, while connecting humankind to the cosmic environment.

What it comes down to is a manipulation of images. As opposed to blurs of sense impressions or stimuli that evoked only conditioned or instinctual responses, the emergence of images in consciousness as distinct entities with which one could have varied and considered relationships must have been coeval with language. Language offered tools for the separation of one image from another, "markers" for retention of distinct images in memory, and a logic for constructing the grammar of rational response to them in the mind. Spoken words also enabled the communication of images, making them social as well as private entities.

Images are of three orders. First are the images created in the mind by sensory data, whether from the cosmic environment or one's own body—the images making conscious what is seen, heard, felt. These become clear retained images insofar as one gives each a separate name and stores it in memory for future reference.

Second are the images both outward and subjective, created by art or voice, also (of course) communicated through the senses. But these images have a very different impact on our minds and feelings than do the straight sensory. To see, hear, feel, taste, or smell what we know was made for the purpose of being seen, heard, felt, tasted, or smelled by another human in order to mediate an interpersonal but socially significant meaning is not the same as getting it "raw," straight from nature. *These* perceptions are retained in mind for the hopes and fears they evoke concerning one's relation to society as well as to the cosmos. So it is: the way we see art or hear music is very different from the way we see the sun or hear the wind; likewise, we taste the food cooked by one who loves us—or one who hates us—differently from the way we taste wild berries.

Third are those images that exist only in subjectivity: dreams, fantasies, visualized cogitations. Needless to say, they are fabricated of material taken from nature or art or society, and they are well admixed with inner feelings; but they are of a different nature in that they remain wholly within the house of the mind.

In addition, intermediate categories linking two or three of these orders exist: remembrances (accurate or otherwise) of nature, art, or subjective dreamlands. We must also mention known facts and abstract ideas that may well be carried in the mind under some sort of image. As Owen Barfield has commented, abstractions are but decayed metaphors.[14]

Religion, of course, may plant itself in any of these three orders of images. Explicitly religious images, in the sense of altars or gods or other symbols of transcendent reality, may be seen "naturally" in the outer world (the "cathedrals of nature"), they may be created by art, or they may arise in subjective consciousness. But the great function of religion is that it *connects* these three orders, providing bridges among them and thus overcoming the isolation of subjectivity from the world or the alienation of the human from the natural. Gods once seen on mountaintops or treetops may be fashioned of wood or stone as art, and they may then socially be imputed rule over sky and sea and inwardly given sovereignty over the tides of human feeling. Sources of natural power, such as sun, moon, or wind, are assigned meaning compatible with human subjectivity. Peter Berger has written that "religion is man's audacious attempt to see the whole universe as humanly significant."[15] That is certainly at least one side of the truth about religion, one that points to its close affinity to language.

Language is that which connects meaning to meaning, inner to outer, and outer to inner, thus humanizing the cosmos insofar as it names it, though not to the extent of religion when it both names and personifies the cosmos or the power behind it. Nonetheless, we again see religion as a form of language, or perhaps more profoundly, we see language as a form of religion. On different levels of intensity and personification, both language and religion define and interpret the images in their orders, connecting human subject and cosmic object.

To pursue further the matter of the origin of religion, we need now to look at the origin of humans in more precise anthropological terms. When did humans become human? Paleoanthropologists speak of hominid species in the evolutionary chain leading to modern man as *Pithecus* and *Homo*, ape and man. Characteristic of the protohuman Pithecus stage is *Australopithecus afarensis* of some four million years back; one star of the *A. afarensis* set is "Lucy," discovered and described by Donald Johnson.[16] The evolutionary transition to the protohuman state represented by Lucy, who walked more or less upright, was gradual and marked by three early characteristics: bipedalism, brain development, and use of tools. At one time, it was thought that these three emerged more or less together. But the discovery of the small-brained, toolless, but bipedal Lucy and her kin pushed bipedalism back a million years and, in the eyes of many authorities, made evident its priority over the other two features.

Why was bipedalism the first major step toward true humanity, the one upon which the growth of a large brain and the use of tools apparently depended? The answer may have intriguing connections with the question of religion.

Nonbipedal primates use two main means of locomotion: they are either branch swingers or knuckle walkers. Another important feature of most nonhuman primates is a low birthrate. Females generally raise only one child at a time, spacing them over several years. They also have only occasional estrus; and when it occurs, the males in the local band become highly aroused, fighting in a general free-for-all for the privilege of mating with her. These chaotic arrangements are largely responsible for the low numbers and poor prospects of most primates in the world, despite their intelligence and social organization. The low birthrate makes survival an always-precarious affair, and the sexual infighting inhibits social evolution by periodically disrupting cooperation and harmony.

C. Owen Lovejoy has suggested that one branch of the primate family, the protohuman, found its way out of this box. It prospered sexually and socially through three interrelated evolutionary developments: bipedalism, the pair bonding of one male and one female, and continuous sexual contact resulting in much more frequent births.[17]

Bipedalism was the key. This new mode of movement meant, first, that a female with a child was relatively tied to one place—home—since a bipedal child does not cling to its mother like a monkey but is carried in her arms. The male, on the other hand, is free to walk out and find food, and he has free arms with which to bring it back. The prospect of sex, as well as emotional bonding to mate and offspring, motivated him to return with provender, and this incentive increased the birthrate. These interconnected adaptations, according to Lovejoy's ingenious theory, developed over millions of years and led up to *Australopithecus* and finally *Homo*.

All this development probably took place in the context of climate changes in Africa, humanity's first home, some four to five million years ago, when drying changed much of the continent from forest to savanna. That shift in climate doubtless increased the value of bipedalism by making our distant ancestors taller and thus able to spot food or predators farther away, and by strengthening mobility in open terrain. Like Lucy and her folk, they probably ranged in family groups or small bands in the vicinity of lakes and streams for gathering and foraging.

The next stage was the emergence (some two million years ago) of *Homo habilis* and *Homo erectus*, early man, still short of *Homo sapiens*, contemporary man. At this time, hunting and the associated making of bladelike tools became important. This in turn probably meant formation of male bands who continued the ancient work of bringing home food, but now often by means of cooperative quests for game. The cooperation needed for bringing down and preparing large animals undoubtedly facilitated human social development, and the manufacture of tools for killing and dressing the prey encouraged technological advance. No less important was the gathering and preparing of plant foods by women, as it is done in Africa today by continually talking or singing female groups. All this development went hand in hand with mental expansion—the coming of language and the large brain.

And religion? According to conventional theology, protohumans would have become *Homo* upon being infused with a soul, an immortal spiritual part distinct from body and mind, capable of knowing God, and in acute interaction with supersensory reality. We have absolutely no way of knowing how Lucy and her folk thought, much less whether she knew God, nor have we any better idea of the real status of thought or God for *Homo erectus* a couple of million years later.

But if the foregoing hypotheses are correct, we can well imagine some sort of sanctions in the mind enforcing pair bonding, the nurture of children, and the loyalty of hunting bands. They may also have dealt with emergent feelings of joy and grief. Inner sanctions must have arisen simultaneously with the outer social and emotional developments, and they must have taken verbalized form much later as language appeared, reinforced with conceptualized mental images. Images must have linked subjective consciousness and outer social need through words as soon as language itself presented that intangible tool kit. For, again, these images are what the linkages and distinctions language makes are all about.

We ourselves know all too well that our first impulses are not always in the direction of loyalty to mate and community good; we need not think our remote ancestors were any different. The crucial areas of family and tribal bonding, of sexual control and subordination of self to hunting and work group, of altruism to the point of self-sacrifice when necessary—still underneath all else the vital arenas of religious sanction—must have required some inner discipline, as well as social discipline, capable of overriding "natural" impulse when need be. The symbols used could only be those that—by sign or metaphor, by the image linkages made—indicated a dimension within which human life operated other than the ordinary outward, visible, and natural.

The sociobiologist Edward Wilson has convincingly argued the superior survival value of communalism and of the inculcation of altruism within the community. Among verbal creatures, he further argues, religion is the supreme vehicle for this stern but necessary teaching.[18] The fundamental sociobiological point is that human behavior, including worship and morality, ultimately derive from biological natural selection designed to ensure group and species survival.

As a full explanation of religion, this case may be one-sided; in my view, at least, religion has probably always answered to a human capacity for poetic vision and a yearning for ultimate understanding, as well as provided sanctions for behavior with species-survival value, including loyalty and altruistic self-sacrifice. Sociobiology, in fact, presents a first-class example of metanarrative rank with subtexts about the privileged position of the scientific observer and progress toward enlightenment and emancipation. Like so many other metanarratives, it is finally undercut by its inability to explain itself in a way congruous with the way it explains everything else. If sociobiology can explain religion and the rest of human society merely as ploys wrought by the cunning of the gene, where did sociobiology itself come from? How do we know it is not also just another plausible myth, foisted on us for some survival value that our masters deep within the cells have decided it holds, though it is really no more true than any other fable? Perhaps some evolutionary élan vital is now shifting its human bets from religion to science, assuming—an awesome assumption—that science now holds the greater survival value, and so this world-soul is now implanting the appropriate tales. But does that make them *true?*

These issues are, however, something of a digression from our investigation of the origin of religion. We do not doubt that a major function of the earliest human religion—whatever else it may have been—was to offer necessary sanctions as part of its role as a language's making distinctions between good and bad, or ours and theirs. As with all scientific narratives that emerged out of the rational unity of knowledge and the narrative of modern emancipation from myth, a basic problem with sociobiology is its inability to countenance fully that early religion, like language, may have truly had more than one "origin," insofar as it served more than one end and that faith was not (as it appears to emancipated moderns) a well-defined, detachable, and therefore dispensable segment of human life.

But if what we call "religion" began as language's linking inner and outer images, the point is that it was really nothing special and therefore nothing about which dispensability as an issue would arise. The modern question of whether one could be a "good person" without being religious would not have arisen in the same way as today, for the requisite categories of thought were not in place. No concept of "religion" as a separable, voluntary, detachable area of human life from that of the community and its corresponding subjectivity obtained; at the same time, no language other than the protoreligious—mythical models, taboos, and the like—existed for talking about goodness—though, of course, as always, individuals may have been more or less amenable to the claims of goodness, for even the "primitive" are complex as persons.

"Religion," without the word, was simply a way of thinking, a vocabulary, for dealing with essential commitments and necessities of human social life—and perhaps increasingly for maintaining inner equilibrium in the face of fear, the need for deferred reward, and the inevitable tension created by conflicting obligations. The question of whether it was the *best* language would not arise until language had advanced, or decayed, sufficiently to produce abstract as well as personified metaphors, and so allow a choice between them. Then, finally, some decision between the "religious" and the "philosophical" ways of handling such matters was available. From the beginning, however, varying degrees of emotional relation to religious images was no doubt found.

At some point, we know not when, humanity made the ultimate discovery: death. Avoidance of death—or seeking it whether for altruistic or suicidal reasons—was then not merely based on instinctual fear; rather, it was compounded by conscious awareness of what death was and extrapolation from the sight of death in others. Death, too, came under the canopy of religious language, for death above all had to be dealt with in a way that fused inner feelings and their images with outer, observed realities.

Primal religion was then a way of thinking and talking about such things, unselfconscious in its use of symbol and metaphor as tools of language. That phenomenon is nothing remarkable, for such use was not discontinuous with the symbolic character of all language and acts, human or animal. In the context of social relations, use of symbol and metaphor expresses mind to mind what is not fully consummated at the moment or what is to be completed in subjectivity, from the raised fist and the stroking gesture to the courtship dance.

Early humans, *Homo erectus*, moved onstage a million or so years ago. *Homo erectus* was, in all likelihood, responsible for several immensely important steps in human development: the dispersion of the race outside Africa, the taming of fire, cooking of food, cave dwelling. Did they also move ahead in religion? Most sites leave nothing that seems susceptible to a religious explanation—no burials, no sacred art, nothing but the most severely utilitarian hearths and stone tools. This lack of evidence does not, of course, mean there was nothing at all, for what has survived so many thousands of years can only represent a tiny percentage of *Homo erectus'* total culture. Whatever was made of sand, wood, or skin is forever lost, not to mention all the songs and all the stories insofar as they communicated in human sound. Nonetheless, in the absence of any positive evidence to the contrary, we must conclude that *Homo erectus* had not yet found the capacity to express subjectivity in the symbolic forms of art, although—since animal parallels exist—we may well hypothesize such articulation through voice and gesture, and even dance.

The most oft-cited evidence of religious practice by *Homo erectus* involves two of the grimmest activities in religion's repertoire: head-hunting and cannibalism. These are particularly associated with the remains found at Chou Kou-Tien in North China ("Peking Man"). Here human bones have been broken and splintered as though to eat the marrow, and skulls are detached from bodies and collected. Further, the skulls show damage at the base of the cranium in a way that would allow the brain to be extracted; in fact, recent head-hunters of Borneo and New Guinea have ritually removed the brain of a victim in a similar manner and eaten it as a way of assuming the deceased's name and identity.

Some authorities, however, have questioned the head-hunting and cannibalism interpretations of such *Homo erectus* finds, pointing out that in recent cultures, such practices are inevitably associated with Neolithic (archaic agricultural) societies rather than the most primitive. Johannes Maringer, for example, has held that the evidence would also be compatible with a far more benign explanation: the practice of some of the most primitive peoples on earth, such as the Andaman Islanders, of removing, cleaning, and carrying about with them the heads of departed loved ones as tokens of remembrance and vessels of their protective power.[19]

Either way, we need not doubt that these earliest hints of some kind of ritual activity with the heads and bones of the dead of their own kind had a connection with that dreadful discovery already mentioned. In some vague but powerful way, perhaps, *Homo erectus* sensed a lingering—or enhanced—invisible energy in the dead, which could be appropriated by the living, directly or indirectly to challenge their own deaths, in rites by which one symbolically faced and mastered the last enemy.

It was during the fourth glaciation, or Würm glaciation, some seventy-five thousand years ago that Neanderthal, an early *Homo sapiens*, appeared. With him came the first unambiguous evidence of religious life. In both Europe and the Middle East, this powerfully built race attained the highest level of culture known thus far. The Neanderthals provide the first clear instance of intentional burial, with the remains treated in a way unmistakably significant: smeared with ochre, the color of blood and life; the burial of family groups together; the placing of new tools and pieces of meat in the grave with the deceased. Neanderthal religion was not restricted to human burial rites; purposefully placed skulls suggest a bear cult, such as has been practiced by circumpolar peoples down to the present, in which the remains of that mighty adversary become guardians of home and hearth. Yet, again, the remains we do have indicate that, above all, it was the mysterious threshold between life and death that focused whatever spiritual imagination these folk enjoyed.

The question is, however, what sort of imagination *Homo erectus* and the Neanderthals possessed. Some scholars would not wish to overemphasize the explicitly religious significance of their funerary and related practices, in the absence of much further evidence of religion or religious consciousness. It may be that burial was, at least in part, merely sanitary or a caution against predators, or maybe it was even done in only a partly understood imitation of the next human development, *Homo sapiens*, with whom the Neanderthals lived in contact for many millennia.

The great creative explosion, above all in art and symbolism, appears with *Homo sapiens*, the Aurignacians and Cro-Magnon peoples famous for their cave art some thirty-five thousand years ago in Europe, though *Homo sapiens* arose much earlier in Africa, then migrating around the Mediterranean (there are important sites in Israel) and into southern Europe. They are the first humans that are virtually indistinguishable from present-day folk in appearance, in use of language (many believe), and, it would seem, in intellect. Their cave and rock paintings are the first major human works of art and of undoubted, though enigmatic, religious significance.

These illustrations were not mere picture galleries, nor were they the decorations of homes. They are in sanctuaries obviously reserved for sacred activities, located far underground, away from living areas, accessible then as now only by arduous and dangerous journeys through narrow passageways. After such a subterranean trek, the light of the Cro-Magnon's torch would fall on the bright colors of game animals painted on the walls and even ceilings of a hidden inner chamber, with animals painted over and over, often one superimposed on another.

We can only imagine what those familiar yet mysterious forms would have meant to those who saw them freshly hued. One purpose certainly had to do with hunting magic. By painting and perhaps ritually slaying the underground animals, their counterparts in field and forest might also have been made susceptible to the tribesmen's spears. But the meaning may go beyond this. It is not unlikely that the caves were places of initiation.

In one, footprints in a room by the gallery recall the stomping or dancing of many childish feet before the last ice age; they may well derive from an initiatory scenario.

John E. Pfeiffer, in *The Creative Explosion: An Inquiry into the Origins of Art and Religion*, has proposed another possible meaning of cave art, as suggested by patterns in more contemporary Australian and African San (Bushman) rock paintings—that they are aids to mythic memory and storehouses of tribal wisdom.[20] However chaotic the dense packs of cave pictures may seem to the modern observer, the stylized formats and the arrangements of the paintings in particular caves may tell stories important to the people responsible for them, encoding events from mythology, history, and festivals; perhaps they also map sacred geography. (Australians, for example, learned and remembered the lay of their land through stories of mythic events believed to have taken place at various important sites.) Since it is customarily in initiatory ceremonies that such secret and sacred lore is imparted, it would not be surprising if meanings like these were contained in the art ornamenting the scene of cave initiations.

Now we clearly see the rebounding reflections of the image so characteristic of human society. In the picture caves, we find what had been seen in nature, and perhaps also in dreams and visions, reconstructed in art. What is first revealed is its human meaning, as possible tokens that recall myth and geographical orientation; second, its magico-sacred meaning, as instruments of power and initiation now. Perhaps the Cro-Magnon caves, like so many later caves, were portals to the Other World, associated with gods and the dead. In any case, the full-fledged discovery of art they symbolize surely opened countless Gates of Horn to true dreaming both sacred and profane, unveiling ranges of human self-awareness and empathy with nature heretofore sealed off.

Another feature of archaic religion that unquestionably also exposed fresh frontiers of human subjectivity and sacred consciousness was shamanism. How far back shamanism goes is not entirely clear, but it may well have been associated with the Cro-Magnon caves and their culture. Many have assumed that the famous human figure dressed in animal skins and horns of the Trois-Frères cave in France, known as the sorcerer and thought to be some twelve thousand years old, is shamanistic. All that can be said for certain, though, is that shamanism appears to be among the oldest strata of spirituality that the history of religion can trace, well established in many recent tribal societies upon European contact, and offering innumerable clues of its presence in the deep background of the literate religions as they moved into history.

What is shamanism? The term refers to the role of specialists in the sacred who possess direct control of or partnership with spirits and access to the Other World of gods and the departed and who are thereby able to heal and divine. Mircea Eliade, in his classic work titled *Shamanism: Archaic Techniques of Ecstasy*, offers a vivid and richly documented account of the shaman's call from the gods, his "initiatory psychopathology," expanded awareness and vocabulary, role as psychopomp, and capacity for "earth-diving," or marvelous flight.[21] Claude Lévi-Strauss has vividly shown how shamans heal, first, through diagnosis that interprets the cause of illness or misfortune in terms of the society's world view—that is, a lost or stolen soul, invasion by evil spirits, violation of a taboo—which makes it understandable and therefore manageable; and, second, through correcting the dysfunction in the same terms by acting out the recovery of the soul, driving out the malignant entity, and atoning for the taboo breakage.[22] Shamanism can be seen as virtuoso handling of religion as a language's linking subjective images and cosmic/physical realities; it dramatically and forcefully compels their convergence through spectacular symbols and consciousness-altering "techniques of ecstasy." This scenario is nothing more nor less, of course, than what culture does through all sorts of media. The archaic shaman may rightly be considered the spiritual ancestor of various later religious specialists (the prophet, priest, mystic, and heaven-faring savior) and of various other specialists as well (the artist, poet, singer, and psychotherapist).

Not all shamans in all societies have played all the roles we have cited. But in all genuine cases, images of that which is more than biological and aligned to the realm of dream and vision break through in the shaman. To him or her, the human and the god who personifies that other realm become visibly linked as coworkers and mutual visitants; they even become identical if the shaman is possessed and acquires, as often happens, the visage and personality of the deity. Both the human and divine are enhanced through the shaman's mediation. The range of human experience is vastly, one might even say infinitely, expanded by the capacity to contain godhead; and the divine, by taking on entranced human face and form, becomes familiar and thus gains the attributes that may be transmitted down through the centuries in art and song.

David Lewis-Williams, in *The Mind in the Cave*, has linked shamanism and Aurignacian cave art in an intriguing way. He argues that what really distinguished *Homo sapiens* from his Neanderthal and *Homo erectus* predecessors was the ability to induce, experience, and intentionally remember altered states of consciousness, such as those brought about by drumming, rhythmic actions, and intense concentration—all shamanistic techniques—as well as reverie, fantasy, dreaming, and hypnogogic states. These experiences often include bright lights, tunnel-like settings, and perceived shapes that can become of high significance to the subject's mind. To Lewis-Williams, the shaman was the adept at this new breakthrough in consciousness, cognitive awareness of altered states. Speleological art was the attempt to reproduce the worldview of altered states for future reference, especially in connection with initiatory scenarios, in a suitably suggestive setting, the tunnel-like cave—though it must not be forgotten that much noncave rock art is broadly similar in character.[23]

To be sure, the symbolism of Paleolithic religion, like that of religion today, can be complex and many-layered. While the animals of Aurignacian cave art—mostly large herbivores like the bison, ibex, auroch, and horse—may have had visionary origin, they may also have sociological significance, representing perhaps the totem animals of different clans; their interrelationships and superimposition one on another indicate intricate outer societal patterns. Or, perhaps, they may be a kind of language, even an alphabet, telling long-forgotten myths of the tribe, or like some Australian rocks outlining the mythic geography of their terrain.

The Nobel Prize winner Gerald Edelman has proposed two levels of consciousness: primary consciousness and higher-order consciousness.[24] Primary consciousness, probably shared by most mammals, is a consciousness that is aware of the world at the present, based on the mental image of it created by sensory input. It enables the person or animal to react appropriately to that world. But it lacks awareness of similar images from the past, what might be called "remembered presents." It also lacks an explicit notion of a personal self; an ability to imagine long-term past or future as possible continuations of the present primary-consciousness world; and the self as an actor with various possible choices relevant to past or future in that world. Of course there are levels on which the entity does "remember," but they are not conscious imaginal memories, only "lessons" expressed through conditioned fears or desires.

Higher-order consciousness, on the other hand, has all of these conditions. It entails awareness of the subject as personal, as having past and future based on imaged memories and projections, and as a conscious awareness of ability to make choices. These abilities in turn make possible symbolic memory, language, communication, and more complex forms of social organization as made up by such intercommunicating selves. *Homo sapiens* is the only species that has higher-order consciousness, and the evolutionary emergence of this kind of consciousness is, of course, what can be postulated for the leap from *Homo erectus* and Neanderthal to *Homo sapiens*. Such a model would explain much: speech in the full human sense involving abstract, metaphorical, and memory-based expression, as well as "primary" responses; the ability and need to aid the memory of significant experience through pictorial and other symbolic signals, in this case of shamanistic altered-consciousness experience; and highly differentiated social organization. In the midst of this revolution must be placed the origin of religion as we know it, though it must be stressed that it also was *not* the origin of religion *as we know it*, as a separate detachable segment of life; rather, it was just part—if not the essence—of the symbolic world being created in, with, around, and under the primary consciousness world by the new way of thinking.

It is clear that the Paleolithic society, like the Paleolithic consciousness, of *Homo sapiens* was much more complex and stratified than that of its predecessors. Its burials indicate as much: cave goods show some remains interred with very elaborate body ornaments, undoubtedly symbols of high status. In fact, a boy buried in Russia as much as thirty-two thousand years ago was covered with no fewer than 4,903 strands of beads and a belt containing more than 250 canine teeth of the polar fox, as well as goods of ivory from mammoths; a girl buried beside him was accompanied by 5,274 beads and other objects—it is estimated the goods would have taken over thirty-five hundred hours to make. Though children, these were clearly persons of consequence.[25] It is hard to imagine that such dedication to death and burial, and such extravagant honor paid to two young persons, could not have had immense religious importance.

After the world of the Paleolithic hunter came that of the Neolithic archaic agriculturalist. The invention of agriculture brought a profound social and religious revolution, one that shaped the nature of practical and spiritual life more than any other factor virtually to the present. The city is no more than an extension of the sedentary village made possible by planting, and until the twentieth century the average person almost anywhere in the world was a peasant whose values and way of life were closer to that of the Neolithic farmer than they were to the contemporary computer programmer. It may be that now, some twelve thousand years after the discovery of agriculture, conditions of human life are changing radically enough to suggest religious change as far reaching as that which separated the Paleolithic hunter and the Neolithic farmer.

What were those Neolithic changes? First we may cite those that affected the connection of inner and outer images, the latter now grounded significantly (not directly) in nature, but in nature as modified by the human hand. Neolithic religion gives renewed importance to the earth, frequently personified as feminine—Mother Earth—and to feminine fertility symbols in general. The turn of the seasons, with anxious prayers at seedtime and joyful thanksgiving as the harvest is gathered in, punctuate the sacred year. The sedentary nature of agriculture makes especially important permanent sites of the sacred: the holy mountain overlooking the fields, the altar in their midst. A darker dimension of the sacred comes forward as well, for the discovery of agriculture seems to have brought with it a new sense of the relation of death and life; a seeming death, like that of the seed buried in the soil, or an actual death, like that of a victim who fertilizes it, can bring abundant life to many in the end. It was in the Neolithic period, not before, that practices such as animal and human sacrifice and head-hunting most flourished.

Socially, the Neolithic revolution not only changed the pattern of human life for most by making it sedentary, but it also typically produced enough surplus wealth and energy, despite great population growth, to make possible homes, granaries, and public buildings such as temples on an unprecedented scale. It also permitted at least a small number of people to pursue public roles as rulers, merchants, priests, and even philosophers rather than directly engage in production. For better or worse, religion, like the statecraft with which it was closely intertwined, was professionalized.

Together, that elite of rulers, priests, and merchants living on the surplus produced the next great political–spiritual event—the ancient empires, with their sacred kings and elaborate national cults and their busy commerces affording broad intercultural contacts. These three also pioneered the invention of writing, with all its immense consequences down through the centuries.

Theirs was the world of the ancient empires and their peripheries, a world whose soul was still profoundly ruled by shamanistic and Neolithic values; it was a world that now knew the power of the written word to chronicle and consolidate; it was also a world shaken by new discoveries and new terrors. It was a world during which the next powerful epoch in religion appeared—the Great Religions. Their rising was itself a great moment in religious history, and our religious era still belongs to them. Yet it must be seen that they themselves are but the final culminating stage of the religious revolution wrought by the discovery of agriculture.

That last stage was marked by another tremendous event, the discovery of history. To it and its meaning, we must now turn.

CHAPTER THREE
RELIGION AND THE DISCOVERY OF HISTORY

How did religion get from its primordial and timeless symbols represented by nature and the human self—the animal, the plant, the soul surviving death—to the focus of the historic Great Religions on the archetypal person, generally the founder, and the single pivotal historical moment? Continuities there may be, but impressive also is the distance between the cave painting of Trois-Frères or the archaic open-air Shinto shrine facing a sacred mountain or waterfall to an altar bearing the image of Christ crucified or the Buddha in meditation. No less momentous is the gulf between those faiths whose calendars revolve around seedtime and harvest and those that celebrate a second creation in Wesak—the day of the Buddha's birth and enlightenment—or Christmas and Easter.

Before proceeding to these reflections, let us review again our understanding of the meaning of religion. Religion is fundamentally a manipulation of images. Above all, it establishes connections among three great orders of images: those created by sensory data from the outside world, those humanly created in art and manufacture, and those from the worlds of dream and fantasy and cognition, which—though perhaps inspired by outside forms—truly exist only in subjectivity. As a kind of language, religion connects these realms, saying that the wind or sun is akin to powers or domains within and so may be personified in art and ritual or by gods of the cosmos affecting one's dreams and visions. Some authorities believe that true human speech came late, certainly only with *Homo sapiens*, perhaps only with Cro-Magnon man. But if so, the same connections might have been felt and articulated long before through sign and gesture as rooted in animal sound and ritualism. The history of religion is a history of these connections, especially as they are embodied in the major constellations of images that serve as models for interpreting the world and for human behavior.

The image constellations live in interaction with human society. They are generally pluralistic, yet certain sets of images will articulate, more than do peripheral images, what is seen by a society to be the source of power; therefore, the images become a society's major touchstones of interpretation of the humanly significant world. In primordial hunting society, as evidenced by cave paintings and bear sacrifices, the animal in life and death was clearly the dominating image—giver of meat, tester of human strength, embodiment of mystery. The hunter not only wants to challenge his prey, but he also wants to "be" the bear or deer. After the agricultural revolution, the main images center on the plant, whose drama of life, death, and new life becomes the archetype of so much else: sacrifice, head-hunting, initiation, the savior.

But around the fifth century B.C.E., the focus changed dramatically and, in historical terms, suddenly. This is the period called the "Axial Age" by the philosopher Karl Jaspers.[1] We shall speak of it preeminently as the era of the Discovery of History, and we shall focus on the spiritual crisis it entailed and the resolution produced in the form of the major religious founders with their Great Religions. For the Axial Age was an era of the emergence of large-scale literate and historical cultures, empires, and world religions. Elsewhere, Jaspers has written that there is a "sense of history only if events are understood as the objective premises of our present existence and at the same time as something else, something which has been—and in having been, was for itself—singular in time and unique in kind."[2] Behind the changes of the Axial Age lay a new awareness of time, or more precisely, a new kind of time. One could only have the existential awareness of history requisite to establish spiritual (and cultural) forms to deal with it after one had grasped the one-way character of time: events have happened that are unique, they have passed, and they will not come again; yet they affect the present and indeed are its foundation.

The Great Religions that arose in this era were centered not on beast or grain, but on the sacred person—the prophet, the enlightened one or savior—and the sacred book. Both emerged in a moment of historical time deemed to have special, pivotal significance for all human experience. As Mircea Eliade has shown, for the "cosmic religion" of early hunters and agriculturalists, the *illud tempus*—the mythical time when the gods were supremely active and the ultimate meaning of the world was revealed—was the time of creation, typically reenacted at New Year's, with its ritual return to chaos and renewed order.

For a Great Religion, however, a moment *in* time—the time of the Buddha, the Christ, or the Prophet—becomes the moment of a second and even more powerful creation. In practical sacred importance, it exceeds the first creation; it is the centerpoint when "the hopes and fears of all the years are met" in a great new divine event associated with the work of an ideal archetypal person, together with the generation of a sacred text bearing witness to the event and the truths associated with it. Rather than the plant or animal, the master images of religion are now the person, the text, and the historical time in which divine purpose is worked out. Insofar as religion means images connecting inner and outer, we may think of the formation of the Great Religions as the emergence of a single image—the founder, savior, enlightened one, prophet—or a closely knit cluster of related images—his saints and symbols—at the center. All other images are in subordination to these.

The image can be usefully understood in terms of the archetypal psychology of James Hillman and his premier interpreter, Roberts Avens.[3] For them, the image is that which dwells in the "imaginal realm," in the term of Henry Corbin, the distinguished scholar of Islamic mysticism. Imaginal reality lies between the material plane on the one hand, and the intellectual or spiritual (in the sense of ultimate reality) on the other. This imaginal realm must not be taken to have the negative connotations of "imagination" as the mere fanciful construction of ephemeral entities in the mind, for it discovers ways of knowing our pluralistic universe appropriate to our ultimate instrument of understanding, consciousness, or psyche. The old gods may inhabit this terrain, but so do the half-conscious images and mythologies that activate the rationalist and the atheist, the scientist and the logician, the sensualist no less than the ascetic. For do these not also enter their life roles in response to seeing a picture of an archetypal embodiment of the rationalist or scientist in the mind?

The imaginal realm is not imposed on the world; rather, it is one with our knowledge of the world; it is *how* we know, as we make what we know relevant to ourselves. The religious image then, again, is crucial to religion as a kind of language that links the three orders of image—nature, art, subjectivity. As Owen Barfield has vividly put it, it is erroneous to think of early man's making myths and gods by "always projecting his insides onto something or other," as though the world were dead until we gave it a fictive life. The truth is rather the reverse: "It was not man who made the myths but myths or the archetypal substance they reveal, which made man."[4] For man perhaps had no "insides" until myth and religion, working in profound exchange with the sense data of nature and the raw feelings, gave them to him.

The imaginal way of knowing is inherently polytheistic, and therefore so also is primordial human nature. For imaginalism handles in consciousness terms the "working" world of pluralistic reality. To it, the ultimate unity—whether represented by a king of the gods, Zeus or Amon, or a more abstract principle, Brahman or Ma'at—is in effect just another image associated with a particular state of awareness, that of mystical oneness with the All.

But the rise of the Great Religions meant, in the imaginal level, the establishment of a single image as sovereign and the subordination of all other images to it, or else their expulsion as demonic or nonexistent gods of wood and stone. Yet the newly sovereign image is still a word from the primordial vocabulary. Again, Barfield has put it interestingly: "Every man, certainly every original man has something new to say, something new to mean. Yet if he wants to express that meaning . . . he must use language—a vehicle which presupposed that he must either mean what was meant before or talk nonsense."[5]

Certainly, if our talk is not nonsense, religion is a language par excellence. Never did religion have anything more radically new to say than in the inception of the Great Religions, when heavensful of gods and spirits were brought under one true God, or one unified state of consciousness, like that of the Buddha under the tree of enlightenment, or the one Tao of which the Chinese sage spoke. But the language was still that of religion. This meant that into the new unities came all the baggage of religion, not to be trashed but to be rearranged around a single center, to which all the rituals and myths and hierarchies would point. What would not fit in that pattern was, of course, discarded. Often it did not go quietly, leaving demoted gods and rites as the familiars and magic of popular religion; more consequentially, it left voiceless yet lingering images in the psyche. No question about it, advancing only one image to the throne of heaven can be done only by main force, and by doing so, there is bound to be wreckage, some of it strewn with shards and sharp splinters, and some of it not quite dead.

Yet the birth of the Great Religions was inevitable; one can hardly imagine it not happening in the course of human events. There was, of course, preparation. The background of the discovery of history was the growth of archaic agricultural states and, in particular, the ancient riverine empires based on large-scale hydraulic works. Interestingly, however, the great Founders tended to come not from the imperial centers, but from smaller pastoral or farming territories on their fringes: Lumbini, Lu, Galilee, Mecca. For most of their people, the ancient empires were peasant societies offering only marginal sustenance. They afforded augmented division of labor, which led to some sense of unique individuality and a role for an elite; the agricultural empires also produced some surplus wealth to support religious and intellectual specialists—priests, contemplatives, and philosophers who could offer models of the ideal spiritual person and so advance the ideal of the adept as an archetype, an image that became more and more deeply embossed on consciousness.

For everyone, the very existence of a complex society suggested the possibility of significant individual choices. The growth of technology increased trade and travel, thus bringing exposure to other cultures and ways of worship. So did wars of conquest, with armies marching back and forth and the taking of slaves. All in all, the ancient empires meant countless people uprooted from familiar village and shrine, thrown into burgeoning urban centers where they had neither roots nor familiar gods. In such a situation, one is left to oneself to find images that work and to seek experience that is convincing. Just before the dawn of the Great Religions, we find the idea of individual salvation as a personal project rapidly growing in Egypt, Greece, and India.

Another important idea in the ancient empires was the sacred king, who would as in Babylon ritually fight the forces of chaos annually, or as in China plow the first furrow to begin the agricultural year. He too represented the life of humanity and the forces of the cosmos concentrated in one archetypal person. So, in another way, did the prophet, the voice of the gods in the world and in the lineage of the archaic shaman. Significantly, Jesus, the supreme religious founder, is prophet, priest, and king in traditional Christian theology.

Despite the subterranean current flowing in another direction, however, the age of the ancient empires was overtly the heyday of polytheism.

The pantheons became more and more packed as the many peoples and tribes who conjoined to make up vast empires added their deities, and the bureaucracy of heaven expanded to match the increasing complexity of society below. Yet the contrivance of many polytheistic systems doubtless brought them subtly out of synchronization with the natural images of the psyche within. No such overloaded pantheon could truly match the psyche of any particular individual. True, imperial polytheism, through its patronage of art and story, often enhanced the individuality of the gods. But that did not belie the deep-seated urge for some pivot, some sovereign center of meaning and supreme image, which would bring all things into order. Before that transition could happen, with all its gain and loss, the ancient spiritual crisis had to be exacerbated by the discovery of history, which made the old chaos of gods seem not only confusing but menacing.

Like that of the scriptural text that was to become so prominent a feature of the Great Religions, its direct background was the invention of writing. At first, script may have been mostly of commercial use, but in time, it recorded history and sacred words of power. Combined with ancient oral traditions of holy myth and mantic formulas, whose very sounds held transcendent energy, writing captured the words surrounding the pivotal moment of sacred history. To this day, the most sacred power of the text, though written, is oral and auditory: the solemn reading of scripture in religious service, the chanting, recitation, or singing of Bible, Veda, or Koran. Yet the application of writing created the religious icon of the sacred text, a locus of the sacred that, though perhaps dimly foreshadowed in the pictograph or the hieroglyphic charm, is essentially coeval with the Great Religions.

The discovery of history was a consequence of record keeping. Though at first perhaps no more than a succession of kings and victories, even the most primitive records would have engendered a sense of things changing and not changing back. Recorded events were always in danger of moving beyond mythical models to become unique and irreversible events in our time which must be handled by us for our day. Even a chronicle of kings can tell us that our kings are but epigoni of great progenitors, but they can also tell us that those predecessors lived in a time within history like ours, not in some mythical *illud tempus*.

Whether recorded or not, the disruption of local patterns by empires like the Greek or Roman or the time of the warring states following on the decline of the Zhou dynasty in China could not but bring home to ordinary people the vicissitudes of time as now experienced and remembered. Human life, needless to say, has always been uncertain, but now its disruptions came from peoples much farther away than the next valley, people of queer tongue and strange gods, who might carry off captives or demand that the community plant new crops and give the first fruits to an alien lord. Such events would be unique, and unique events—whether conquering armies, plague, or famine—were usually bad for ordinary people. The discovery of history therefore carried with it on many levels (from dislocation in the realm of psychic images to disasters with which one had to cope) what Eliade called the terror of history, the fear of onrushing irreversible time, full of uncertainty and probably horror. It was this with which the custodians of the sacred now had to contend.

The maintenance of religion in the ancient empires was essentially the province of the priestly/bureaucratic class responsible for the state's orderly functioning: the scribes of Egypt, the *shih* of old China. Honoring structure and continuity above all, it pleased them to place above the personal gods an eternal regulative principle. Ma'at, Rta, or Tao ordered the universe, even as particular kings were but the shadow of the principle of kingship. In the ancient imperial cosmogonies, creation and apocalypse were clearly less welcome than order; to creation, they significantly preferred in practice a primal metahistorical era of model kings or sage emperors who represented imperishable paradigms for the present. But now, time as change threatened to run out of control, off the regulative tracks, and destroy the timeless.

The discovery of history was thus a crucial challenge to religion, at least as crucial as that posed millennia earlier by the discovery of agriculture and the new orientation of humanity to the earth. Religion had, as always, pointed to realities transcendent over self and world, realities before which those entities could only be contingent. In earlier cosmic religion, time was itself contingent, a matter of cosmic religion's "eternal return." Now that the temporal process was seen as one-way, irreversible, time itself became nearer to the center of reality, whether divine or demonic. Religion then had to handle in some way the reality of irreversible time and its correlate, the possibility that humans can make individual, irreversible choices within it or, conversely, suffer its unpredictable terrors involuntarily.

Moreover, as historical religions, the founder faiths are intended to carry out purposeful action in history, and purpose means choice. They are well aware that as they fulfill their purposes, some historical forces are with them and some are against the divine or cosmic mandate; the world is divided, and one must choose. This historical dualism, and the need for radical choice by nations and persons, is taken to a new level by the Discovery of History religions; it goes with their new understanding of history as the arena of revelation and salvation. This concept is important to comprehending their role in the history in which they live and which in large part they have themselves made.

Like the earlier agricultural challenge, historical time was profoundly unwelcome to religion, threatening its most fundamental structures and seeming to open the door to its oldest and greatest enemy, cosmic chaos. It implied a world wherein no law or god was in charge, and anything, however bad, could happen without reason or regard to moral deserts. Indeed, so awesome was the terror of historical time that most ancients could not, or did not, face it full and put in place a counterfoil to its horror. They reacted without entirely realizing what the enemy was. Nonetheless, an examination of important features of religion in the Discovery of History era, the Axial Age, suggests the nature of the age's deep-seated spiritual crisis. Responses to history follow four main strands, sometimes separate alternatives and sometimes intertwined: epic, ritual, the religious founders, and wisdom.

Epic

One response is to accept history but to see it as the unfolding of divine purpose—the triumph of a particular people or dynasty, the defeat of the powers of darkness by God. Thus history, with its wars and tribulations, is granted reality, but its terror is defanged by transcendent purpose. Much of the great narrative literature of the era of the Discovery of History has this basic motif: the historical and prophetic books of the Hebrew Scriptures, the Kojiki in Japan, the Aeneid.

Ritual

Another response is to keep certain rites, such as those of a court, a city, or an official priesthood and its shrines, unchanged as a sort of frozen perpetuation of the past before the discovery of history. Thus, representing one area of experience untouched by the ambiguities of historical time, timeless ritual becomes a counterweight to history. In ancient Rome, the institution of the vestal virgins and the sacrifices of the city's official priesthood remained virtually unchanged through all the historical vicissitudes of the empire until the triumph of Christianity. In ancient Japan, an imperial princess was sent far away from the court to the Saigu, or abstinence palace, near the Grand Shrine of Ise, the Shinto shrine of the imperial ancestral deities. There she avoided all Buddhist practice and even words. She thus represented in her Shinto purity and ritual acts the court not as it was, but as it would like to be seen by the primordial gods.

The Religious Founders

The most consequential response to the Discovery of History, however, and the most momentous religious event of the millennium beginning around the fifth century B.C.E. was the life and work of the great religious founders. Only a half-dozen or so persons have filled this awesome vocation, becoming the pivotal figures of religions embracing hundreds of millions of persons, washing over vast geographical areas, and lasting fifteen to twenty-five centuries. They are Zoroaster, the Buddha, Confucius, Lao-tze, Jesus, and Muhammad. (Others, especially the Hebrew lawgivers and prophets, and the Vedantic sages of India, have had a comparable role within their traditions.) Although their stories are encrusted with myth and legend, with the possible exception of Lao-tze they were undoubtedly real persons, and all incarnate in the way in which the person—though he may point beyond himself—has become the central focus of the new religious style. Three of them—the Buddha, Jesus, and Muhammad—knowingly or not, went an important step beyond the others by founding the world's three major missionary and transcultural religions, faiths that went far outside the boundaries of their homelands to draw the bulk of their adherents from distant places and become the foundational religion of many otherwise diverse cultures.

In all cases, the founder represents a fresh response to history. The other responses are little more than a special case of characteristics of primordial religion, but the major religious founder is a new development, and so far as we know, one unique to his millennium, unknown before and since. At the dawn of history as we know it, he represents a person who, while living in a discrete, identifiable moment of historical time, exemplifies or communicates a reality far greater than it, to which historical time is subject. The message is encapsulated in scripture and perpetuated through sacred gestures, acts, and institutions: sacraments, forms of prayer, ethical values; sangha, church, ulama, mandarins.

By making the life of a single individual the pivot of history, the founder religions acknowledge history's irreversible movement and at the same time give it a sharply focused central axis. As they emphasize the drama of a single and unique life as the bearer of revelation, they show that now, in the more complex, diversified, and uncertain life of a "modern" society, the significant individual—and not just tribal custom—is what counts. This is reflected all the more in the fact that these religions, although much fortified by institutionalization, have in one way or another given recognition to the importance of individual response to their claims. The new personalism is displayed in the prominence given to such themes as karma or judgment: each individual is held individually accountable for his or her faith and life, and receives individually appropriate reward or retribution. In earlier religion, such individual reckoning was usually far hazier, more likely a tribal matter than truly personal. With the advent of the saving person as the central religious symbol comes the corresponding reality of the individually accountable person's responding to it. We will return later to the theme of the religious founder.

Wisdom

Another way of transcending the onslaughts of historical time is through absolutizing states of consciousness or philosophical realizations in which the timeless manifests its incomparable superiority over temporality and history. Thus, mysticism and mystical metaphysics, emphasizing the oneness of all things with the Absolute and the illusory nature of conditioned reality, were potent forces in the period of the Discovery of History. In India, at approximately the same time as the emergence of the founders, sages in the tradition that was to become Hinduism produced such works as the Upanishads and the Bhagavad Gita. In them, the central theme is the inner unity of the individual self, who seems to suffer the vicissitudes of time and history, with the supreme Self, who changes not. In the West, philosophers such as those of the Platonic and Neoplatonic movements offered broadly comparable visions, declaring that inwardly blending the self with the One like two rings conjoining was better than clamoring after the empty glories of empires rising and falling with the tides of history. In time, their contemplative vision was itself to be joined with the historical stream of Judaism and the Western founder religions, Christianity and Islam.

In the founder faiths, a reaction in favor of mysticism and wisdom tended to set in long after the founder's day in the second stage of a religion's development, the Wisdom/Imperial stage. The wise came to urge a perspective that stressed the timeless, divine essence behind the temporal career of the historical founder. Thus, in Buddhism, the Mahayana movement tended to downplay the historical Buddha in favor of realizing one's own buddhahood through oneness with the eternal Dharmakaya, the universal essence. Christianity, especially in the Greek theologians and mystics, and Islam also, moved through a "wisdom" stage in which the deepest emphasis was on grasping with mystically illuminated insight the eternal reality of God that underlay the particulars of the revelation through Jesus or Muhammad.

The founder religions and what they implied about the human carried the day. The other responses to the crisis of the Discovery of History, in the end, were largely incorporated into them or into their Judaic and Hindu equivalents. The founder religions made use of epic, especially as prolegomena showing how God or destiny prepared for the supreme revelation in the sacred person—as in Christianity's use of the Hebrew Scriptures or the Buddhist popularity of the Jataka tales, stories of the founder's previous lives. Each founder religion generously employed ritual with its sacred time and space to perpetuate the memory of the founder and indeed to recreate spiritually the time when his holy feet walked the earth. As we have seen, these faiths also acquired mystical dimensions.

The ruling image was the founder, the transcendent with a human face. Millennia after the obscurity of the few human beings who shared the cave paintings with magnificent animals and the potent yet stereotyped roles of shamans and sacred kings, sacred revelation emerged in the form of a person of distinctive character and appeal, capable of saying or doing unexpected things that nonetheless made surprising sense when all put together.

The rare founder vocation calls for an especially comprehensive religious personality. The founder must himself be an image that mirrors and brings together in a convincing new pattern the diverse spiritual needs and aspirations of his day. Characteristically, he appears at a time when important changes are afoot in his society, through powerful intercultural contact like that of Aryan and Dravidian in the Buddha's day, or the Hellenistic mix in Jesus' time, or through dynastic decline and civil war, as in Confucius's and Lao-tse's era. The old order is seen by many to be outmoded; events have shattered its framework and splintered its light. In times like these, religious language and symbol are still effective, but a half-conscious awareness has come that they must be shaped into new configurations, illuminated from a fresh angle and reinforced by a powerful new symbol of legitimacy and authority to work today.

At the same time, the new religion must maintain enough symbols of continuity with the former established religion to be able to draw on its legitimacy, as did Christianity with Judaism or Confucianism with the old "Sinism" of the *Book of Rites*. It must not offend the many for whom too sharp a break with the spiritual past, at least on the level of symbol and practice, would be highly disconcerting. Rather, the new founder faith does best when it can show that the new does not reject but instead fulfills the old, bringing out its plenary but thus far unspoken potential so that people can say, "This was really true all the time, but we didn't realize it till now." The Buddha, therefore, did not directly attack the brahmins or the Vedas, but instead implied that what he taught merely perfected what was already a tendency within Hinduism, to emphasize inner enlightenment rather than priesthood or rite.

The effective founder, then, must follow a very delicate tack, one neither too radical nor too conservative, revealing something significant that is new while maintaining a sense of meaningful continuity with what went before. Like Jesus, he must fulfill rather than destroy the Law and the Prophets; like the Buddha, he may teach his listeners to be lamps unto themselves, finding their own salvation through meditation and the unblinking analysis of the Four Noble Truths, while exercising discretion in his relations with authority and following the familiar ancient way of the wandering ascetic and sage.

Likewise, the founder must be spiritually accessible to a wide spectrum of the people. Again, like Jesus and the Buddha, he must be able to appeal to the poor and voice some of their concerns, while also winning friends and supporters among the elite, even among the established priestly class. He must have a message both for the general public and for a loyal, closely knit band of disciples who will be a nucleus of the institutionalization of his work. He must have something for those of the activist and contemplative temper. He must appeal to both men and women.

All these imposing qualities were necessary for the founders of the Axial Age in their great task of transforming religion from its archaic cosmic, communal nature to the Great Religions of history. At the same time, we must recognize that the founder does not so much radically innovate as redirect and revalorize religious motifs already present. He himself is but a "super" version of the immemorial shaman and priest; his scriptures are but a written extension of archaic myth, chronicle, chant, and god-possessed mutterings. Indeed, at least some of his scriptures, like the Confucian classics and the Hebrew Bible known to Jesus, already may have been written and canonized. Few specific symbols and practices of the Great Religions are wholly new to them. Like the cosmic religion themes of Christmas, they simply take on new meanings and slightly new configurations while maintaining the overtones of the old.

Nonetheless, the Great Religions make a new departure. Besides centering on a new way of the individual person, both of the founder and of those who individually turn to him as the focus of spiritual power and revelation, they embody a constellation of distinctively presented, if not entirely novel, features that cast a long ray of light down the religious future. These are a sacred moment in historical time, a single central personal symbol, a definite canon of scripture, a definite process of salvation, and definite models of human nature and ultimate reality.

A Sacred Moment in Historical Time

As we have seen for the cosmic type of religion, whether it is the old Babylonian and Egyptian or Shinto today, the major festival is New Year's. Its celebration suggests a symbolic return to primordial chaos and a recapitulation of creation, the ritual defeat of the monster of chaos by the hero or the lighting of a new fire. The Great Religions, while acknowledging the first creation, make central the second creation, the time of the founder and the saving events associated with him. Distinctive events in historical time define these religions' experience and mark their sacred calendars: Passover;

Wesak, commemorating the Buddha's birth and enlightenment; Christmas and Easter; the Islamic month of the hajj. The events behind them are akin to the creation of a world, and in a sense they are even greater than that primal act, for they are both the culmination of the creation and the rectification of what went wrong with it.

A Single Central Personal Symbol

We have already discussed the transformative significance of the emergence of the archetypal person as the supreme medium of revelation, of making the universe humanly meaningful, in the Great Religions. We must emphasize that even the appearance of gods as beings full of "human" personality and capable of emotional interaction with humans (as in Hindu bhakti or the variegated Taoist pantheon) rather than as one-dimensional archetypes or centers of sheer numinosity was broadly speaking a product of the same Axial Age that produced the founders, or even a consequence of it.

A Definite Canon of Scripture

Precursors of the role of scripture in the Great Religions of course exist, such as the Pyramid Texts of Egypt and the orally transmitted Vedas of India. The place of texts in the Great Religions, however, is special. They are not timeless power formulas or myths, but words coming directly out of the sacred event, whether narratives leading up to or embracing it, or the discourse of the founder himself, or letters and tracts of his close disciples. Characteristically, in the Great Religions, the canon of scripture is more sharply defined than in even those archaic faiths that were literate; in the former, one knows precisely which texts are "in" and which are "out."

This definiteness is of a piece with the Great Religions' drive toward a high level of self-definition in many areas. They want to make clear who is a member of each and who is not, who is saved and who is not, what is true and what is heresy, where the boundaries are on all dimensional planes. Scripture confirms that the right doctrines, practices, and institutions are not merely subjective or ambiguous realities, but can be demarcated publicly and verbally. Further, it shows they are clearly connected to historical events—the same events that produced the founder and the subsequent canon—and that they clearly define one's role as a physical or spiritual soldier in the armies of light.

Although views regarding the exact nature of scriptural authority vary both within and between Great Religions, all believers would grant that their sacred texts possess a unique authority setting them apart from all other books and requiring that their words be received with special reverence. As both parent and child of such a unique book, the authority of the Great Religion itself is ratified. Indeed, the whole issue of authority in religion is raised to a new pitch as the authority of priesthoods (or ministeriums) and scriptures intermix; the assertion of objective truth in religion often rises to high prominence as well when the Great Religions define themselves as truth and authority versus error and chaos.

Definite Process of Salvation

Similar to the enhancement of scriptural authority in the Great Religions is the process of the definition of teaching concerning salvation. First we must note that, unlike much tribal and archaic religion, the Great Religions tend to emphasize individual salvation in this life and the life to come. A growing trend in this direction in archaic religion—whether in the soteriology of the Hellenistic mystery religions or the growing stress on karma and reincarnation in India—is part of the background of the great faiths. The Axial Age, with its crisis of emergent individual awareness, posed the question before submitting the final answers.

As in the case of the terror of history, the full dimensions of the abyss of radical individualism opens up, with its potential for ultimate choice and ultimate aloneness, only to transcend them in the same thought: in heaven, in nirvana, in the Tao, in the Confucian good society. The Great Religions have thus centered on single simple sure keys to salvation out of the terrors of history and individualism: faith in Christ, love of God, submission to God's will, meditation. Techniques have varied within religions themselves, involving controversy and different practice on the role of sacraments, bhakti devotionalism, or lay and monastic versions of Buddhism. But the individual believer is usually presented with a clear path to salvation, if he or she chooses to follow it, by priests and preachers.

Definite Models of Human Nature and Ultimate Reality

The path to salvation in the Great Religions applies an equally definite model to the relation of human and divine nature, though its doctrinal articulation may undergo development. A fundamental model or root metaphor will appear: the human being as child of God, a wave on the sea of infinite reality, the product of karma. God will be seen in corresponding terms, as personal deity, as impersonal Absolute, as the negation of all conditioned reality.

These concepts, like the others, help define the religion and set it over against others. Obviously only one teaching on such final and urgent issues can be correct; those who believe wrongly about God himself do so at their own peril. At the same time, religious beliefs concerning human nature have a powerful—though frequently convoluted rather than straightforward—interaction with the cultures in which they dwell. Art and literature may reflect some aspects of the spiritual view of human nature, engaging with such themes as the moral responsibility of the child of God or the plasticity of the expression of divine infinity; but they characteristically explore it to its ultimate limits and even react against it, yet they may not quite be able to free themselves from the fundamental human image of their culture.

The emergence of the Great Religions entailed spiritual loss as well as gain. Cosmic religion possessed an equilibrium and nuanced sense of the sacred scattered through the universe at an opposite pole from the Great Religions' tendency to focus around single events, symbols, centers of value. The old polytheism was a matter of quality as well as quantity, seeing the divine in a different way from monotheism. It perceived discrete gods in a diversity of places, moods, and persons; in violent and calm, new and old, male and female. Inevitably, something of this quality crept back into the Great Religions in the culti of saints, angels, and heavenly pantheons, yet even those benign principalities and powers were subservient to a single Lord or spiritual path, servants of one who, like the Buddha, was "teacher of gods and men." The Great Religions sacrificed equilibrium for purpose. Rather than answer to all needs or fulfill all potential symbols, they chose those that fit the historical destiny each saw for itself.

A good example is the relative role of male and female. Despite later pious claims to the contrary, in virtually every instance, the rise of the Great Religions meant a marked lessening of feminine presence in spiritual life, on both the symbolic and practical levels.[6] Goddesses, priestesses, and shamanesses alike were displaced by a new faith whose founder was inevitably male, whose disciples and successors in the leadership of the movement were also male, and whose scriptures were written by males.

The social order envisioned by the new faith was also thoroughly patriarchal. In this respect, it did not, to be sure, usually differ from its predecessor, but the male-dominated order was now reinforced by a male deity or equivalent above, whose chief earthly representatives were likewise male. In China, the rise of the Confucian order was marked by decrees against the practices of female shamanesses and "witches"; in the West, the rise of the great monotheistic faiths militated against the cults of Isis and Ishtar. Monasticism, a prominent feature of several of the Great Religions, was likewise antifeminine insofar as it implied the potential completeness of male spirituality and spiritual authority without significant contact with the feminine. The ideal held up even to nuns was usually the overcoming of all that was female and physical in order to approximate, at least, the spiritual male.

Another loss was the sense of reciprocity among religions that characterized cosmic and archaic religion. Although one divine patron might send his clan into war against another, there was a sense in which it was recognized that all gods were more or less the same. One worshiped the gods of wherever one went, and some went so far as to perceive, as Apuleius did of the Great Mother, that they were one going under many names: Isis, Ishtar, Cybele, or Aphrodite. But as we have seen, the Great Religions brought a greater exclusiveness. Faiths were decisively right or wrong. That realization could, of course, be taken as advance insofar as it represented a heightened respect for consistency. As such, it doubtlessly went with the heightened meaning of free, separate individual existence. One defines oneself, at least in part, through consistent behavior and regard for objective truth. Yet some might feel that the older religions better appreciated the limits of logical rigor in exploring the world of the spirit.

To balance off the losses, however, was a great new reality. Religion was now set on a relatively fast and irreversible course of historical development. Each Great Religion began with an implicit program, a history ready to unfold expeditiously. The plus was that the religion then had some capacity both to vigorously make history and to adjust to changing historical circumstances; the danger was that its program might be exhausted, its coinage all spent, well before the end of world history. But for better or worse, embedded in each Great Religion was the presupposition that (in the postmodernist phrase) a "Grand Narrative" was to be narrated as the religion actively took on its task of doing the will of God, converting the world and building the ideal society.

CHAPTER FOUR
THE DEVELOPMENT OF THE GREAT RELIGIONS

Once the Axial Age religions emerged, what changes did they go through, and why did these changes occur?

Religious change is governed by two basic forces, pressure internal to the religion and pressure external to it. Needless to say, they are in complex interaction. Yet, to analyze them, we must first separate them, then consider them both historically as well as individually. We need to try to discern when or in what ways a religion is changing because of needs inherent in its own structure and history, and when it is responding to forces in its environment. Admittedly, the issue will rarely be simple in practice. Religions may be forced to respond to outside circumstances that they themselves had a hand in creating, and a changing world may affect deep subjective feelings that the experiencer believes are purely religious. However, on both individual and historical levels, the effort needs to be made to sort out internal and external pressures. Religions have their own internal developmental agendas, which are based on the program implicit to their basic vision; in addition, they respond to changes in the world around them.

The social scientific study of religion has tended to emphasize the role of the external force. In the study of new religious movements, a long tradition assigns their origin to intercultural tensions and conditions of repression, or "relative deprivation." As far back as 1913, Alexander F. Chamberlain wrote of "new religions" occurring as a product of the meeting of native and "higher" peoples. The new faiths, he said, make use of incompletely understood ideas brought by traders, settlers, missionaries, and colonial officials.[1]

In 1943, Ralph Linton described "nativist movements." In contrast to the attempted assimilation of Chamberlain's "new religions," nativist movements are "any conscious, organized attempt on the part of a society's members to revive or perpetuate selected aspects of its culture" when the society is undergoing rapid change; as in the Native American Ghost Dance, the perpetuated cultural features are of highly symbolic (if not magical) value.[2] Anthony F. C. Wallace presented what he called a "revitalization movement" typically started by a charismatic prophet to construct "a more satisfying culture" in times of cultural disorientation.[3] In the same way, Neil J. Smelser's "value-oriented movement" arises in times of ferment and stress and when alternative—that is, nonreligious—means for reconstructing the social situation are perceived as unavailable.[4] These perceptions of new religious movements, like many others that could be cited, presuppose a "crisis-response" view of their generation and, more broadly, a view of religion as a passive but fluid entity only responding to external pressures.

This understanding, however, leaves some unanswered questions regarding new religious movements and religion as a whole. First, it does not explain why some crises or stress, some situations of rapid social change, and some apparent discrediting of old values produce new religious movements and others do not. Japan's devastation and defeat in World War II, for example, is widely held to have set the stage for Japan's postwar exfoliation of new religions, yet no comparable phenomenon took place in its erstwhile allies, Germany and Italy.

On the other hand, some new religions appear to arise spontaneously or out of opportunity, rather than from any discernible crisis much beyond the normal anxiety of human affairs. One thinks of the rise of Spiritualism, Adventism, and communal movements in the young American republic of the 1840s, or the growth of new religious movements in the "youth culture" of the 1960s, which—despite tension over Vietnam and civil rights—was not a time of trauma comparable to that suffered by colonialized peoples or Japan in 1945.

Several critics have pointed out that crisis-response models fail adequately to take into account that religious movements are, after all, *religious*. Bryan Wilson writes that although the preservation of a threatened culture or the creation of a new society may be implicit in a religious movement, it is not usually the group's own main intention or principal feature. In the religionist's own mind, the *religious* objectives of giving salvation, magical power, or heightened mystical experience have preeminence.[5]

H. Byron Earhart, writing on the new religions of Japan, argues that a religious tradition has long-standing needs and drives of its own that cannot be overlooked in understanding why a movement derivative from it has arisen or taken the form that it has.[6] We would agree, noting that this case is particularly congruent with the long histories of the Great Religions. Although their origins certainly express potential latent in religion from the human beginning, they may rightly be understood historically as a response both to the crisis engendered by the discovery of history and to all the secular factors that went into the enhancement of individualism—noting with Wilson, however, that their own conscious intention put it in the form of salvation and sacred experience. But the religions' subsequent history is surely as much an exploration of potential forms of expression implicit in the faith from its inception as it is a response to external vicissitudes. The real pressure is very often from within, much like a balloon being inflated; the outer circumstances may shape its form, particularly by setting limits to what is culturally acceptable.

Buddhism, for instance, began as a religion whose central practice was the concentration or meditation that stops the suffering/desire syndrome. The implicit question was therefore: What is meditation? Is any practice that stops mental action and so frees one from the mental roots of suffering and desire meditation in the Buddhist sense? The historical answer came as Buddhism explored several "at the limits" possibilities: the quasi-magical rituals of Vajrayana, the simple act of faith of Pure Land, Nichiren chanting.

Religions explore "development of doctrine" possibilities such as these not only because various interpretive options may be more or less congruent with the several cultures into which the faith moves, but also because individuals attracted to the faith are eager to know what it can do. They want to discover what new kinds of experience it can offer and what classes of surety it provides. Honen, the Japanese father of Pure Land Buddhism, said that he had read the Buddhist canon of scripture five times, but found no peace until, through faith in Amida Buddha's vow to save all who called upon his name, he depended on *tariki,* the power of another, rather than *jiriki,* one's own power. It was, to be sure, a time of strife and change in medieval Japan. Yet for this quiet, reclusive monk the battle was inward and involved a search toward the far limits of Buddhist meaning. For him, *tariki,* though not meditation in any customary sense, most adequately fulfilled its promise for him because it expressed, through depending on another rather than on oneself for salvation, the ultimate meaning of Buddhist negation of the ego. Salvation through faith was therefore truly at the heart of Buddhism, though it took the religion many centuries fully to realize this, as we have noted in connection with Newman's development of doctrine idea.

Religious change is basically induced when subjective experience is found dissonant with the religion's practical reification. Honen, like Luther, came to experience his religion's ritual and institutionalization to be at odds with what he inwardly knew the same religion to mean. As we have seen, religion is fundamentally the story of images linking the subjective world with the social reification of the same, in rites and public ideas and in institutions dealing with the transcendent and the human place in the cosmos. But what happens when distance appears between inner and outer, whether because of social change or the individual's own need to explore?

Change must then take place to get them together. The person may first try to change subjectively; but if this does not work and if pressure does not relent, he or she will be driven to change the outer instead, thus shaping it to fit the subjective model. Often the extent of change can be minimized, and many innocuous symbols of continuity can be maintained; at other times, major rearrangements are called for, since it has become important not only to tinker with the outer expressions of reality but also to adopt a new flag—to symbolically stress invigorating change rather than reassuring continuity. Either way, change takes place, and change makes history.

The Great Religions are *religions with a history*. They have a history not only from the point of view of the outside observer—from which all religions, however "cosmic," have histories inasmuch as things have happened in them over time—but they also have a history because the idea of history is inherent in their own inner experience. Their scriptures, shrines, chronicles, churches, and temples all posit as their reason for being events that happened in real historical time. Perhaps some of those histories are mythical, but they are nonetheless significant for the view of time they assume. The Christian cult of the saints, which replaced the polytheistic gods and goddesses of archaic Mediterranean religion, differed from what went before in several important respects. The saints represented the sacred in human flesh, not divine nature, and moreover in the flesh of persons who had acted significantly at specific times and places in human history—as martyrs, apostles, bishops.[7]

One must realize that history is not a given, nor is it a work of nature unaided. It is a human phenomenon, a product of human consciousness both as process and as awareness of that process. Just as history as we know it unveils the expanding scope of human awareness and ability as we move from one tier of civilization to another, so thinking of the process *as history*—as irreversible and accelerating change—is a way of thinking associated with one stage of that process. In other words, there is a history of history. Like religion, it is an image relating the human to the ultimate, grounded in subjectivity and projected on the world as it interprets the world.

Marxism may be the last and most rigorous attempt to reify the history image as objectively true in the outer world just as it is in its subjective sources and in reflection. But the Great Religions have gone in the same direction, perceiving irreversible divine purpose in the drift of events. We have noted how deconstructionism and postmodernism have endeavored to counter that perception, arguing in effect that in fact the universe, including the human universe, is naught but radical pluralism. It is a diverse collection of happenings and human experiences with no more than free-associational links from one to another. But by believing in their own histories, the Great Religions have made history, both as fact and as concept.

It is interesting to compare the Great Religions' unitary view of history and of ultimate reality with the pluralism of such post-Jungians as James Hillman and Robert Avens, whom we have already mentioned and who are clearly linked to postmodernism. Here human consciousness is a labyrinthine cavern of images with neither beginning nor end, though the light may shift from one to another. In the eyes of the post-Jungians, as therapists of the soul, the great human temptation is to see, or rather force, unity (monism) that subordinates one entity for the sake of another, instead of seeing and living each image just as it is. Hillman has argued against the constricting role of the idea of an ego, which he identifies with the hero figure, conquering and overcoming. As heroes, we "ascend" at the cost of not fulfilling potential for multiplicity and diversity, and ultimately our conquests are futile, as the human ego, however heroic, in the end goes down to Sheol. Wholeness, for Hillman, is not this sort of sterile ego integrity; rather, it is a self at home with a multiplicity of imaginal presentations, each received with joy in its own time. It envisions a human life as the embodiment of a sequence of many gods. Hillman declares, "Polytheistic psychology would not suspend the commandment to have 'no other gods before me,' but would extend that commandment for each mode of consciousness." [8]

Understandably, Hillman is skeptical of ideas of "spiritual growth" as a project of the imperial ego, as he is of the notion that we ought to keep "growing till we are in the grave." This idea is merely a fixation on the maturation process of childhood and youth. Adult life is not progressing "to" anything; rather, it is ideally the subtly and infinitely varied rounds of experience afforded by fulfilled relationships and fertility on both the psychic and biological planes.

In this light, the Great Religions are adolescent religions. Indeed, that image illuminates much about them: their thirst for truth and commitment, their need to organize the world, their preoccupation with the ego-self and its problematic, their view of historical and personal time as an area for "growth" and the attainment of success up to the ultimate conquest of all rivals. The Great Religions, like "moderns" of all stamps, want to perceive in history, especially religious history, a unity of direction in what may really be an infinite array of image events in jumbled relation to one another. Such events are not exactly random, yet neither do they move in anything so simple as "straight-line" cause and effect.

Careful history itself brings out this jumbled diversity of cause and effect. "Grand Narrative" styles of historical writing, like that of Gibbon, have assumed that the Christian cult of saints was a replacement for the old polytheism. Detail work shows that the saints were not always old gods with new names. Although the assertion may contain broad truth, as Newman recognized in *Our Lady*, saint-honor developed differently in different places and was consciously more closely related to Roman concepts of friendship and patronage than it was to polytheism.[9] It was an animation of new ranges of faces in the cavern of images as much as the replacement of old with new in the same ranks.

The unity of history is itself an image, as real as any other in the imaginal world between spirit and flesh. But like all images *in* human history and like most in individual human life, it has its mysterious rise, its development by association with other images, and its decay. The last stage, the Folk Religion stage, is represented by the final collapse of a religion into remnants, isolated myths, and folk practice—the breakdown of a unified image into separate images as the unity is no longer sustainable, presumably because the religion is no longer the focal symbol of a unified heroic ego in a sufficient number of believers. For example, in folk religion in China, few people "are" Buddhists or Confucianists in the sense many Christians are Christian; that is, they do not exclusively hold heroic images of the Buddha or the Sage as the central focus of their inner lives, though certainly fragmented Buddhist and Confucian stories, practices, and attitudes remain potent. (In the same way, certain images in one's personal life—about oneself, one's relationships, one's beliefs—may fragment as disconfirmations accumulate and alternative images arise.)

Great Religions sink down to Sheol because of such an exhaustion of their original unifying language. They are ordinarily unable to accept nonunifying language by permitting themselves in polytheistic manner to be only one image of the sacred among many, since their original and ruling rationale was to unify subjective and outer images in one master image, one sovereign God, savior of all, or "teacher of gods and men." As we shall see, the last stage of a Great Religion evolves as Folk Religion when, though unacknowledged, the master image has fragmented and when the bonds linking religious imagery and the major institutions of society have also frayed or snapped.

Although the Great Religions have a sense of history, revelation, and mission in history, they are open as well as closed to historical change. A conservative mandate, desiring only to maintain faith with the original revelation, can be found in all, and it is expressed by factions often labeled "traditionalist" or "fundamentalist." But such a mandate must coexist with another notion inspired by the original opening: that new revelation *can* come in historical time, at the right *kairos.* A sense that religion can and must adapt to changing conditions while remaining true to its sources goes with acceptance of history, and it must therefore consort with the limiting principle that only a certain amount of protean flexibility is latent in that fidelity. This point is the source of endless conflict, and no one will know what a faith's full potential was until a its last drop of life has drained into the sands of time. But since it stemmed from a single historical moment and a single definitive revelation, presumably each Great Religion had some limit to how far it could adapt and still be itself in any meaningful way. Do all religions reach a point where they can adapt no more?

Before dealing with this question, we must turn to the story of the Great Religions themselves and their historical vicissitudes. Our study of the history of the Great Religions will be based on a model that proposes they develop through five stages over a historical trajectory of some twenty-five hundred years, though the length of each stage may vary considerably. These stages are Apostolic, Wisdom and Imperial, Devotional, Reformation, and Folk Religion. As we have suggested, progress through these stages, although deeply affected by external conditions, is not wholly governed by response to them; it also follows an internal logic of religious history.

They are, in our view, the natural succession of ways a religion, fundamentally a response to the Discovery of History crisis, develops the potential for expression latent in itself. All the stages refer back in some way to the problem of historical time, but they also deal with a dissonance left unresolved by the preceding stage, that is, a sense that the earlier stage's potential has been exhausted.

At the same time, all of these religions carried over a great deal of sacred baggage from previous religious eras, going back to the Paleolithic. They *are* religions, and they emerged in a time when religious ways of thinking and symbol making were not widely questioned. The "dialectic of the sacred," the impingement of the supernatural on human life, the efficacy of rite, the power of holy scripture, and the necessity of state religion—all were powerful in the affairs of king and peasant alike in the Discovery of History era, despite Greek skeptics and cynics, Chinese "legalists" and hedonists, and Indian Carvaka materialists. Though a new kind of religion, the Great Religions nonetheless easily slipped into traditional forms of expression, albeit with new messages and new particulars, while providing foci around which all manner of things new and old, from sacred wells to metaphysical models, could be consolidated. As they accomplished this task, they permeated their environing society, then they inevitably generated a new kind of society and a fresh cultural wave that changed the old and went on to bring vast new populations into history.

The supreme examples of this kind of religion are the three great truly international and cross-cultural faiths, all also founder religions: Buddhism, Christianity, and Islam. In addition, the traditional Chinese religious system—with Confucianism as its elite expression and its further mix of Taoism, Buddhism, ancestrism, and local culti—also has founders and in large part shares the same paradigm.

Historical Hinduism must also be considered a Great Religion for our purposes, though unlike the others, it has no historical founder and therefore it is impossible to pinpoint a moment of origin. For our purposes, it is best to regard it as having started as a Great Religion, comparable to the others, around the first century C.E., at about the same time as Christianity. This was the era of the texts that have set the tone of all later Hinduism: the later Upanishads, the Bhagavad-Gita, the Laws of Manu, the yoga Sutras. To them, the earlier Vedas are a sort of Old Testament. This period was the high point of Buddhism in India, against which Hinduism as a religion had to define itself, and it marks the early roots of bhakti and the lore of the great salvationist gods—Vishnu, Krishna, Shiva—who were to color medieval and modern devotional Hinduism so deeply.

On the other hand, no attempt will be made to fit Zoroastrianism, Judaism, and Shinto into the model. The evolution of Zoroastrianism does agree with the pattern for its first thousand years, but its career as a Great Religion was abruptly cut short by the triumph of Islam in its Persian homeland. Judaism and Shinto (and also the smaller Indian religions, Jainism and Skhism), not having become the long-term predominant religion of large culture areas, have had a very different sort of history. Surviving tribal religions also do not fit in, of course. But at least 80 percent of the human race now has, at least as the religion associated with their traditional culture, one of the five for whose destiny this model will be proposed—Buddhism, Chinese religion, Hinduism, Christianity, and Islam.

A special note may be inserted of Judaism. This ancient religion has had a history that is truly unique in the annals of religious history, being ancestral to and therefore in a real sense the equal of no less than two of the five "great" religions. These two religions now embrace nearly half of humankind. Moreover, Judaism succeeded in maintaining its own identity without a homeland, imperial or otherwise, for some two thousand years. Its importance for the history of religion is in certain respects comparable to that of Zoroastrianism, which probably also influenced Judaism's concepts of the afterlife, divine judgment, and the cosmic antagonist of God, and through it Christianity and Islam. Yet Judaism has had a different history from the Persian religion as well, as we have seen. In chapter 11, we return to the pivotal role of Judaism in religious history and the current religious world.

Though the "big five" all came out of the problems and prospects of the Axial Age and thereby reflect a unique era whose like had never come before nor will come again, the five faiths did not arise simultaneously. Buddhism and the Chinese tradition are five hundred years younger. The development of the five has therefore been staggered in relation to one another. They are not all at the same stage of internal evolution, one factor that has not always been taken sufficiently into account by promoters of interreligious dialogue.

If our hypothesis is correct, then in the twentieth and twenty-first centuries we are seeing the effective demise of Buddhism and Chinese religion as major world religions; Christianity and Hinduism are entering their Folk Religion stage, surviving as popular faiths without a corresponding living Great Tradition; and Islam is just entering the Reformation stage, corresponding to the Christianity of the age of Luther, Calvin, and Loyola. Much of the contemporary religious scene does indeed seem to bear out these bold-sounding assertions. We shall return later to a reading of the current religious situation.

As we have indicated, our perspective requires that we take very seriously the self-propelling internal dynamics of a religion, even of a religion lasting as long as twenty-five centuries. We have dealt with the issue of external versus internal stimuli of religious change. In thinking of stages of development of a Great Religion, we need to give due attention to the fact that a religion's response to environing conditions may be different at different times because of internal dynamics in the religion's own history. The extent of a religion's previous history, for example, conditions its self-image and therefore its appreciation of what its options are.

The immediate stimulus for religious change may therefore be external. It is likely to be something in a society's outer world that first suggests the dissonance between inner and outer that requires rectification. But the *way* in which the religion responds will surely be shaped by where it is in its own history. A religion has an internal need to do several things: to explore its full philosophical potential; to engender and interpret mystical experience; to connect with as much as possible of the human emotional range; to inspire art and rite; to offer homely symbols of its power in the humbler walks of life; and finally, when all this becomes too weighty, to find a capacity to reform and simplify itself. These are not needs imposed by external conditions; they are an internal agenda set by the mere fact that the movement is a religion, and it is in the nature of a religion to want to engage such areas of human experience. All have in common that they touch, or are believed to touch, the frontier between the human and the Transcendent, building symbol-laden bridges between the two; no religion worthy of the name could overlook establishing numerous bridgeheads along that boundary, though it may not be able to erect the bridges all at once.

The particular historical stage will determine whether the response to an outer need for change is, say, an increase of its emotional spectrum through devotionalism or the self-simplification of reformation, or *finally* withdrawal to the Folk Religion level, when all the major creative responses inherent in the faith's original charter seem played out.

When a religion is in some alignment with the other major institutions of society, as it was in the medieval situation around the world, its challenge is to complement external hegemony with control of the entire subjective empire. Hence, it advances the wide emotional range of devotionalism—Bernardine and Franciscan piety in Europe, bhakti in India, Sufism in Islam, Vajrayana and Pure Land Buddhism farther East.

When rapport with the other institutions—political, economic, educational—begins to slip from a religion's hands, first subtly yet always felt, the response will be for reformation that seeks simplification, both to regress the overextended complexity of the devotional expression and to give it greater adaptability with the world. Through reformation, faith wants to recover full power in at least part of its world, which was the task of the Protestant Reformation in sixteenth-century Europe, Kamakura Buddhism in Japan, and the current Islamic revolution. It is a complex process of seeking to reestablish the religion's hegemony in a gradually secularizing world through simplification and return to its roots (as understood by the reformers), through purification of society, and by emphasis on faith and will to make faith a force even as outer conditions change.

By way of example, one might consider devotional stage religion in late medieval England and the coming of the Reformation to that land. Eamon Duffy, in *The Stripping of the Altars*, has given us a sympathetic and incomparable picture of the "old" religion and of its systematic destruction under Henry VIII, Edward VI, and Elizabeth I.[10] Duffy argues that, far from being "decadent," as some Protestants have asserted, the old faith was vibrant and vital right up to the time of the break with Rome in the 1534 Act of Supremacy; indeed, despite the rarely popular political imposition of a different kind of churchmanship, it lingered half-underground in local religion at least up to the end of the sixteenth century.

Certainly much in the old "devotional era" faith was colorful, charming, and often deeply moving: Chaucerian pilgrimages; tender devotions to the Blessed Virgin, the saints and the Blessed Sacrament; well-crafted votive offerings and impressive works of charity. Above all, Duffy brings home the close-knit, communal aspect of the pre-reformation parish. One feels little warmth toward the high-handed Tudor functionaries and harsh Protestant divines who, following autocratic orders, desecrated much-loved saints' shrines, forbade popular festivals and folkways, and mocked deeply held beliefs.

Yet at the same time, one cannot but sense that this religion was less than a total expression of all that was potential in Christianity. Like most late devotional-era religion, it tended toward extreme fragmentation toward many different expressions of the sacred: toward this saint and that, the various sacraments and shrines. There was a certain calculated quality in its many lists of sins and virtues, and in the emphasis on the hour of death, requiem masses, and indulgences. Duffy makes a striking and convincing case that the doctrine of purgatory, though itself only medieval as an effective force in popular religion, by the fifteenth and sixteenth centuries was a mainspring of religious life. Aided by accounts of vivid and often horrific visions of purgatorial fires—compare Dante—it summed up the ages' powerful religious imagination, deep anxiety about the afterlife, sense of retributive divine justice, and belief that through a combination of penance and pardon there was ultimate hope. Those who yearned for a more deeply experiential or philosophical expression of religion could turn to the age's rich mystical literature by such writers as Walter Hilton, Julian of Norwich, or the author of the *Cloud of Unknowing*.

This material, profound as it is, was essentially grounded in Christian Neoplatonism, and that was not the only perspective from which the Christian inner life can be seen. Medieval Neoplatonism, like Sufism, Zen, or Advaita Vedanta, pierced the mystic clouds above their religions' respective devotional eras. These interior castles were perhaps loftier and certainly more universalistic than the Reformations and counter-Reformations to follow. They strove to surge into the divine mystery beyond all names and concepts. Reformation-era theology, however, focused instead on those names by which prayers are heard and by which salvation is given—that is, names to be written in one's heart by grace and held there by faith, to the exclusion of all others.

Yet this experience was one the religion needed for its own completion. It was the necessary historical counterbalance to devotional diversity, and it was the grounding of mysticism in the knowledge of a single simple sure key to salvation. This key, unlike mystical excursions, was available to everyone anywhere: the peasant in his fields, the shopkeeper at his counter, even the soldier in the field of battle. Its use required neither pilgrimage nor masses nor even developing in oneself adequate devotional fervor. It had to come.

Late-medieval Christianity itself was unconsciously preparing to explore new ways of being Christian. Certain novelties were emerging in prereformation England alongside the old Catholic faith. There was a growing interest in preaching. Famous preachers drew large crowds and were much adulated. Abetted by the invention of printing, the publication and reading of religious literature grew, including some desire for Bibles. On the spiritual fringes, "heretical" groups like the Lollards openly criticized the institutional church and agitated for reforms along "biblical" and later Protestant lines.

Certainly the English reformation could have been done much better than it was One feels, however, that it was also part of an agenda within Christendom itself for further exploration of the religion's potential, one not only externally imposed by the king's marital problems, which could lead to a new kind of inwardness, centering on the "one-pointed" experience of faith and grace and answering (is it did for Luther) to unresolved late medieval anxieties, while in the process destroying much that was fair. Yet one can hardly imagine England without the kind of religious experience eventually given voice by John Bunyan and John Milton, George Fox, John Wesley, and William Temple; or the religious world without the diversity of denominations that went out from England to North America and around the world.

It seems to be a law, of a piece with the overall irreversibility of historical time, that once a certain response has been massively implemented in a Great Religion's history, it cannot be tried again in the same way, no more than one can step into the same river twice or return to an earlier stage of one's life. The present author himself was raised in the sort of Anglo-Catholic Episcopalianism that sought to create a highly romanticized version of as much of fifteenth-century English religion as was possible in the gritty cities and windswept plains of mid-twentieth-century America. Perhaps it was along the lines of Henry Adams' famous chapter, "The Virgin and the Dynamo," in his *Education of Henry Adams*, in which he seems to argue that since the United States, as a child of the Enlightenment, has no direct connection with medievalism, for that very reason medievalism's utility on this side of the Atlantic lies in the escape it provides from the harsh realities of the modern world. An inner, spiritual medieval realm was, for Americans, a place in which to locate the antimodern self that we must all have for our own sanity as we live outwardly in the world of the dynamo. I myself, in the fairyland atmosphere of Anglo-Catholicism, with its soft candles and sacring bells, have felt powerfully and poignantly the appeal of this case. Nonetheless, it must be acknowledged that such religions of romantic reaction rarely succeed for long. It seems not enough simply to hold the virgin and the dynamo as thesis and antithesis; eventually there must be either a Hegelian synthesis at a higher level or, as in the Axial Age, some new kind of religious center altogether.

Later we shall speculate on whether Christianity or Buddhism could undergo a second reformation, though one based on a different central focus than the justification by faith of the last reformation of both; this would be as close as one might come to a repetition of a religion's history. More broadly, once history is discovered, it becomes a part of the human way of being in the world, and there is no stopping its momentum. In time, then, all the responses to historical circumstances and to its internal needs that are possible within a religion's finite potential, as defined by its identifying structures, are exhausted.

The legitimacy of such a view of history based on predictable stages needs to be addressed. From Hegel to Marx to Spengler and Toynbee, those who have subjected history to schematization and stages have played to mixed reviews. Like the earlier Joachim of Flora and the late prophets of a "Greening of America" and an Aquarian Age, they have in the end usually been seen as revealing more about the hopes and fears of their own age than about the veiled future. As we have seen, such schemes can also easily be identified (though I think not quite accurately) with the

Grand Narratives condemned by postmodernists.

Nonetheless, the pattern of stages in the history of a Great Religion advanced here differs from the foregoing by depending on no grand mystical idea of meaning in history or the evolution of Absolute Spirit, but on rational, empirical observations of how religions work and by extrapolation will work in historical time. They are generalizations, to be sure, and to this extent hypotheses, but they are based on a reading of history and not a priori theories.

Finally, for those who have ears to hear it in this way, I would like for this scheme to be received as a prophetic utterance in the biblical sense: a prediction of the future of religion as it will be if forces in motion continue to work themselves out, but a future that can be changed if enough people want it changed and decide to change it. I am not a historical determinist; I believe persons and groups can take decision that can make the future whatever they wish it to be. But I also believe that the social forces constructing history are powerful and will not change unless they are opposed with great conviction and force. To stand against the tide is difficult for an individual, and more so for a group or nation, but it has been and can be done.

Many people (both East and West) will undoubtedly be distressed by the indication in the schema that Buddhism is about at its end as a Great Religion. First, let it be emphasized that this does not mean there will be no more Buddhists; it only means that the religion will no longer have the Great Religion role on the world stage as in its golden age. To Buddhists, one could say *(a)* that the diminishment of the faith in this age of the world is only what has been long predicted in Buddhist doctrines of the decline of the Dharma, and *(b)* that Buddhists can decide to perpetuate their religion as long as they wish to do so.

Such "decisions," contrary to what would seem historically "natural," have been made before. Shinto, as a religion of a basically archaic agricultural type, should perhaps have given way entirely when the Great Religions Buddhism and Confucianism came to Japan, as did its polytheistic equivalents, the pre-Christian religions of Europe and the Mediterranean, before the rise of Christianity. But Japan collectively "decided" to preserve the older indigenous faith alongside the continental imports, and it is still there today. The tenacity of Judaism almost everywhere it has spread in the face of immense pressure is well known and can surely serve as an inspiration to all who wish, despite great adversity, to preserve an ancient faith. I suspect some future Christians will feel this way about their faith. Nonetheless, let the prophecies of this book be taken in the spirit with which all prophecy in a nondeterministic world must be taken: if things remain as they are, this will happen. But if we decide to change the present, the future will also change.

We shall now examine the stages of the historical development of the Great Religions, according to our hypothesis. We may recall that each stage *averages* some five centuries, but in practice, each individual stage has varied as much as three or four centuries from that norm.

CHAPTER FIVE
BEGINNINGS: THE APOSTOLIC STAGE

We start with the world religions before they became world religions—as they were during the lifetime of the founder and the first few generations, when empire, millions of believers, and many centuries were hardly imagined. This period is pre-Constantinian Christianity, Buddhism before Ashoka, Confucianism in the "Hundred Philosophers" era before its adoption as an official ideology, post-Vedic Hinduism in its formative period before the Gupta dynasty, Islam—in which this period was very short—prior to the caliphate.

Two principal tasks are incumbent upon a religion in this first stage: first, to create the definitive presentation of its special revelation and teaching, usually in the form of a distinctive new scripture, such as the New Testament, Qu'ran, or Tripitaka, the Analects and related post-Confucian classics, the Bhagavad Gita and other major texts of post-Vedic Hinduism; second, to establish the regularized leadership of the new faith in a manner prepared to last until the consummation of the age—the emergent Catholic church order in Christianity, the Ulama of Islam, the Sangha, the Mandarins, and the gurus and priestly brahmins of Hinduism. The first stage mandates other important tasks as well. Nonscriptural but authoritative writings must be gathered: words of the apostolic and subapostolic fathers, the *Hadith* of the Prophet, the puranas and tantras. At that point, the religion makes beginning steps in the direction of understanding and if possible regularizing its relation to the surrounding intellectual, cultural, and political worlds, though these are the major concerns of the next stage.

During this period, the religion also goes through certain common experiences that do much to shape its sense of heritage and provide benchmarks against which to mark the troubles and triumphs of subsequent eras: the persecution of early Christians under Rome, alluded to continually by later preachers; the radiant joy of the early Buddhist monks and nuns, as suggested in documents like the Dhammapada; the fading memory of the founder and of the excitement of his presence, recorded though imperfectly in such texts as the gospels of Christ and the *Hadith* of the Prophet. In those days, so different from the times of its imperial role, the religion is an "underground" competitor in the spiritual marketplace. But, at least in later memory, it was in those sunrise days filled with fervent faith and confident hope for a splendid future.

Several distinctive features mark a religion in this beginning phase as it sets about those all-important tasks. The new religion is a gestating faith, sometimes persecuted and precarious, dwelling within the womb of an older spiritual culture. It represents both continuity with it and an alternative insofar as it is also an adaptation of the old-to-new conditions. In its latter aspect, it may well look less "religious" and more concerned with this-worldly problem solving than its spiritual surroundings because the new faith has not yet taken up an elaborate metaphysical worldview or developed a wide variety of devotional practices. It has, however, instead offered a few simple but sure new techniques and easily understood principles that deal with what are widely, if perhaps only half-consciously, perceived to be the "real" life-problems of the times, to which the older spirituality was anachronistic.

The new faith's appeal, despite its socially and politically marginal status, rests in this perception. The older religion was richer in gods, philosophy, rituals, and piety, and it commanded no small respect; but it seemed too cosmic and mystical to deal with the immediate spiritual and ethical problems faced by many Axial Age people. The older cults may have also appeared too closely tied to a social order perceived as passing away and toward which an increasing number of persons felt alienated or marginalized—perhaps they were persons rising in effective if not fully legitimated economic and political power.

The social order that the old pre-Axial faiths inhabited was perhaps that of the ancient riverine empires, whether of the Nile, the Tigris and Euphrates, the Indus, or the Huang He. These irrigation-based societies were, at least ideally, hierarchical, stable, closely tied to sacred places and the ritual turn of the seasons, and so susceptible to experience of dissonance when there was slippage between sacred cosmos and earthly reality. This was increasingly the case as population movements and historical change accelerated after 500 B.C.E. In such a situation, the times demanded enhanced attention to the needs of the individual high and low for spiritual therapy and salvation. Reconstruction of the ritual cosmos in a way that took into account both nostalgia for the old hierarchy of heaven and earth and the new religious individualism was necessary; the successful new Axial Age religion accomplished this combined task more than adequately and became what we now call one of the great religions or world religions.

The new religion—as simplified, personalized, and in a sense, this-worldly alternative to overpopulated heavens and overwrought temples—is evident in early Buddhism. The Enlightened One's own Dharma and that of the pioneer renunciants were almost more a pared-down psychotherapy than the equivalent of the Brahmanical rites and thought of its day. Those the great spiritual physician clearly regarded with disdainful silence, insisting his only concern was suffering and the ending of suffering, which could be realized by each person individually and inwardly. In this quest, caste and gender, though not entirely disregarded, mattered far less than in the Brahman world. Disciples of varied backgrounds are reported: Upali, a low-caste barber; Sariputra, a brahmin; Ananda, like the Buddha himself, a kshatriya or nobleman; Yasa, of a wealthy merchant family.

If the *Therigatha*, songs of nuns from the earliest period of Buddhism, are any guide, many women found themselves well liberated in leaving the world for the order. One who had abandoned an unhappy marriage sang:

> O woman well set free! How free am I
> How thoroughly free from kitchen drudgery—
> Me stained and squalid 'mong my cooking pots,
> My brutal husband ranked as even less
> Than the sunshades he sits and weaves always.

Both men and women enjoyed the new life of the samgha as equals, at least in the sisters' eyes:

> We both have seen, both he and I, the woe
> And pity of the world, and have gone forth—
> We both are arahants with selves well tamed;
> Cool are we both, ours is *Nibbana* now![1]

The path of those forth-goers clearly addressed an unmet need for personal spirituality accessible to diverse persons in an India that was becoming increasingly complex. Indo-European and Dravidian cultures mixed, commerce was growing, and political ferment was in the air. Socially, tension was increasing not only between male and female (possibly stemming from clashes between hierarchy-minded Aryan culture and the gender-freer Dravidian, with its mother goddesses and agrarian way of life), but it also was happening between priestly brahmins and the Buddha's martial kshatriya caste.

As for the latter, the rulers' reluctance to give unqualified spiritual authority to the priests is also reflected in early Jainism (its founder, Mahavira, like the Buddha was a kshatriya) and in the Bhagavad Gita. Like active rulers and warriors everywhere, the kshatriya had little time for monkish mysticism and metaphysics, much less for sacerdotal privilege, but they did yearn for a "do-it-yourself" religion that could calm the mind and affirm one's individual significance in the midst of a busy, tumultuous life.

At the same time, the soldierly self-discipline on which they prided themselves made them willing to test their spiritual prowess by attempting harsh ascetic practice, out of which they might hope to emerge, like the Buddha or Mahavira, a *jina,* or hero—as a conqueror not of an earthly foe, but over the self and its spiritual torment. The early Buddhist answer was radical: be lamps to yourselves, work out your own salvation; if you don't do it for yourselves, it won't happen—and anyone *can* do it regardless of caste or character.

So Buddhism, like Christianity and Islam, started out as a religion highly individualized in comparison to the old civic cults of its environment. Individual faith, individual salvation was at first independent of king or community—though union of throne and altar arrived soon enough as the new faith *became* the religion of kings and cultures, the Wisdom and Imperial stage function. A new Axial Age religion was a religion made by and for *the* age of the radical discovery of the individual and of history, but we first must understand what made the new religion stand out as a new way to liberation for free individuals living in historical time, in their own time rather than out of the immemorial past.

Confucianism was likewise at first an ethical and political system for the new Axial Age that kept the gods of the older cults at a distance. The sage from the state of Lu saw himself preeminently as a political counselor, desperately eager for some prince to retain him. He dwelt in a deteriorating situation, in which the fragile social fabric wrought by the old Zhou dynasty was badly fraying, as warlords rampaged against their neighbors. Confucius, like any other of the "hundred philosophers," was compelled to search deeply for a social antidote.

The answer required no elaborate pantheon of gods, but only an appeal to live in conformity with the way of "heaven" (meaning less a personal God than Nature in its widest and profoundest sense) and with one's own true, innermost nature. That true self was social in character, requiring the honoring of one's given relationships (as ruler of subject, parent or child, spouse, brother, or friend) and a spirit of reciprocity ("Do not do to others what you would not have others do to you"). One had to make this choice for oneself. No supernatural, postmortem sanctions were offered, but only the conviction that *ren* (virtue), the way of the *junzi* (superior person), was its own reward.

Confucius was also a profoundly conservative philosopher, believing first that society could best get back on the right track by honoring the teachings and practices of the ancient sage kings and by taking seriously the lessons of older books regarded as "classics." The practice included the performance of rites *(li)*, not so much out of fear of the gods to which they were putatively addressed, but for the social coinherence value of ritual enactments. The rites the Sage enjoined were already recognized instruments of society.

Confucius was clearly less a religionist in the otherworldly sense than a public ethicist or social philosopher who wanted to call his compatriots' attention to a way of life that really ought to recommend itself through enlightened self-interest. A society based on right relationships and reciprocity solidified through *li* should be one in which everyone would prefer to live rather than in one based on mutual greed and conflict.

Hinduism in the corresponding period in the first centuries of the common era, in contrast to the culturally powerful but increasingly metaphysical Buddhism, presented a face of greater concern with the practical issues of a religiously legitimated social order. The subcanonical *smriti* literature, including the epics and the Bhagavad Gita, together with *dharmasastras* (legal texts) such as the important Laws of Manu, tell as much. Though without an individual "founder" or apostolic period as such, the Vedic/Hindu tradition responded to the same questions as did the founder faiths. In texts from the later Upanishads to the Gita, the new Hinduism made its central tenet individual religious experience, whether it be mystical realization of the atman, the divine within, or loving bhakti toward a personified deity. At the same time, it recognized that a fully formed religion must provide not only for inwardness, but also must outline a divinely sanctioned social order. The Laws of Manu thus sanctified the classic Hindu social structure, laying down the order of *varnas* (castes), offering a rough but ready resolution of the problem of one's dual responsibility to the social order and individual liberation. That was through Manu's model of *ashramas* (stages of life), which encouraged the householder at the right moment to give up the duties and privileges of the householder for the life of the recluse and finally sannyasin.

The styles of the apostolic period in Judaism's twin offspring, Christianity and Islam, contrast greatly, but one can see how, each in its own way, the two organized doctrine, scripture, worship, and institutionalization for the long haul. The Founder of Christianity wrote nothing, nor so far as we know was anything written about him in his lifetime. But he did have followers who, whatever their conscious intent, were precursors of institutionalized Christian religion. If the Book of Acts, together with implications in the Epistles of the New Testament, are any guide, the earliest Christian communities were under the supervision of apostles owing their authority to their having been immediate disciples of Jesus or who, like Paul, received apostolic charisma directly from Jesus through a visionary experience.

They exercised individual authority over churches that each had planted—which legends scatter from Britain to India—or that acknowledged apostolic leadership. If the apostles gathered together, as in the council recorded in Acts 15, they made decisions by consensus announced by senior elders like Peter and James. At the same time, the impressive variety of teaching and practice available in early Christianity indicates that the apostles, their disciples in turn, and many other claimants to Christian authority went in different directions in every sense of the word.

All sorts of Christians passed up and down the Roman highways and seaways writing and visiting churches. Denunciations in the canonical scriptures leave no doubt about this, nor does the extant library of noncanonical writings, including Gnostic texts such as those discovered in the twentieth century at Nag Hamadi in Egypt. Some alternative texts, especially the famous Gospel of Thomas, are regarded by authorities as no later than the canonical gospels.

As we will see in a moment, it seems likely that models—one might say potential containers—for a messianic soteriological faith were in place before Jesus. To become Christianity, they needed only the first-generation bare minimum of a name, a eucharistic rite, a cross, and a resurrection (which is virtually all of Jesus' life that is spoken of by Paul and other first-generation writers).

In this "cafeteria" of various roles for Jesus, one could first find the relatively conservative Jewish interpretation of him as the Christ or Messiah, "Anointed One" or King. The title "Christ" is a literal Greek translation of "Messiah," and anointing was the way of making a king in ancient Israel; in view of his death on the cross, Judaic believers now conjoined the Messiah image with the poignant passages in Isaiah about the "suffering servant"—the hero who saves his people not by military victory but by undergoing excruciating pain, baring his back to the smiters, his cheek to those who pluck out the hairs. For them, he was also "Son of Man," a title from Daniel that Jesus reportedly used of himself and that referred to a mysterious judge who would descend on clouds at the last day.

More in the Greek spiritual orbit, others thought of titles like "Lord" or "Son of God," used of Hellenistic kings and deities alike; or contemplated the role of saving gods from the mysteries like those of Eleusis, Orpheus, or Mithra; or even reflected on philosophical concepts such as the Logos ("Word" or "Principle"), describing the creative energy of God at work in the world, in connection with the enigmatic and unforgettable man from Nazareth. For Gnostics, who were as close to Jesus in time as any other Christians, he was more a figure who had stepped out of cosmological myth than he was a historical person, a transcendent actor in human guise who briefly came into this material world—created by a lower demiurgic god who had bungled the job—to save those belonging not to the bungler but to the light.

Apostolic Christianity consciously or unconsciously negotiated this diversity by pursuing several effective tactics at once. First, it emphasized the authority of apostles and of churches, like Rome, with natural prestige and believed to have been founded by one of the twelve disciples, or by Paul or his own disciples. This emphasis meant that scriptures and doctrines traced to an apostle and a major church had priority. Second, the new faith developed an emergent set of scriptures and doctrines that gave some allowance to moderate versions of many bands on the interpretive spectrum, making for a rich Christian mosaic suitable to persons of varied spiritual predilections.

At the same time, as the process advanced, definitive lines were drawn against what seemed to be distortions outside the apostolic consensus. Charges of heresy were heard, and the religion's mainstream enjoyed both the benefits and limitations of a crystallizing, clear-cut theological worldview. This process developed in interaction with the regularization of mainstream church order. It exfoliated out of the foundational authority of apostles, apostolic churches, and churches in major cities in time for imperial-era consolidation into the fourth-century creeds and hierarchy of patriarchs, archbishops, bishops, and parish priests. The authority of the entire lineage ultimately derived from the great apostolic sees to work its way down to villages in the recently converted countryside.

But early Christianity was an experience of salvation and a relatively austere ethic, still feeling its way toward full theological and ritual expression. The extent to which it embodied otherworldly soteriological experience as over against "secular" concerns is the subject of much controversy, some of it perhaps projecting backward issues affecting the world of modern scholarship and making distinctions that might not have been perceived in the same way in the first century. Suffice it for now to say that the messianic faith conjoined individual sin and salvation with an egalitarian view of society, related to Axial Age individualism that covertly undercut the hierarchy and particularism of the Judaism and Hellenism of the time. The process was not even. In the gospels and epistles, one finds painful tensions between universalism and acceptance of predetermined roles for slave and free, men and woman. Yet even in the latter case, subordinates are still viewed as individuals capable of divine love and salvation, and early Christian communities seem to have contained a diversity of persons.

In the ancient world, "religion" was hardly the kind of distinct social entity we envision today. Aspects of what we call religion could embrace everything from the *pietas* of patrician Romans through the mysteries and

Neoplatonic mysticism to ethnic and folk culti. In this context, the spreading community centered on the name of Jesus could perhaps best be called a liberation movement on several levels, from intrapsychic to social—though like all liberationism, it was forced at some point to define its own boundaries.

The process in Islam is essentially comparable, but it appears different because it is much more compacted in time and because the religion much sooner controlled the political world within which it completed its regularization. Like Jesus, the Prophet of Islam wrote nothing; his revelations were oral, given from God through the archangel Gabriel. They were largely retained by memorization on the part of the Prophet's hearers and followers, a process common in traditional societies, although some segments of the sacred transmission may have been jotted down. The scripture-in-formation was not entirely canonized by the time the imperial era began.

Even before the Prophet's death, complaints arose that different versions of his words of divine revelation, the Qur'an or "Recitation," were in circulation. Disputes amongst them could have led to serious schism. This situation of excessive diversity, comparable to that in Christianity before the canonization of the New Testament, was unacceptable and, as in the case of Christian doctrinal disputes, it found resolution through the combined authority of sacred emperor and religious scholars.[2]

Although earlier collections may have been made, the definitive collecting and editing of the Holy Qur'an (according to tradition) was carried out under Uthman, the third caliph (r. 644–656 C.E.), some twenty years after Muhammad's death. The commission in charge of this important task was headed by Zayd ibn Thabit, who had been the founder's secretary. The four scribes who constituted that body found the texts that would become the holy book of Islam transcribed on various surfaces: "pieces of papyrus, flat stones, palm leaves, shoulder blades and ribs of animals, pieces of leather, wooden boards, and the hearts of men."[3]

As in the case of Christianity, establishing the final text of the faith's core revelation was carried out in the context of burgeoning diversity in the religion and increasing administrative centralization. The last years of the Prophet's life, called from this point of view the "period of apostasy," were marked by the appearance of a number of rival prophets in Arabia, some perhaps imitators inspired by Muhammad's success. The most important was Maslamah (or Musaylamah), who was slain in battle by a Muslim army in 633. Other rivals were the Kahinah ("Prophetess") in the north and Dhu-l-Himar in the Yemen.

These and other mavens in that time of strife were based in tribes and regions. Like the Muslims who would in the end be successful, their partisans sent armies forth under sacred banners, dealing with issues of theology and religio-political authority in the field. This resolution, hardly different from what would soon enough be the case in Christianity (e.g., the Thirty Years' War, originally between Catholic and Protestant states), occurred early in Islam. It occurred because the Prophet had united Arabia—apart from these disruptions—into the prototype of an empire in his own lifetime, for he understood that the divine will was to be carried out no less in the political realm than in the spiritual.

Islam's second, or Imperial stage, could well be said to have commenced with the "Year of Deputations," 631, the annum before Muhammad's triumphant return to Mecca and death. In 631, representatives of tribal rulers arrived from all over Arabia to accept Islam from the Prophet. In a real sense, then, Muhammad was both founder and first emperor of his world faith; the caliphate per se began the next year, 632, when Abu Bakr, the Prophet's close friend and father-in-law, was selected by consensus of Muslim leaders to succeed the founder/ruler as the movement's temporal head.

The caliphs, despite challenges, maintained a center for the Islamic community, upholding its jurisprudence and patronizing Islamic scholarship. Umar II (r. 717–720 C.E., a century after the Prophet) ordered the gathering of the *Hadith*, or stories of Muhammad retelling his sayings and indicating his responses to various situations. This order was done with the help of impressive analysis of the reliability of various texts and lines of transmission. Those considered authentic have appropriate authority in Islamic thought. But by now, we are moving well into the religion's Wisdom and Imperial stage.

Early Islam was then as much a powerful political movement as it was a religion, greatly concerned with the regulation of life in this world. The Arabia in which it emerged was a "no-man's land" among three great empires—the Byzantine, Abyssinian, and Persian—two Christian and one Zoroastrian; it also harbored a minority of Jews. The new faith offered a catalyst for Arab unity and assertion as a world power that was equal to—

and soon to be greater than—those older and vulnerable regimes. The catalyst was monotheism, clearly in the seventh century the ideological foundation of successful, world-class powers. But for Islam, it was both the basis for individual "submission" to the will of Allah, and for the creation of a community—the House of Islam—ideally as unified here below as God was above. Islam has always believed that true faith in one God means a corresponding seamless unity in the world of the faithful—that the sovereignty of God should be recognized in all parts of life, including the political, legal, and familial, as well as in such strictly "religious" areas as how one says one's prayer.

Apostolic religion generally dealt with the problem of the isolated, historically aware individual in the Axial Age, not so much by offering him or her a full-sailed metaphysical bark, as by providing—the Buddhist term—a ferry to the other shore which is sturdy but simple, takes some effort to row, and gives a journey with this-worldly as well as other-worldly benefit. At the same time, it should be noted that the "apostolate" of the new religion is actually an adaptation of preexisting social and ideological structures, reconfigured sufficiently to appear newer than they are, as though the new organization were nothing but the lengthened shadow of the founder. Yet the founder, or more accurately the persona of the founder, does not make new so much as see with fresh eyes what is there, and he communicates effectively that new perception. The founder, in other words, becomes an authoritative spokesperson for an existing, but perhaps uncrystallized and emergent spiritual ideology and practice embodied in a class or group that *already* is socially defined and that possesses some structure.

This point may be significant. Let us look again at our five religions with it in mind.

The Confucian mandarin class of scholars, priests, and administrators, the Ru, though putatively the successors of the Sage's disciples, were also very much a continuation and refinement of the preceding Ru class of learned and skillful persons, custodians of the arts and literary classics, which Confucius "edited" but preserved as the foundation of the new tradition.

In Buddhism, the samgha may be in direct apostolic succession from the Enlightened One's own circle of disciples—impossible to prove or disprove at this remove; but certainly the ancient order was inspired by even older existing structures. It is said, in fact, that the Buddha's first five disciples were of the group of extreme ascetics he himself had earlier joined, then left in disillusionment. Bands of ascetics of diverse schools thronged the roadways of old India in that Axial Age time of spiritual ferment. Probably like the Buddha himself, not a few were based in the kshatriya rather than the brahmin caste; we know this to be the case with Mahavira, founder of the Jains and the Buddha's near contemporary. Hence, their emphasis was on inward ascetic and meditative practice rather than Vedic rites and learning. It was as if to show that what the priestly house could do with the help of lineage and performance, kshatriya could realize through inward praxis.

In the mirror image situation of Upanishads-to-Puranas period Hinduism, the preexisting group, the brahmins, maintained control and continued performing their particular rites, but—as the Bhagavad Gita makes evident—were compelled to admit equal spirituality more and more to kshatriya like Prince Arjuna, to yogic styles of practice, and to feeling-oriented devotional as well as liturgical forms of worship.

In the case of Christianity, the relation of the early Christian church to preexisting structures is perhaps more controversial. At a minimum, though, it seems possible that groups who were focused on Jewish messianic and apocalyptic belief, perhaps related to the Qumran community, could be found throughout the diaspora in the Roman world, providing a ready audience for the gospel of missionaries like Paul.[4] It may be that these groups already had organizational and worship structures, such as recognized roles for the likes of apostles, elders, and deacons, and a sacred-meal precursor of the Christian Eucharist, into which the new wine could be poured.

Or else the enigma remains that has long puzzled students of the New Testament: why do the earliest Christian writings, the epistles of Paul as well as Gnostic texts like the Gospel of Thomas, seem to presuppose a very advanced soteriological and Christological faith, together with a working church structure, yet seem innocent of any substantial information, beyond the saving events—the incarnation, cross, and resurrection—about the actual life of Jesus? That answer was not provided until the gospels appeared decades or even a generation later. One is also perplexed as to why the eucharistic liturgy became the mandatory central act of worship in the early church and indeed up to the Reformation, on the basis of what is actually rather meager explicit support for it as the major Christian rite, especially in its full liturgical expression, in the scriptures themselves. Was there also a pre-Christian Eucharist, waiting only for the name?

Perhaps details of the life of Jesus, beyond the cross and the empty tomb, were not offered in the Pauline era because existing communities already knew what they needed to know and do about an apocalyptic messiah; all the apostle had to supply was the name and the decisive soteriological event. Those could then be connected with the preexistent messianic cultus and probably also on the basis of previous reflection, with the philosophical Hellenized Judaism of Philo (e.g., in the Johannine literature) and "prophetic" passages in the Bible—some of which were later, not always convincingly, associated with the birth, life, and death of Jesus.

This is not the place for further digression into speculation along these lines. Whatever the specifics, it seems that Christianity, like other "founder" religions, must be granted continuity as well as discontinuity with its environing culture.

Islam likewise displays both sides. Although much is new in the Prophet's revelation, the faith itself affirms that he is but the "seal" of a long line of prophets of true monotheism; in addition, symbols like the Ka'aba in Mecca and the star and crescent clearly derive from prior Arabic religion. A group of people called Hanifs, not well understood but mentioned in the Qu'ran, seem to have been precursors of Muslims as Arab believers in one God.

Moreover, Islam's obvious connections with Judaism and its Semitic style of religion indicate another broad and deep background. Both religions are based on revelation through prophets, encoded in written scriptural texts; both give importance to religious law, including comparable dietary regulations; and in the past (Judaism) or now (Islam), both have offered sacrifice and made pilgrimage to one central temple in a holy city. Much common mythic background history obtains: the primal role of Abraham (Ibrahim), Ishmael (Ismail), Enoch (Idris), as well as Jesus (Issa). The last points to Islam's fraternal relation to Christianity as well. That Abrahamic faith shares some (though not all) of those marks of "family resemblance" with Judaism and Islam.

Indeed, one is inclined to think that something of this lore, though in noncanonical form, may have been more widely dispersed through the Arabian peninsula than is often supposed to provide the Prophet with "containers" into which to fit his final fulfillment of the Semitic spiritual heritage. It seems unlikely the religion could have flourished as rapidly and successfully as it did had the names and notions borrowed from Judaism been entirely novel, imported wholesale from the north in the luggage of his caravans. Perhaps, as the existence of the Hanifs suggests, many of Muhammad's contemporaries felt a tension between the ancient astral worship and prophetic religion of the Judaic sort, including Jewish legendary and cultic content. It was the Founder's task as prophet not so much to introduce wholly new elements as to present a vision in which the two newly fit together as a seamless whole, offering completeness rather than tension.

At the same time, new faiths must also offer convincing symbols of novelty to have proper authority. They do well to focus on a new authoritative scripture as a central symbol. First, as we have already indicated, the very fact that the sacred texts are in writing, the latest Axial Age communications technology, rather than immemorial bardic oral tradition, of itself says that they are new and contemporary. They are a word from the Highest issued sometime *since* the beginning, in the context of human history. On top of this, at least some of the new scriptures include references to datable events: for example, "there went out a decree from Caesar Augustus."

Thus, the new scriptures: the New Testament, the Qu'ran, the Buddhist Tripitaka, and Mahayana sutras; the texts of the new Hinduism (Bhagavad Gita, Yoga sutras, Laws of Manu, Puranas, and Tantras); the Daodejing (Tao te ching) and the post-Confucius "classics" (Analects, Mean, Great Learning, and Mencius). They all proclaim the separate and consummate authority of a new tradition, being ascribed to the founder (except for Hinduism) or his immediate apostolic era. A little later comes the development of distinctive doctrinal statements supplemental to the scriptures and, finally, theological works.

A new and authoritative organizational structure is no less crucial. Its requisites are twofold: first, the need to distinguish the authentic lineage of successors of the first disciples and ultimately of the founder; second, to maintain the tradition against the persecution or conflict all too likely in the apostolic stage. The first few generations of a new faith are bound to present widely diverse interpretations of its meaning. Rules have not been laid down, and many possibilities beckon to be explored. A religion in an apostolic period is in a state of flux as it finds it way from charismatic to routinized hierarchical leadership and hammers out its norms of doctrine and practice. What will later seem heretical extremes, such as Gnostic Christianity and Xunzi's naturalistic Confucianism, may appear briefly as options for the direction the faith will take and indeed may be covertly incorporated into its mature form.

That sort of chaos is not likely to appeal to those who have received the mantle of leadership. For most people with leadership instincts, order and limits are important to the construction of a world. More and more lines are drawn: between Gnostic and Catholic Christianity; between the Jû tradition and any other of the hundred philosophers; and between the Sthaviras versus the Mahasamghika in early Buddhism.

Those leaders are not necessarily wrong; some degree of intellectual and organizational firmness and line drawing to the point of blood-witness seem necessary to the long-term survival of a religion in a pluralistic world. However well one may regard the intellectual virtues of Gnostic Christianity, it seems likely in the end that it was weakened by its flexible accommodationalist attitude toward Roman persecutors; while for the lineage priding itself on bishops in apostolic succession, the blood of martyrs was the seed of the church. For survival in tough times, the imperative of organizational authority outweighs intellectual expansiveness. Thought ranging wide and free within the ecclesia flourishes best when a religion feels itself culturally dominant and unthreatened, as in the heyday of liberal Christianity.

If the religion is going to last over centuries and millennia, the apostolic period inevitably completes its foundational scriptural and regulatory tasks and draws to a close. Three continuing needs become increasingly insistent: institutional stability, doctrinal consensus, and political legitimation. Religionists thereby acknowledge that initial enthusiasm cannot succeed in conquering the world, or even in long sustaining itself, without conceptual and institutional unity, together with support from a powerful state that the faith in turn undergirds spiritually.

By the end of the apostolic period, the new religion usually has shaken out a stable, working institutional and leadership pattern, whether under bishops, a caliph, or monastic order. It is probably already in the process of producing a definitive version of the scriptures and of theological definition. The apostolic age comes to an end as two things happen, usually more or less simultaneously: the adoption of the faith by a powerful empire

(Ashoka's, Han China, the Gupta dynasty, Constantine's, the caliphate); and the establishment of doctrinal agreement by the faith's institutional leadership aligned with the imperial patron. Often this consensus is reached by formal council, such as Nicaea, the other Christian general councils, and the early Buddhist councils; or a parallel process may be followed, such as the production of the definitive edition of the Qu'ran under the third caliph, Othman, and the "seeking of the Hadith," a systematic locating of the Prophet's words and acts to form the basis of Islamic law, a task completed by the end of the third century after his death.

To become a Great Religion, then, a faith needs a political and geographical base of imperial dimensions, an authoritative institution, and a received scripture, as well as the rest of a religion's forms of expression. Those that have attained this highest destiny have, by the terminus of the first of their five eras, consolidated those requirements or are well on the way to securing them.

CHAPTER SIX
EMPIRE AND WISDOM

What becomes of a faith, then, when it acquires an imperial alliance and becomes dominant in a major society and culture area? Its attitudes, praxis, and institutional life must adjust to meet this novel second-stage role. Becoming a "church" in the Troeltschean sense,[1] it endeavors to maintain its integrity while making countless adaptations to meet the spiritual expectations of people of varying cultural background, from peasants to philosophers and emperors.

An empire is a large, politically unified landmass encompassing diverse nationalities and cultures, drawn together by trade and cultural diffusion, but among which, one people and their culture are supreme both politically and economically. The empire is ruled by a bureaucracy largely drawn from that people, under the sovereignty of its titular ruler. The dominant nation, particularly its aristocratic and mercantile classes, benefit most from the imperial state. Their spiritual, political, and cultural values are most likely to be widely disseminated throughout it and, by way of its prestige and influence, even past its frontier posts. Yet influence flows from the subordinate regions to the center as well, increasingly as history advances. It is also true that certain classes of outland peoples under the center's hegemony profit from the imperial arrangement. They enjoy an era of relative peace, prosperity, free commerce, and opportunities to share in a common culture of world importance; and if the empire is not inordinately tyrannical, these benefits may be widely appreciated.

This period is where the Great Religion adopted by the empire fits in, for in a traditional society, it will above all be the legitimizer of imperial rule and the vehicle for defusing the common imperial culture, in addition to being a propagandist for its virtues. The religion, now defined in a clearly demarcated textual and doctrinal way, also has a definite professional hierarchy that slips easily into the empire's bureaucratic structure so that church and state reinforce each other.

The religious leadership *is* the bureaucracy, as was the ideal in Confucian China; it at least manages its educational and social service functions; or, lastly, its dignitaries, like Christian bishops, have recognized bureaucratic rank. The state in turn assumes important reciprocal functions in religious administration. The emperor Constantine presided at the Council of Nicaea as it worked out very important and controversial theological definitions, and he and his mother were canonized as saints in the Eastern church.

The religion must present itself as new to indicate that a new spiritual era has arrived; it must also present itself as old, to show that it is disarmingly only the fulfillment of what has gone before. While of course these were also challenges facing the apostolic period, now they must be dealt with on a much larger scale. The new religion, as world-faith, must legitimate, complement, and complete the ideal world-historical role of the empire. It must similarly show itself the consummation of all previous philosophy and (selectively) of the previous dispensation's religious life.

While establishing its unquestioned spiritual supremacy, the newly triumphant faith borrows and assimilates rites and ideas from its environment with a free hand. Now it needs with acute urgency not only symbols of continuity, but the full panoply of popular religion to meet all that is expected in such an age of a dominant faith: seasonal festivals, pilgrimage sites, imposing rituals, the ceremonies of sacred kingship, wayside shrines, charms and amulets. Through such means it does much to bring ordinary people gently into the faith, and the imperial order.

Some of this religious impedimenta the austere monks and apostles of the earlier age might have scorned. But because this is a time when many kinds of religious language still speak, the religion cannot do otherwise than assimilate the paraphernalia of the common culture without losing all viability at the moment of its greatest apparent success. The emergent new shapes are opposed only by a minority of purists, some of whom may express their protest by becoming ascetics or sectarians. This was also the age when Christian monasticism, Islamic Sufism, and various rigorist "heresies" appeared.

By and large, though, the religion's initial emphasis on a pivotal event in history, the foundation of its initial missionary proclamations, is now considerably diffused by reversion to cosmic, sacred-and-profane patterns. On the popular level, festivals such as the Christian Christmas and Easter, though retaining their historical reference in principle, go far toward becoming eternal-recurrence seasonal rites. Rites of regular worship—such as the Mass, the Muslim Friday prayers in the mosque, or Buddhist temple offerings—soften their original sharp sense of commemorating one who lived once for all in historical time and died a human death. They focus rather on the new religion's founding revelation as but the first in a continuing series of manifestations of the timeless within time, as they ritually evoke the founder and the eternal together through the continual creation, day after day or week after week, of sacred space and time.

Intellectually, the same is reflected in a trend that gives this stage part of its name, an increasing appeal to the motif of universal wisdom rather than to the more historical and existential dimensions of the faith's early years. The historical task is, for the moment, accomplished by the emergence of an empire of believers. The religion's social program must now be to move that empire out of history, as it were, to become an unchanging reflection of timeless reality now under a ruler who (like the Byzantine or Chinese emperor or the caliph in Baghdad) is Son of Heaven or Shadow of God, whose obligation is to innovate nothing but to preserve all things as ordained from above.

Philosophically, the corresponding trend is toward ideas and literature that grow more out of mystical and less from salvation experience and that minimize the unique historicity of the religion in favor of its primordial and universal truth. Older and probably more universalistic conceptual motifs will be brought into the service of the new truth, at the same time tilting it in their direction. In the end, the new religion, though triumphant in name, will be intellectually a subtle synthesis of old philosophy and new doctrine.

The foundational imperial age for Buddhism was that of the last great Mauryan emperor, Ashoka, 274–232 B.C.E. With his enlightened reign dawned a golden age of Indian art and a rarely equaled time of tolerant and humane religious policy. That renowned ruler's famous pillars—on which are inscribed his decrees as well as significant biographical information—make no explicit reference to enlightenment or Buddhist philosophical doctrine, nor do they even identify the monarch as a Buddhist in any strict sense. But they tell of his sanguinary conquering of the Kalinga country (modern Orissa state) in the eighth year of his reign, and of how then, sickened by the carnage that was the price of his glory, he turned to the dharma and the ways of peace. Ashoka determined to live by dharmic principles, to teach them to his subjects, and to send envoys to present them to other kings. These actions he termed a new policy of "conquest by dharma."

To this sovereign, *dharma* meant Buddhist ethical virtues of nonviolence, honesty, and compassion, including harmlessness to animals. He posted edicts promulgating these values on his pillars, and personally traveled his kingdom preaching them to his people. (In the west, the later Constantine likewise issued much legislation intended to reflect Christian values, such as abolishing death by crucifixion and mandating Sunday as a day of rest.)

Ashoka's patronage of the dharma is indicated by his endowment of monasteries and his strenuous efforts, like Constantine's, to prevent schism. To eliminate sectarianism, Ashoka called the third Buddhist council of 247–246 B.C.E., which made the Theravada school orthodox and expelled many heretics from the order—a move reminiscent of Constantine and Nicaea. He gave his enthusiastic support to missionaries sent to distant lands, including his own son and daughter, who went to Ceylon.

It was during this reign, as is appropriate for the Imperial stage, that Buddhism grew from a small sect in India to spread throughout India and beyond. The emperor enjoyed discussing the Buddhist faith with scholarly monks, like Constantine who similarly spent hours in learned conversation with bishops and theologians. Yet Ashoka (also like Constantine, who was baptized only on his deathbed) publicly embraced only the ethical and institutional life of the religion whose historical destiny he so affected, and maintained a policy of tolerance toward all religions. The Christian triumph in the west was considerably less pacific; but not until Theodosius (r. 379–395) did the new faith become the exclusive religion of the empire and pagan temples were destroyed.

As another expression of the Buddhist Wisdom/Imperial stage, mention should also be made of the Kushan empire (c. 50 B.C.E.– 220 C.E.), which ruled over much of northwest India and what is now Afghanistan, reaching its height under Kaniska I in the first century C.E. He and other Kushan rulers supported Buddhism, promoted its spread through central Asia, and most important, encouraged Mahayana, the "Wisdom" version of the faith that fitted well its imperial as well as its popular role.

Ashoka has long been remembered as the ideal king. Mauryan emperors subsequent to him, however, were ineffective. In 184 B.C.E., a zealous champion of Hinduism, Pushyamitra of the Sunga house, overthrew the last heirs of the dharma-sovereign and, according to Buddhist records, burned and looted monasteries of that faith. Although the next few centuries were times of political confusion, they were also a religiously fertile era: the rise and flourishing of Mahayana thought in Buddhism (the "Wisdom" component of the Wisdom and Imperial stage); the recrudescence of Hinduism through such signs of its new relevance as the Bhagavad Gita, the Laws of Manu, and early forms of bhakti and Vedanta.

Mahayana crested a little later than the Mauryan imperial period, but it can be properly considered its spiritual consummation so far as the wisdom aspect of the era is concerned. Its broad emphasis was on the universal Buddhahood of all beings rather than on the historical Buddha. Mahayanists often worshipped Prajnaparamita, the "Wisdom That Has Gone Beyond," an initiatory goddess. The exent to which the wisdom of the new religion was but a revamping of old wisdom in the culture is shown by the obvious links between Mahayana and Upanishadic/Vedanta thought. Even more important, the universalization of Buddhahood and wisdom characteristically undercut "apostolic" historical particularism in favor of an outlook that emphasized the eternal, ahistorical aspects of the religion's philosophy and the equally ahistorical diversity of its popular culti. As a great text of wisdom-era Mahayana, the Lotus Sutra made clear the historical Buddha was but one of countless illusory manifestations of the timeless, eternal buddha-nature of the universe, and the paths to enlightenment he reportedly taught were but provisional techniques necessary only to those still laboring in the world of conditioned reality and relative truth.

If we take the inception of Hinduism to be around the first century C.E., we can say that Hinduism, in its own Wisdom era as a Great Religion, was in turn influenced by Mahayana Buddhism. This is the Hinduism of the Gupta empire (300–500 C.E.), often regarded as the golden age of classical Hindu civilization; it has been compared to the Elizabethan period in England. No doubt in partial response to the challenge of Buddhist thought, Gupta Hinduism updated its own armory of religion expression. Although their roots were certainly earlier, it was a time of the final redaction of classic Hindu texts such as the Yoga sutras, the Laws of Manu, the Brahma Sutras, and of the development of Vedanta thought prior to the great Shankara. (The last is a highly monistic and universalistic philosophy stressing the presence of the One, Brahman, in all things, a realization attained by mystical experience.) It was also the age of the Puranas, mythological texts not without considerable theological insight, through which the culti of great populations were brought into the formal Hinduism by identification of their gods and myths with those of the Great Tradition. They became basic to the next stage, the Devotional.

The Gupta golden age of this new Hinduism—its Imperial and Wisdom stage—was founded around 320 A.D. by Chandragupta I and enhanced by his son, the great Samudragupta, who united north India under his peaceful and prosperous reign. (The empire lasted until it was destroyed by the invasion of the White Huns c. 550.) Samudragupta inaugurated his rule by celebrating the ancient *asvamedha* (horse-sacrifice), a Vedic rite that proclaimed the ruler's orthodox Hinduism. Buddhism had objected to this custom, and it had been disused for five centuries. Caste was reinforced, and the religion of the Buddha gradually declined, though the Gupta rulers themselves were reasonably liberal and tolerant. The art, architecture, and literature of the period, including the poetry and drama of the great Kalidasa (fl. c. 400), was patronized by the court, as was astronomy and mathematics, with innovations in the latter field that included the zero and decimal numbers.

The Chinese Buddhist monk Faxian, who visited India in the days of Chandragupta II (r. c. 380–415), was able to praise his peaceful kingdom, noting that the people were prosperous, "paying no head-tax and unharassed by officials. . . . The kings rule without corporal punishment, but criminals are fined. . . . Throughout the land the people abstain from taking life or drinking wine, and only Chandalas (outcastes) eat garlic or onions."[2] While this account scarcely accords with an alternative tradition alleging that this monarch acceded to the throne by arranging the assassination of an elder brother, other accounts support the general picture of a strong, capable sovereign ordering a peaceful, successful government while endowing learning and dispensing charity freely. Moreover, the Chinese pilgrim well conveys the overall image of benign splendor the Guptas have projected through the centuries, and in the end, the lingering image of a religion's imperial era is religiously as important as any actual facts.

It was in the era of the Gupta contemporaries of Constantine and his Byzantine successors that, even as the Trinity was emerging to the west, Hindu theism took visible shape. The Hinduism of bhakti and personal theism that was manifested in the ancient deities Brahma, Vishnu, and Shiva, worshipped separately but metaphysically considered a *trimurti* or trinity, acquired in Gupta times much of the art, architectural, and expressive bhakti worship with which devotion has been associated ever since. The Guptas were devout Vaisnavas; it was during their era that most of the Vaisnava Puranas (mythological/ theological narratives) and Tantric samhitas (esoteric texts) took final form. It was also in this period that the worship of the goddess emerged in full force. By such means, the traditional Vedic religion was assimilated to countless popular culti—the process of "brahmanization" or "sanskritization"—to emerge as a timeless, ever self-renewing pantheon that revealed the even more eternal Brahman or Vedantic nondualism. This wisdom/imperial consolidation shows social order, yoga, the gods, temples, and scripture as taking concrete expression in an "ideal" Hindu state and in actual religious practice from palace to peasant hovels.

Sharing in the same Hindu stage was the Pallava kingdom's controlling much of south India circa 350–880. Fervent Tamil devotional poetry contributed much to Hindu revival in its bhakti form, and it was also in this area that the great Shankara (c. 788–820), the pivotal figure in Advaita (nondualist) Vedanta philosophy as well as a monastic founder, lived his short and outwardly austere life.

Turning to China, we look at the Han dynasty (202 B.C.E.–220 C.E.) for the wisdom/imperial expression of the Chinese tradition founded by Confucius and the more legendary Laozi. The "Han synthesis" version of Confucianism incorporated Taoist and other traditional motifs into the thought of the Great Sage and his lineage with a generous hand, making it more metaphysical, imbued with doctrines of correspondences interweaving man and nature, and fashioning as Confucian rites those by which the emperor coordinated his practices with the turning seasons.

Coming to power after the collapse of the totalitarian Qin dynasty (221–206 B.C.E.), which had burned Confucian books and covertly favored Taoism, the first impulse of the founding Han ruler, Liu Bang, better known under his imperial title Han Kao-tsu, was to move in a different direction. He sought consensus and tried to govern on the principle that the state exists to serve the people; thus, he and his early successors minimized laws, reduced taxes, and promoted decentralization. The country prospered, enjoying much cultural and economic development.

While later Han emperors reverted to a standard imperial style, religiously these contemporaries of the imperial Romans presided over a similarly syncretistic spiritual world. In their case, it was a result of deliberate policy. Early Han, although pragmatic and nonideological in spirit, was Taoist insofar as its laissez-faire policies reflected a Taoist spirit and its leaders often indulged in the magic and esotericism that was increasingly associated with Taoism. But the Han emperor Wu (r. 141–187 B.C.E.), whose reign represented the high point of Han prestige and power, officially encouraged Confucianism; in fact, the state established Confucian schools and universities. Thereby began the tradition of administration by Confucian-trained mandarins, whose bureaucracy was aided by the invention of paper, also a Han achievement.

At the same time, Han Confucianism was far from the relatively simple, this-worldly ethics of the Sage and his immediate disciples. Wu was under the influence of the leading Confucian scholar of the time, Dong Zongshu (c. 179–104 B.C.E.). He combined traditional Confucianism with the eclecticism, often Taoist in a broad religious sense that was current in the Han era. That worldview was expressed in the ancient *Yijing (Book of Changes),* but it was more firmly established in later "wings" (appendixes), which were added to it in the Han period. It was a worldview that was highly complex, but centered on the cosmic polarities yang and yin (primordial masculine and feminine forces, also heaven and earth) and their correlates throughout the universe, together with the five elements: wood, metal, fire, water, and earth. Out of this raw material, philosophers like Dong developed elaborate patterns for understanding and ritualizing seasons, emotions, music, humanity's relation to the universe, the role of the emperor as son of heaven, and much else. The typical Wisdom/Imperial combining of things old and new to produce what appeared to be an eternal, cosmological portrait of the universe is evident, as is its disseminating it through a bureaucratic structure that is at once imperial and spiritual. From then on, Chinese popular religion was at the same time Confucian (in ethics and state rituals), Taoist (in much else from poetry to exorcisms), and later Buddhist.

In Islam, the Wisdom/Imperial stage was the five centuries of the Damascus and Baghdad caliphates and no less of the Cordova caliphate in Spain (755–1236). These years were a cultural golden age when Islamic philosophy, drawing from the Greek heritage and the experience of Sufi mysticism, came to stress the timeless character of both God and the Qu'ranic revelation, culminating in the inward universalism of the philosophers al-Ghazali and Ibn Arabi. In the Sunni tradition, the caliph was the temporal successor of the Founder, acceding to all his roles except that of unique prophet of God. The Muslim ruler was entitled Commander of the Faithful, Vice-regent of the Prophet, and even Vice-regent of God. The first four caliphs, called the Rightly Guided, were elected by recognized leaders of the Muslim community and ruled from Medina; they were succeeded by the Ummayad dynasty in Damascus and, after 749, by the Abbasids in Baghdad, who reigned until 1258, when the Mongols sacked that ancient city.

The great age of Islamic civilization has rightly been acclaimed. Learned Arabs of the Baghdad and Spanish caliphates preserved classical Greek and Roman scholarship during the dark ages of Europe, and they transmitted it (including the concept of the zero in mathematics) to those then-backward lands from farther East. They also made substantial advances in such varied fields as astronomy, medicine, chemistry, geography, and history. The caliphate reached its apogee under the celebrated Harun ar-Rashid (r. 786–809), whose opulent court is idealized in the *Arabian Nights Entertainment*; those vivid stories well suggest the combined wealth, exquisite culture, and cruelty of his reign.

Of greater religious interest, however, is his son al-Ma'mun (r. 813–833), a monarch inclined toward philosophy and the sacred sciences. A story tells us that this ruler had a dream in which Aristotle appeared to him and, after some philosophical discourse, told him to treat scientists as gold and hold to the Oneness of God—an appropriate parable of the imperial age's need to conjoin the best learning of the ages (including the preexistent intellectual tradition) with the heart of the new religions, divine unity. Al-Ma'mun, perhaps overly influenced by Aristotle, favored a rationalist school of Islamic thought called the Mu'tazila, which held that reason is equal to revelation and superior to tradition as a source of truth. This philosophical party conceived of God as a pure spirit who always acted rationally for the best; it also taught human freedom and responsibility rather than emphasizing the absolute sovereignty of God. Mu'tazilites explained away anthropomorphic language in the Qur'an, asserting that scripture was created in time, in opposition to those who said it was the eternal word of God.

Al-Ma'mun tried to impose this interpretation on Islam in his empire as he granted it greater political freedom, but his sudden death in 833 was taken by his opponents as a sign of divine displeasure. Preeminence shifted to the Ash'arite theology, which lectured in a more mystical Platonic style that God is simply absolute power and grace, is more mysterious than reasonable on the human level, and is to be adored and obeyed rather than explained. The Ash'arite spirit led toward the mysticism so developed spiritually by the Sufis, who tended to see God as the sole reality under the varied appearances of the world; Ash'arism and Sufism were brought together by al-Ghazali (1058–1111), perhaps the greatest of Islamic philosophers, who used reason at preliminary stages of philosophical, theological, or legal discourse, but ended in mystical vision.

Both schools, however, moved away from the historicity of the earliest Islam to place the central truths of the faith in a timeless context—the essence of the Wisdom/Imperial move. In effect, truth was now known as much by direct reason or ecstatic insight as it was by historical reference back to the Prophet. Timeless truth also supported the authority of an empire whose sovereign was sometimes called the "shadow of God" and to whom obedience was owed as if it were granted to the heavenly sovereign whose viceroy he was.

In Christianity, the Wisdom and Imperial stage is that of Constantine and his imperial successors, and of patristic theology. The Greek and Latin fathers greatly stressed such timeless, universalistic aspects of the faith as the Trinity and the eternal Logos incarnate in Christ over against historical particularism. The liturgy also, in both Eastern and Western branches, became a hieratic service that seemed less the memorial of a historical event than an eternally recurring breakthrough of the timeless, paradisal realm of the Trinity and the saints into time. According to Augustine's *Civitas Dei*, a book written amid extremely tumultuous conditions on the worldly plane, the ideal for society was timeless perfection rather than the pursuit of a historical destiny.

The reasons for the triumph of Christianity in the Roman Empire around 312 are not readily apparent, even though Armenia had become the first officially Christian country in about 300. Although the faith of Christ was by now well established in the empire, it was still a minority in most places and had no greater prestige than the Neoplatonic mysticism favored by philosophers, by the Mithraism popular in the army, or by the ancient polytheism nostalgically upheld by patrician traditionalists. Moreover, only a few years before, in 303, the aging emperor Diocletian had begun a new persecution of Christians. One of his commanders, however, had another destiny—Constantine, who became supreme after a long struggle for power following the former's abdication in 305.

Deep psychological currents favorable to Christians apparently ran through the complex mind of Constantine. His mother, Helena, had become a Christian. And at the famous battle of the Milvian Bridge, where he defeated a rival in 312, it is said that he saw a cross in the sky and the letters *IHS*—the Greek beginning of the name Jesus, or the Latin initials for *In Hoc Signo*, "By this sign." The result was the so-called Edict of Milan, which decreed toleration of Christianity in 313. After Constantine finally became sole emperor in 323, he established his capital at Byzantium, later named Constantinople (modern Istanbul), and pursued policies favorable to Christianity, as we have seen.

In 325, he sponsored a council of bishops at Nicaea, which endeavored to establish Christian orthodoxy and reduce the prospect of schism. No less important was the way in which this occasion made clear the emperor's temporal sovereignty over the church, for he himself had convened the council; the church's hierarchical nature, for it was the bishops in council who determined orthodoxy; and the transcendent, timeless nature of Christian doctrine, for the creed's main point was that the Jesus of history was in fact the transcendent, unchanging Son of God ("eternally begotten of the Father . . . of one substance with the Father"). The doctrine of the Trinity, of three "persons," Father, Son, and Holy Spirit, in one God, was generally accepted in the same era. The elegant structures of trinitarian theology enveloped the historical Jesus even more firmly within that eternal heavenly reality, out of which he had only once and then only temporarily come down to earth "for us men and our salvation."

The definition of the Trinity was especially the contribution of the three great Cappadocian fathers: Basil of Caesarea (c. 329–379), Gregory of Nazianzus (c. 329–391), and Gregory of Nyssa (c. 335–395). The Cappadocian fathers were not only deeply influenced by Neoplatonism, but they were also in opposition to the Arian heresy that sought to define the Son and Holy Spirit in ways that made them lower than God the Father. The Cappadocians emphasized that God, or any "person" of God, is infinite and hence beyond limiting definition; the three "persons" are therefore infinite and coequal and can only be understood in relational terms. Gregory of Nyssa went on, particularly in his famous allegorical interpretation of the Exodus as a model of the spiritual path, to paint the human capacity for change and growth as also infinite and salvation as an endless journey into the infinity of God.

Pseudo-Dionysius, the influential fifth- or sixth-century mystical writer who so powerfully sums up the wisdom of Christianity, speaks in *The Divine Names* of transcendent Oneness manifesting itself as the Trinity and then, out of love, entering the world of many things in the Incarnation:

> In a fashion beyond words, the simplicity of Jesus became something complex, the timeless took on the duration of the temporal, and, with neither change nor confusion of what constitutes him, he came into our human nature, he who totally transcends the natural order of the world. This is the kind of divine enlightenment into which we have been initiated by the hidden tradition of our inspired teachers, a tradition at one with scripture.[3]

Wisdom clearly subsumed the historicity of the Old and New Testaments into timeless reality, in which an individual human life increasingly participates as it grows into God, all of which is quintessential wisdom-era religious thought.

It is too easy, however, to stress the history of ideas in the church and forget that changes of similar immense consequence were going on in worship and social organization. Indeed, as always, for the uneducated majority what was seen to be done in worship, and the sociopolitical role of religious institutions, was much more influential than the discussions of theologians.

As the church moved out of the spiritual underground of the great cities and into spacious buildings, typically modeled on the basilica or Roman court of law, or into the rural world of peasant and lord, the liturgy, or pattern of worship, also changed. It became expressive and ornate. The clergy wore symbolically colored garments and moved with slow ritual, accompanied by music and incense, to present and bless the bread and wine. In the West the language of the service was Latin, in the East, Greek. These tongues in their archaic, liturgical forms, especially Latin, quickly became "sacred" languages, like Sanskrit in India. For the ordinary worshipper, the atmosphere created by such worship as this suggested less a historical memorial than the presence of an eternal, transcendent reality that deigned weekly to descend into the holy places of this earth. The relation of the church's chief shepherds to the imperial establishment no less indicated that ecclesia and empire were linked as putatively timeless and unchanging vicars of that unquestionable sovereignty above. Thus, Christianity—like the other great religions in the Wisdom and Imperial stage, through all its words and symbols—endeavored to show itself not so much as a historically conditioned institution than the Absolute abiding on earth.

The Wisdom and Imperial era fully establishes the Great Tradition of a Great Religion in both its social and intellectual dimensions, placing an elite of thinkers and hierarchs in powerful positions at royal and imperial courts and in monasteries and universities. These persons go to great lengths to orient the new religion toward the whole accessible heritage of culture and thought, especially those monistic and mystical dimensions of the life of the mind that stress the timelessness of what can be known or intuited at the outer limits of realization. By the same token, the religion almost spontaneously created popular forms that admit peasant masses into its ambit, retailing the faith on the level of folklore and village temples, identifying it with what seems to be the no-less-timeless ancient lore and sacred places of hearth and field. But the culture-shaping, feeling-enhancing potential of a rising Great Religion is not exhausted by the structures of the second stage.

CHAPTER SEVEN
MEDIEVAL DEVOTIONALISM

The assimilative Wisdom and Imperial stage gradually issues into another stage, with a fresh set of attitudes and central practices. This next stage is Devotional, which in most of the great faiths is broadly associated with the Middle Ages. To modern viewers, medievalism has ever seemed both fascinating and impossibly distant. Finding it difficult to recapture the ordinary humanity of most medieval folk, we tend to think of it and its people in overgeneral and often contradictory stereotypes: it was an "age of faith" and of torture, of splendor and squalor, of saints and sinners, of icons rather than the "real people" who are quite present in the likes of Chaucer's *Canterbury Tales* or the Lady Murasaki's *Genji Monogatari.*

In regard to such icons of the intellect, it is always salutary to reflect on such words as these from Aldous Huxley: "The past is not something fixed and unalterable. Its facts are rediscovered by every succeeding generation, its values reassessed, its meanings redefined in the context of present tastes and preoccupations. Out of the same documents and monuments and works of art, every epoch invents its own Middle Ages, its private China, its patented and copyrighted Hellas."[1]

Because the Devotional period corresponds broadly with the medieval in most cultures—stretching out the Middle Ages to cover, say, 500 to 1500 C.E., or even later in some places—it is easy to see in it a common worldwide medieval style of spirituality, rather than a stage intrinsic to each great religion.

Of course, much can be said on behalf of a world-medieval point of view. Contact between the world religions was certainly sufficient to encourage cross-cultural imitation of devotional styles, and we can glean certain parallels from such relationships. An interesting example is the rosary.

Probably originating in the Middle East in the early centuries of the common era, the devotional practice of saying prayers or mantra on a string of beads spread during the Middle Ages through several religions and from Ireland to Japan. Or consider a very different religious manifestation: Tantric attitudes and practices (e.g., the sacramental use of sex), which appeared in the early medieval centuries in Hinduism, Buddhism, and Taoism. Although the first two are certainly related, debate continues as to whether the arts of the *Fang-zhong shu*, a text frankly explicating its Taoist version, was originally an import or an independent development.

Pilgrimage and devotion to tombs of saints was also very important in medieval Christianity, Islam, Hinduism (the *mahasamadhi* of God-realized saints), Buddhism (consider the numerous stupas to relics of the Buddha and other holy ones, even the *miira,* "self-mummified buddhas," of northern Japan), or Confucianism (where the honor given the tomb of the Sage and other worthies was like an extension of ancestrism). But the cultus of saints' tombs is so pervasive that one finds it difficult to say it began in one faith and then spread to others. Rather, it seems inwardly incumbent on a religion at this point to explore as wide as possible a variety of sensory, conceptual, and emotional ways of focusing attachment to the religion, among which hagiolatry would be an obvious prospect. Practices that are available for our consideration include those that are visual, audial, relational (i.e., connections to holy persons), and tactile (e.g., kissing relics and the like), with appropriate feelings to go with them. Within these parameters only so many possibilities obtain.

That is seen to be especially the case when certain medieval "ground rules" are recognized. By grace of the world's historical conditions from 500 to 1500, all the great religions generally dwelt in a situation wherein:

- The majority of the population was illiterate and so in need of visual aids—pictures, statues, symbols—and tactile actions to complement oral communication.
- The majority were sedentary agriculturalists, and their spiritual lives tied to the local church or temple and its village; such travel as there was for most people was linked to war or pilgrimage.
- As a fruit of the Axial Age, beneath the formless One the sacred was pictured primarily in human, not animal or abstract,

form, at least in its manifestations on earth. Even the angels were essentially human! That is, the sacred appeared as gods, goddesses, buddhas, bodhisattvas, immortals, saviors, and saints living or deceased. These were the forms (unpictured, of course, in Islam) to whom devotion was characteristically directed and to whose shrines pilgrimage was made. Such human–divine beings were in turn sources of illumination and miracle. (Miracle was certainly important in medieval religious lore, but we must not forget, as we noted in the first chapter, that medieval skepticism was also possible.)

- Finally, it is interesting to recall with Aldous Huxley in his *Heaven and Hell*, the importance of color and pageantry for the medieval world.[2] Contrary to the sentimental view of some moderns that the Middle Ages were days of technicolor splendor, for most people the medieval human environment displayed drabness most of time: wattle and dung homes, earth-colored garb, utensils of unfinished wood or stone. The more splendid paints and dyes were rare and expensive, and even the mighty had, by modern standards, but few proud paintings, tapestries, brocades, golden or silver or even pewter plate, or jewelry to soften the dark gloom of a medieval castle, in which no manageable illumination was brighter than a candle. Consider, then, the impact on the average medieval man or woman of a brightly hued statue of a deity, savior, or saint; of a gleaming altar or resplendent procession, or a solemn liturgy with tapers and incense. In our day, saturated as we are with cheap color and canned drama, it is difficult fully to recapture the medieval power of such rare brilliance or the significance of its being associated with religion and the transcendent.

Given this context, we are not surprised to find the Devotional age's manifesting itself as an age of statues, temples, and pageantry, and of focused feeling-laden prayer to saints and saviors, not seldom in their imaged or localized forms. For it was a time of search for diversity, color, and feeling in religion and life, but a search under constraints: some limits were a result of the times, such as those already mentioned; some were of the particular faith, such as the Muslim ban on images. Yet within these parameters, a tremendous range of image and feeling was brought forth: the rosary, sacred dance, pilgrimage, prayer to a great diversity of human forms of the One.

The image of the person capable of giving and receiving love is the keynote of the age, embracing both divine personalities and their human devotees. Love thus becomes both the supreme symbol of the divine and the locus of the human relationship with ultimate reality. The word *symbol* is used here in the Tillichian sense of that which participates in what it symbolizes. Devotionalism emphasizes personality—the personal as capable of distinctive traits of character, of giving and receiving love, of acting spontaneously and unexpectedly, of manifesting what is really most important about the Transcendent.

By the same token, devotion emphasizes that it is the person with these qualities who best worships God; what God treasures most in his lovers is the spontaneous gesture of unconditional love, such as the dance steps of bhakti or Sufi saints, marked by the unique personality of the worshiper.

In the Wisdom stage of Christianity, the human personality of Christ was all but eclipsed by his assimilation into such more abstract roles as universal Logos and Pantocrator; in the Middle Ages, however, after the Devotional stage had well set in, his lovable personhood—if not exactly his personality in the modern sense—returns as the divine human. Saint Francis, according significant tradition, made the first Christmas crèche and thereby worshiped divinity formed of infant flesh, and Saint Bernard sang, "Jesus the very thought of Thee, with sweetness fills the breast."

Devotionalism is profoundly reflected in art. Indeed, in most places this stage is the greatest hour of religious architecture and iconography. The exaltation of sacred personhood and sacred feeling within the worshiper naturally summons up the greatest skills of artists to reveal the tenderness, the mystery, and the individual uniqueness of the holy ones.

Intellectually, this age also represents a culmination of the great system-making program implicit in the previous stage, when all of nature and supernature, all the orders human and divine, are brought together in vast enterprises of the mind that show their interconnectedness: the *Summa* of Thomas, the Buddhist syntheses of Tiantai and Shingon. The relation of these Great Tradition works to devotionalism may not be immediately apparent, yet it is there, for they provide the overall legitimation for the particularistic roles of objects of devotion by appropriately placing them in the hierarchy of heaven and earth or the stages of the spiritual life. Gods, buddhas, or saints can, as it were, step out of the mandala or the latinate pages of theology to bless or answer heartfelt prayer, their place intuitively grasped by the simple and understood by the wise.

Politically, this period was a time when the imperial unity of the second stage had given way to a number of feudal states within the religion's orbit, though the memory of empire remains potent. The many kingdoms abet Devotional era tendencies toward religious particularism while emphasizing the religion's inherent universalism as the faith of diverse lands. The corresponding inward plurality of paths and local manifestations of devotionalism ultimately leads into the fragmentation of the next stage, the Reformation stage. For now, however, faith is at once both one and many.

The Devotional stage is, then, the Christendom of 1000 to 1500 with its personal piety to Jesus, the Blessed Virgin, and the saints. This devotion was linked to the spirit of chivalry in aristocratic secular society and is reflected in warm and soaring Christian art from the great cathedrals to Giotto. As the inimitable Henry Adams put it in *Mont Saint Michel and Chartres*, "the Virgin was actually and constantly present" during the labor of medieval cathedral building. One can, this grandson and great-grandson of presidents tells us, sense the difference between a church or a temple built under such direct, personal spiritual inspiration, and one lacking it. "Without this sense, the church is dead." Moreover, "most persons of a deeply religious nature would tell you emphatically that nine churches out of ten actually were dead-born, after the thirteenth century."[3]

That personal presence of the divine in its innumerable representations was nowhere better expressed than in Franciscan piety. Brother Francis himself was awakened to his vocation when he heard the painted lips of a crucifix in a ruined church tell him to "rebuild my church," and toward the end of his life he became so close to the crucified Savior that he shared his wounds, the stigmata. The saint of Assisi also exuberantly participated in the personalized praise of all creation for the Creator: Brother Sun and Brother Fire, Sister Moon and Sister Water, and Sister Death. His popular and effusive style of devotion likewise magnified simple, personal, superficially naive expressions of feeling directed toward concrete, visible objects manifesting the triune God: representations of the Nativity, the Eucharist, the Cross, acts of joyous praise that go far toward making the celebrant seem a fool for God, like Juggler of Notre Dame or Francis himself pretending to play a mandolin before Our Lady.

Medieval Christian devotion was no less directed toward Jesus present in the Sacrament of the Altar at Mass. The nostalgic Eamon Duffy tells us that "as the kneeling congregation raised their eyes to see the Host held high above the priest's head at the sacring, they were transported to Calvary itself, and gathered not only into the passion and resurrection of Christ, but into the full sweep of salvation history as a whole."[4] In the words of didactic verse:

> Then shal thou do reverence
> to ihesu crist awen presence
> That lay lese alle baleful bandes;
> knelande holde up bothe thi handes.

According to the canonist William Lyndwood (d. 1446), for the sake of devotion the canon of the Mass was to be recited by the priest in silence "ne impediatur populus orare," so that the people might not be impeded in praying. John Mirk, in *Instructions for Parish Priests*, tells pastors to admonish their people that

> whenne they doth to chyrche fare,
> Thenne bydde him leve here mony wordes,
> Here ydel speche, and nyce bordes,
> and put a-way alle vanyte,
> And say here pater noster & here ave.[5]

Obviously, the prevailing orientation is toward personal devotion in the awesome presence of the Eucharist, and not the more recently favored active liturgical participation. Individual participation obtained in another powerful aspect of medieval devotionalism, however. William A. Christian Jr. has gathered a remarkable collection of late medieval accounts from Spain of apparitions of the Blessed Virgin, and these also present the flavor of the Devotional era. For example, in August 1458, in the midst of an epidemic of bubonic plague, a vision was seen near Lleida, Catalonia, by several witnesses. One witness, a boy named Jaume Cirosa, said under oath that on the previous Thursday, August 3, at the hour of vespers, he saw a lovely little girl. She had long blonde hair, wore a red cape, and displayed a beautiful cross on her shoulder. She said to him, "Tell the people to make processions and make them devoutly, and to confess and convert and return to the side of God, and if they do, God will forgive them." She added: "There is no child four or more years old whom my son will not reap"—a grim prophecy fulfilled in at least one case, for the witness Jaume himself soon died of the plague.

Like much in the annals of devotionalism, this report may suggest a local folk religion background. The beautiful cross the girl wore was like that on a nearby church altar, and regional peasant belief spoke of *vellatas*, fairies who could take the form of little girls with golden hair. Yet the apparition's words, typical of many admonitions of Our Lady, as well as the indirect reference to Christ as she speaks of "my son," place the vision in a devotional Christian context. As a great religion's sway takes deeper and deeper hold, immemorial folk beliefs will be brought into its orbit and lightly tinctured with its names and forms.

Seeing and hearing the sacred in the mystery of the Mass at a village church; witnessing the familiar fairy/human form by the humble in homely settings; embracing the same with the ecstasy of a St. Francis or St. Bernard: that is Christianity in the era of devotion . . . and like all the eras, it lingers in hearts everywhere even as it shares the center with new developments.

Devotionalism is Hindu bhakti in the same period, a great era of Hindu temples, as it was of cathedrals in Europe. Though the roots go back centuries before, as we have seen in relation to the Gupta and Pallava era, personalized piety's great age was from the composition of the Puranas in the early centuries of the common era to the time of Caitanya (1485–1533). Devotionalism reached its richest intellectual expression in the theology of Ramanuja (c. twelfth century) and was popularized by poets from the Alvars to Kabir and by the dance and sculpture of medieval Hindustan. Its characteristic form is the *kirtan* (or *bhajan* in south India), which comprises the followers' chanting or singing the names and praises of Krishna, accompanied by drums, cymbals, and often ecstatic dance. Kirtan may take place in private homes, in temples, or street processions, and any devotee may take part, though sometimes it is led by quasi-professional musicians. And Krishna is the devotional god of Hinduism supreme.

Krishna is to devotional Hinduism almost what Jesus was to Francis: a charming and irrepressible divine child, God as a divine dancer and lover, a warrior on behalf of right, and finally, if not quite one who suffered the agonies of crucifixion, the victim of abandonment and betrayal by his own.[6] More than any other Hindu divinity, he demonstrates sacred love *(prema),* the beauty of God manifested in human form *(rupa),* and the purposeless yet fascinating and creative divine play *(lila)* by which this wise-child deity made the universe. While the main literary sources of Krishnaism, the Bhagavad Gita and the much later (c. tenth century) Bhagavata Purana (also called the *Srimad Bhagavatam*), are prior to 1000 C.E., it was during the Devotional era that fervent Krishna worship spread widely and took its most effusive form in erotic poems that celebrated the love between Krishna and his consort Radha. Devotees lost themselves in ecstatic dancing and chanting to fast-beating music. Women would place images of the infant deity in tiny cribs and, calling themselves "mothers of the god," rock him back and forth as an expression of love. In services, figures of Krishna and Radha are often put together on the swing the bride and groom share in Hindu weddings and are swung back and forth. Bhaktas always put their practice in terms of setting aside self-restraint and merely asking, "What more can I do to show my love? What more can I do to please the beloved god, to make myself his indulgent mother, lover, or companion?"[7]

The aforementioned Purana, following the Bhagavad Gita, puts the theory of bhakti plainly:

> Neither by Yoga, nor by philosophy, nor by deeds, nor by study, nor by austerity, nor even by renunciation of desires, am I easily attained. Those only who have pure love for me find me easily. I, the Self, dear to the devotee, am attainable by love and devotion. Devotion to me purifies even the lowliest of the law.
>
> Without love for me virtues and learning are unfruitful.
>
> He who loves me is made pure; his heart melts in joy. . . . The bliss in that state is so intense that forgetful of himself and his surroundings he sometimes weeps profusely, or laughs, or sings, or dances; such a devotee is a purifying influence upon the whole universe.[8]

The great Vaisnava theologian Ramanuja (c. 1077–1157) spoke of the importance of divine descents (avatars) like Krishna by which the supreme God made himself present to humanity. As his commentary of the Bhagavad Gita paraphrased chapter 7.1, the theologian said of the devotee, "With the mind attached to Me because it is turned toward Me, his love for Me is so great that if he were to be separated from my essential nature, qualities, actions, or glorious realms, even for an instant, his nature would fall to pieces. Therefore he keeps his mind closely bound to Me." More surprisingly, Ramanuja went on to point out that God is similarly dependent on his passionate devotees: "I consider the jñañis are my very soul. This means that the support for My existence is under their control. Why is this so? Because the jñañi does not have even the possibility of sustaining his soul without me" (commentary on Gita 7:18).[9] Other theoreticians of bhakti, following categories attributed to the apocryphal sage Narada, have developed paradigms reflecting remarkably subtle psychological insight into the devotee's progress, paralleling the winding pathways of human love, toward deeper and deeper love of God, as he or she finds anagrams in the love for the other of a servant, a friend, a parent, a spouse, in the love-deepening pangs of separation, in the ultimate joy of absorption. So it is all love that opens up that within which is greater than any human love.

In Buddhism, the Devotional era is the period 500 to 1000. Under the powerful influence of such Mahayana texts as the Lotus Sutra, that age saw the rise of devotion to buddhas and bodhisattvas—such as Avalokitesvara (Chinese Guanyin, Japanese Kannon), Kshitibarba (Japanese Jizô), and above all Amitabha (Japanese Amida) of presectarian Pure Land Buddhism—gathering strength in China and Japan. It was also the period when the very different but also personalized and experiential Vajrayana took shape in Buddhist India, Tibet, and parts of southeast Asia, with its emphasis on evocational meditation spilling over into incomparable art. From Borobodur in Java to the Hôryûji in Japan, many of the greatest of Buddhist temples derive from this era.

It was the already-mentioned Lotus Sutra, however, that best expressed the spirit of Buddhist devotionalism and influenced its development. Though ultimately deriving from India early in the Wisdom era, its widespread devotional influence can be attributed to the Tiantai (Japanese Tendai) school established at the beginning of the Devotional period by Zhiyi (538–97).

Like devotionalism generally, the Lotus taught prevenient divine grace, falling like rain unmerited upon all—in this case, from the universal Buddha who is the sutra's central figure and who descends avatarlike into all worlds (in ours as the historical Buddha) from out of the realm of eternity. It held simple, childlike devotion—a toddler making a crude clay stupa or presenting a small clutch of flowers in his tiny hand to a Buddha image—to be closer to liberation than the proud achievement of the arhat based on his own mighty efforts at study or meditation. For the latter only reinforces the ego while striving to get rid of it, while the essence of pure devotion is childlike self-forgetfulness before the beloved.

The Lotus wisely tells us that all *yanas* (vehicles for liberation) are acceptable, for all are relative to the needs of persons in conditioned reality; once liberation is realized, one will also realize that there is no vehicle and no path, for liberation is everywhere, and one was already there all the time—it is just a matter of remembering that stupendous fact. It relates the famous parable of a father who, coming home from a journey, sees to his horror that his house, with his children inside, is on fire. Quickly realizing that if he yelled "Fire," they might panic and be in further danger trying to rush out, he shouted instead that he had brought them presents, namely, many small toy carts. Squealing with delight, the children ran out of the house to see them and were thus saved from the fire.

The fire represents, of course, this destructive realm of existence, burning and destroying itself with passion, and the toy carts the many vehicles of Buddhism, relative truths by means of which one can travel beyond this world to the other side. The Lotus Sutra next goes into a long discourse on whether the father was justified in lying—for he really had no toy carts—in order to save his children. It finally concludes that he was, just as preachers are justified in proclaiming Buddhist vehicles supposedly leading to enlightenment even though they are themselves part of the relative, conditioned reality from which they purport to liberate. For until one has traveled far down their vehicular roads, one cannot understand the unconditioned, absolute truth of universal enlightenment accessible to one who sees reality as it appears through the eyes of a buddha or bodhisattva.

Tendai, based on the Lotus Sutra, believing in innumerable noncompetitive paths to salvation, afforded an immense umbrella under which diverse forms of evocation to buddhas and bodhisattvas could be arrayed. Its great Enryakuji monastery in Japan, begun in 788, soon became a vast complex of temples scattered through the deep woods of this picturesque site on Mount Hiei, just northeast of the ancient capital, Kyoto. Not only was it politically influential, but Hiei's numerous sacred shrines made the holy mountain virtually a devotional Buddhist "cafeteria." Here was a shrine to Dainichi (Vairocana), the Great Sun Buddha who represented the essence of the universe; there one to Fudô (Acala), the flame-backed, immovable Buddha of fierce opposition to all the snares of illusion; down the path, a lovely temple to Kannon, the many-armed bodhisattva, or "goddess" of mercy, the responder to simple prayers for help, of whom many tales of miracles are told; and, finally, a large edifice to Amida, the savior buddha who has vowed to bring all who call on his name in faith to the Western Paradise or Pure Land. (However, the polymorphous Tendai approach could not sustain the faith of all as times changed; it was also Mount Hiei that became the foundation for Buddhism's next step, the Reformation stage.)

Like all other devotionalism, then, loving worship in Buddhism was justified theoretically in convoluted yet psychically understandable ways by the sophisticated while serving several broader functions: it offered aesthetically and emotionally satisfying worship to all levels of society where Buddhism had by now been fully acclimatized; it presented gates through which one could enter a path toward liberation; and it suggested ways buddhas and bodhisattvas themselves could exercise wisdom and compassion—their premier virtues—by becoming (on the conditioned-reality plane) gods in heaven answering prayers. This was the Devotional stage through which the dharma, having acquired broad wisdom and imperial prestige, had to pass as it deepened and diversified its inner life, before endeavoring in some places again to simplify it through Reformation—for in all religions there is unceasing tension between the broad and the narrow way.

For Chinese religion generally, the same period (or more precisely, from the fall of the Han dynasty in 220 to the accession of the Song dynasty in 960 C.E.) represents the Devotional stage. It includes the confused but culturally creative Three Kingdoms and Six Dynasties periods, when Buddhism and Taoism flourished, and the great Tang era. Tang emperors patronized both Buddhism and Taoism. It was an age of the relative recession of Confucianism and appropriately of the heyday of personalistic, feeling-oriented Taoist and Chinese Buddhist traditions, with their hierarchies of gods, saviors, and immortals; their splendid art; and their popular devotionalism.

It was during the Tang era that the elaborate devotional hierarchy of Taoist deities took shape to make a heavenly counterpart of the bureaucratic structure below. Sovereign was the Jade Emperor, Yu Huang, attested to by the tenth century with poems describing his celestial court, where he is attended by deities of stars, mountains, wind, and rain. A state cult of this popular figure was instituted in 1017. Also very popular was Kuan Di, the "god of war" (more accurately, of martial virtues), a deification of Kuan Yu, a romanticized hero of the chivalrous Three Kingdoms (third century C.E.) period. He is particularly believed to have control over evil spirits.

The Tang era also witnessed the building of Confucian temples in most communities. These were not places for popular worship but for Confucian scholars and administrators under the leadership of the chief magistrate, a mandarin appointed from above. They remind us that the legacy of the Wisdom and Imperial period has by now become a part of popular devotional religion in the sense that its place is recognized and that its officials have popular religious roles; the chief mandarin was responsible for worship of the city god on behalf of the community and even for punishing him if affairs went badly.

The great bodhisattva Avalokiteshvara's transmutation into Guanyin, the Buddhist "goddess of mercy," is an important story for Chinese popular devotionalism. This compassionate bodhisattva was originally the male Avalokitesvara. However, he possessed some androgynous features, was able to appear in female form as an expression of skill-in-means, and clearly seemed more accessible and appealing to the popular Chinese mind than the Buddha with his austere teachings and emaciated (though oft colorfully depicted) *lohan,* or disciples.

A shift in statues and dedications in the great Buddhist caves of Lung Men, near Loyang in Henan province, bespeaks the opening of the Devotional era. Those made from 500 to 540 show the historical Buddha, Sakyamuni, to be the most popular image. There were 43 dedications to him; 35 to the future Buddha, Maitreya; 8 to Amida; and 22 to Guanyin. Between 650 and 690, however, only 8 were offered to Sakyamuni, 11 to Maitreya, 103 to Amida (no less a center of Buddhist devotionalism), and 44 to Guanyin.[10] He/she was introduced into virtually all Buddhist temples by the sixth century, though as the masculine Avalokitesvara until around the tenth century when, probably under the influence of Taoist ideas about the need for complementary male and female energies, the merciful bodhisattva acquired feminine status to sit alongside the masculine Buddhist pantheon.

Another likelihood no less indicates the way an indigenizing great religion can absorb aspects of ancient popular faith, salvaging them on its own terms. A case in point is Chinese shamanism. It had been politically powerful during the Shang and Chou dynasties. But Confucianism naturally opposed these influential oracles, often women, and their world of irrational male and female spirits, for disciples of the Sage endeavored to base society on ethics, reason, and male domination. During the Han dynasty, the old shamanism had been extensively attacked and ridiculed by court Confucians. It was driven underground, often reemerging as popular Taoism, sometimes in the form of apocalyptic, revolutionary sects appearing among the poor and oppressed rural peasantry, such as the Queen Mother of the West cult of around 10 B.C.E. to 5 C.E. in northeast China, or the Five Bushels of Rice uprising in the second century C.E.

The Queen Mother of the West (said, incidentally, to have been revealed by an immortalized shamaness) is particularly important for the story of Guanyin and devotionalism. The lack of a comparable female figure in Buddhism became painfully apparent after the Confucian attempt to suppress her cult and especially after Taoism and the imported Buddhist faith fell into serious rivalry as vehicles for popular devotionalism. Despite Confucian efforts to rationalize the world, yearning for goddesses lingered on the streets and in the villages.[11]

Buddhism could not fail to respond, and Guanyin changed until she met the need. With her loving eyes, her white robe, and her vial pouring out waters of mercy, she became the recourse of ordinary people in difficulty or danger. The adaptation of Guanyin was not, however, perceived as some calculating or cynical device of priestcraft. Rather, in a way characteristic of popular devotionalism, innovation was by miracle.

In 939, in Hangchow, a monk named Tao I was meditating when he saw a strange glowing light emanating from a nearby stream. Investigating, he found a piece of beautiful wood some two feet long. Hauling it out of the water, he took it took a famous sculptor and asked that it be made into a statue. When the latter took the wood to his workshop and split it open, he found there a perfectly formed statue of Guanyin. Its authenticity was reinforced by a series of dreams in which a white-robed woman appeared and commanded the statue be worshiped. This seems to be the first actual mention in extant Chinese records of a statue of the bodhisattva in female form; the success of the image is indicated by how quickly its temple became a great pilgrimage center thronged with worshipers and how famous it became for its miracles and answered prayers. Indeed, this period, at the very end of the Tang dynasty, saw the building of many Guanyin temples; and when Hangchow became the capital of southern Song dynasty (1127–1279), the original temple received imperial support.[12]

Hardly less popular, especially in south China, is Mazu, the "mother goddess," a deified maiden believed drowned at sea in the tenth century. Immediately storm-tossed fishermen saw her standing luminous over the troubled waters ready to help, and she was endowed with supernatural powers until she herself, like Guanyin, became Queen of Heaven.

The roster of Chinese popular deities, together with their respective shrines and festivals, is well populated. It ranges from deities honored throughout the empire to local city and village tutelary deities of ancient background. Those named epitomize Chinese devotionalism, though, since they represent deities who emerged in the wake of the Wisdom/Imperial ideology as fixtures in a heavenly imperial court, as representations of Taoist and Han synthesized ideas of complementarities and spiritual energy; at the same time, they possess popular appeal and the ability to focus religious emotion.

In Islam, the Devotional period might be said to run from the time of Jalal al-Din Rumi (1207–1273) to the beginning of the twentieth century. Rumi's exquisite mystical but accessible poetry and the Mevlevi order he founded express Islamic devotion at its finest. The order is famous for the dancers known in the West as "whirling dervishes," whose choreographies express a remarkable combination of ecstasy and precision. Although there were earlier sources of devotionalism and earlier mystical fraternities, the high Middle Ages and modern period (by the Western chronology), when the Ottoman, Safavid, and Mogul dynasties ruled much of the Islamic world, saw its greatest efflorescence. In those days, the tomb-shrines of *wali* (saints), their roofs usually domed to symbolize heaven, appeared across the countryside. Pilgrimage to major sites where their *barakah* (spiritual blessing) filled the air often exceeded the *hajj* to Mecca, especially among Shi'ites, for whom sacred journeys to such shrines as

Mashad, Karbala, or Najaf were important experiences of grace and expressions of loyalty. No less significant were *mawlids* (celebrations) of the birthday of a saint or of the Prophet himself. Increasingly, popular piety included devotions of Sufi origin, such as *dhikr* (the rhythmic recitation of phrases), often the ninety-nine known names of God. In more advanced circles, the practices includes breath control and body movements that increase the ecstatic feeling. Also popular is *sama'*, or the use of music and dance to enhance piety, together with the singing of mystical verses.

It would be hard to imagine more impassioned devotionalism than that of Shi'ites during the first ten days of Muharram, the first month of the Muslim calendar, when they honor the martyrdom of Husayn, the third Imam according to Shi'a teaching. The commemoration was initiated in the tenth century. During this festival, Shi'a communities set up black tents with memorial arms and candles to remind the faithful of the martyr, who was said to have been cruelly killed by the forces of the usurping caliph at the battle of Karbala, in what is now southern Iraq. The tragic story of Husayn is recited from pulpits in the tents. Occasionally, groups of men would go through the streets expressing their anguish by wailing, dancing wildly, and inflicting wounds on themselves. At the climax of the commemoration, on the tenth day, a passion play reenacts the hero's death. Brightly garbed horsemen charge and recharge each other, battering one another in sport with wooden weapons. At the climax, Husayn is taken and seen to suffer excruciatingly from thirst as his foemen make sport of him, and the crowd grows more and more excited. At last, he is beheaded.

The ten-volume collection of Sufi lore called the *al-Hilyat al-Awliya*, collected by Abu Nu'aym al-Isbahani (d. 1038), and further elaborated by Abd al-Karim ibn Ibrahim al-Jili (d. 1428), a disciple of the great esoteric philosopher Ibn Arabi, systematically presents the traditional view of divine hierarchies. It parallels a process that also appears in the Devotional era respecting Christian saints; the Hindu Vaisnava and Saiva pantheons; the buddhas and bodhisattvas of the Vajrayana mandala; and the Taoist heavenly hierarchies under the Jade Emperor. The Sufi array of saints, however, is a hierarchy of friends of God on earth. In the Ibn Arabi tradition, it is made up of one *qutb*, or central esoteric "pivot," two "guides," four "pillars," seven "substitutes," twelve "leaders," and eight "nobles." These saints mystically hold the world together; they may outwardly appear very ordinary and, in their humility, may not even themselves know their exalted status in the inner scheme of things. Should they fail, all would collapse.

Islamic devotionalism clearly reflects the popularization of features with roots in the great tradition, whether of Sunni Islam, Shi'a, or mystical Sufism. But these are combined with recurring religious themes with deep folkloric roots. The cult of the saints, their tombs, birthdays, and miraculous powers, though protested by some among the orthodox, was irrepressible and probably is related to a wider and older Asian belief in the man or woman of great spiritual power: the Buddha, the *jivan-mukta* (God-realized one) of Hinduism, the Taoist immortal, perhaps ultimately the shaman. The appearance of Muslim *wali* (saints) and *shaykhs* (spiritual masters) simply inculturated that model into the new faith. Likewise, it is surely no mere coincidence that the Shi'ite wailing of Husayn originated in the same area, the Valley of the Two Rivers and its environs, where the far more ancient wailing for Tammuz, the ever youthful yet ever dying and rising god of vegetation, had been heard long before either Christ or Muhammad. Devotionalism brought all this together between the high Middle Ages and the twentieth century, when the tide of that articulation of Islam began to recede before the gathering forces of the Islamic Reformation.

What are some reasons why devotionalism takes over from the Wisdom/Imperial expression of a Great Religion?

First, as a faith still relatively new to a society in the second stage puts down deeper and deeper roots, sinking into folklore and folk custom, its popular forms naturally become stronger and more self-confident. In the nature of things, these expressions are likely to exhibit protodevotional characteristics or practices such as offerings and pilgrimage, often carried over from earlier religion, which can easily take on the emotional coloring of a great religion's devotionalism. By the religion's third stage, these forms will have worked their way up to acquire Great Tradition sanction; with a patina of great art and poetry, they set the tone of an entire period.

Second and concomitantly, as a religion's expression in art and literature matures, it almost inevitably becomes less archetypally stylized and more person-centered. Great personalizing religious art creates as well as reflects the devotional mood, from the wonderfully human yet transcendent buddhas of Nara to the imbibers of mystical wine in Persian miniatures.

Third and above all, devotionalism reflects the religionists' burgeoning confidence in themselves as persons. This is the result of the religion's having finally made for itself a fairly stable and self-confident civilization in the Wisdom and Imperial stage. Its struggles for spiritual and political–social legitimation are now over; it has won. Its people can take themselves seriously as centers of feeling and meaning.

Yet devotionalism also reflects something opposite, the crisis of defining personhood in a period when outward society is likely to be slowly fragmenting following the imperial age. Thus, Christian devotionalism arose in the wake of Byzantine and Carolingian imperial–wisdom Christianities; Hindu bhakti, in the wake of the Gupta state and, finally, when Hindus found themselves under alien rule; Muslim saints and ecstasy, in the aftermath of the caliphate; Chinese devotion, after the Han; Buddhist devotion under successors to its Mauryan and Kushan patrons.

For reasons of both confidence and fragmentation, then, the self discovers that it can stand on its own before God or Ultimate Reality as a center of feeling, deciding, knowing inwardly, and loving, qualities that God and his lovers can mirror between each other. But the process has opened an inner floodgate that will not rest until its waters have washed with still more power over the fields of history.

CHAPTER EIGHT
REFORMATION

Devotion culminates in the age of reformation. It is a period *averaging* five centuries, the same as the others. For though the first revolutionary upheaval itself may be relatively brief, a matter of decades or at the most a generation or two, it establishes the religion's character and agenda for the next several centuries.

The Reformation era is complex. Spiritually it has roots in devotionalism, for among its salient features is the emphasis on faith, inwardness, and the essentials of salvation, which the previous era had encouraged, but with a new simplification of focus just on those qualities. The elaborate iconography and feeling-tones of medieval devotionalism are relatively downplayed or even rejected altogether. In a sense, reformation is a reverse of the Wisdom period's interpretation of the religion, for where the latter had moved toward timeless and universal realities, reformation narrows expansiveness down to simple, personal issues in crucial respects. If an age is often better understood by the questions it asks than by the answers it gives, wisdom asks and the scholastic wing of devotion further asks, "How can all the entities of the universe and human experience, including the facts of the new faith, be integrated into an immense interlocking system?" Thomas Aquinas, al-Ghazali, Dong Zongshu, Shankara, and the Lotus school of Mahayana Buddhism gave their voluminous, multitiered answers. But reformation sets all that aside to ask, with Luther, "How can I be sure that I am saved?" Understandably, the simpler and sharper the answer to such a question, the better.

Religion still has considerable capital to expend in the era of reformation. It may shift direction, but it remains an immensely powerful historical force. Though the emergence of the Reformation age is itself basically the product of the religion's own internal dynamics, those same dynamics now begin to tilt the balance more and more toward responding to external historical change as well. While benefiting from political alliances and incorporating much from outside during the second and third stages, the new Great Religion still sets its spiritual tone from out of its own essence and was fundamentally in charge of its history. Now we see the cutting edge of spiritual and cultural change occasionally slip from its grasp, though the Great Religion retains plenty of fight and the battle is joined. Yet the battle itself has at least half the nature of response.

If the Wisdom and Devotional periods represent the classical eras of a religion (i.e., its moments of triumph and culture creation), reformation is its first great reaction to a changing world—a response, or rather series of responses, made when the religion still has power to respond on the Great Tradition level, as equal to anything else in the intellectual, educational, political, economic, and artistic worlds at their best. But it is now not the *only* entity in those worlds; it is itself increasingly divided.

As the Devotion period draws to an end, the most obvious backdrop for reformation is likely to be the rise of national governments that lack the intimate relation to the religion of their predecessors, though they would no doubt nominally support it if they were of the same faith. This phenomenon is itself the product of historical forces related to the rise of the Great Religion. Very rare is the human empire, dynasty, or political order that lasts more than two or three hundred years; even rarer is that which, so enduring, does not undergo major modification. By now, the empire that first harbored the nascent religion and put it on the world map is long since gone, and so are the successor states, which, at least initially, probably emulated its policies toward the faith. For example . . .

In Europe on the eve of the Protestant Reformation, the Christian Roman Empire was long since no more than a dream, despite its peculiar afterlives in the oft-antagonistic Papacy and Holy Roman Empire. Instead, national regimes were on the rise, and their rulers, like Henry VIII of England or the princely supporter of Luther, John Frederick I of Saxony, however devout personally, were quite prepared to identify the church in their domains with their own ends and, in Henry's case, as foundations for personal power, rather than standing in awe of the ecclesia's universal character.

In Kamakura Japan, sensitive persons were still nostalgic for the Heian era, when the imperial court was deeply intertwined with the elaborate rites and great monastic establishments of the Shingon and Tendai schools of Buddhism. All that had come to an end, however, with the civil wars of the twelfth century, and the Minamoto house was finally triumphant in 1185. Giving its head the title of *shôgun* (military dictator under the emperor's titular rule), this warrior clan transferred his capital to Kamakura, not far from modern Tokyo. The great reformist evangelists of Pure Land, Honen and Shinran; of Zen, Dogen and Eisai; and Nichiren of Nichiren then spread the news that the old inward trails to salvation were no longer needed, perhaps not even valid. In a new and tumultuous era, one simple sure key—faith in Amida Buddha, faith in the Lotus Sutra, plain Zen sitting—was answer enough to the one all-important question, "How can I be sure that I am saved?"

These rough and ready answers were at home in all ranks of Japanese society. The first two largely disdained monasticism, making saving grace as equally accessible to the peasant in his or her village or to the soldier facing death on the field of battle as to the priest or the learned monk in his cloister. The last, Zen, though monastic, pleased the new military aristocracy because its monks' refined simplicity and soldierlike discipline marched well with their own ideals, and because the Zen orders offered a counterpoise to the excessive political role of the old esoteric monasteries. New socicty, new culture, and new reformed religion all fitted together well in the Japan of the high Middle Ages.

In Islam, the reformation of the twentieth century similarly took place after the end of old imperial regimes—the Ottoman and Persian, and the Russian, British, French, and Dutch colonial empires having dominion over many millions of Muslims. National, and often nationalistic, successor states to those sprawling regimes were fertile fields for Islamic reformative impulses.

Perhaps a precursor of reform was the anticolonialist Caliphate movement of the 1920s, which attempted to unite Muslims on the basis of its universalism under a revival of the ancient Islamic empire. Like the general church councils and various idealistic reform movements in western Christianity before the Protestant Reformation, it did not achieve its goal. The later and often successful Islamic movements of the late twentieth century, sometimes misleadingly called fundamentalist, like the Protestants linked reform based on return to the sources (in this case the Shari'ah or Islamic law, strictly applied) of resurgent nationalism and rejection of outside influences. Yet the universal caliphal empire remains a dream and an ideal. So it was that M. A. S. Faraj—an apologist for the assassination of Egyptian president Anwar Sadat, considered an inconsistent Muslim in 1981—wrote in *The Neglected Duty* that Muslim rulers since the abolition of the Caliphate in 1924 have suppressed the Shari'ah and are apostate, forcing believers to submit to earthly idols.[1] Apostates, of course, may be killed.

Postempire, pre-reformation states like Sadat's Egypt, though nationalistic, are likely to be less congenial toward the traditional, universalistic religion than was the empire, though willing to use it. Thus the Kamakura elite was overall not notably pious though living in a time of religious ferment, and the "fundamentalist"/nationalistic cause arose in Islam only after the hour for secularizing reforms—like that of Ataturk in Turkey or Sukarno in Indonesia, or of tepid, nominal Islam—had come and gone.

Why is this so? First, as the shadow of the past fades, the new states wish less to view themselves as perpetuators of the old holy society, with its alliance of throne and altar; instead, they wish to develop new policies exploring other options, such as greater independence of state from church.

Second, the religion, now fifteen hundred years old, has said much, codified much, and searched out the ramifications of its lore very far. It has, without substantial change in its angle of vision, less and less truly new to say, though new conditions have inevitably appeared on earth. Some secularization appears by default as the religion finds it impossible to remain consistent with its accumulated past and, without radical reform, to respond as flexibly to new situations as it could a thousand years earlier. The Heian regime combined Buddhist piety with Confucian-based social ideology (in Japan, a secular doctrine). Several new twentieth-century Muslim states, considering traditional religious polity inadequate to modern needs, experimented with secular, often nominally socialist, policies before the "fundamentalist" reaction set in. And even those states professing to follow the Shari'ah have not hesitated to use secular Western methods in such areas as petroleum production or military science.

Third, as the wheel of history turns, it is likely that some areas in which the population is of one Great Religion are ruled by a conquering elite of another, as was Hindu India by the Moguls. This naturally means that even the Great Tradition of the popular faith has only limited rapport with the state. This relative alienation of religion and government will have a "spillover" in incipient alienation of religion from other pillars of society, such as education, economic life, and art. These areas in their own way become secular in content and style as the state becomes less interested in patronizing exclusively religious activities and as the court sets an example of comparatively worldly sophistication.

So it was that on the eve of their Reformation eras, we find Buddhism and Chinese religion living under Kamakura and Song regimes fairly unsympathetic to traditional patterns respecting cult and state, and many of their subjects spiritually unsettled and open to new prospects. Hinduism in the days just before Caitanya found itself in an India increasingly subject to Muslim rule, in which the traditional dharma of the social order was often inoperable on a large scale, or adequate to the subjective needs of people opened to spiritual emotions by devotional bhakti. Prereformation Christian Europe was alive with new renaissance ideas and dotted with emergent nation-states restive under feudal ecclesiastical and political patterns, as well as rife with protoreformation "heretical" movements. Islam early in the twentieth century, though subjected either to colonial rulers or to anachronistic regimes, was gathering the will to assert itself and find a new way of being in the world—one with the power of the dynamic first Islamic decades.

Yet religion still had the energy to respond powerfully and creatively to this situation. Its fundamental perception at this point was that the faith must rediscover what its essentials were and press them to the exclusion of all else. The "essentials" will naturally be sought in the context of devotionalism, the motif of the era now passing away. They are therefore likely to be at least in part faith- and feeling-oriented, to hold that true religion means right subjectivity, an inner simplification around that within which is most capable of faith or God-realization. But the reformation quest goes beyond devotionalism in two ways: first, it strives to focus faith on a single object and emphasize simple acts of faith, thereby cutting through the imagistic and emotional complexity characteristic of devotionalism; second, it may in some places attempt to create an ideal religious society, "simplifying" human life by bringing back under religious control political and economic areas of life that seemed in danger of slipping away, as in Calvin's Geneva or the Islamic Republic of Iran.

The reformation response, then, is basically one of simplification, of seeking a simple sure key to the heart of the religion that makes it available anywhere, to anyone, in a changing world, and makes it relevant—whether through social control or inward application—in all arenas of life. The search for a simple sure key often means a deliberate effort to concentrate on what are believed to be the crucial texts, doctrines, and practices, the Bible or *Bhagavatam*, rejecting all else much more rigorously than before. The ideal is to recover the primitive or ideal form of the faith, inevitably presumed to have been simpler than what it has become in the present degenerate times. The process will include a simplification of worship (e.g., Lutheran, Pure Land Buddhist, as over against medieval Catholic or Tendai complexity), of doctrine (e.g., the characteristic emphasis on faith and divine grace in the Protestant confessions or the Pure Land *Shinshu seiten*), and in relation to society (e.g., the characteristic rejection of monasticism and a meditational priesthood in favor, at least in theory, of the spiritual equality of all believers).

Simplification is bound to mean that the faith is relatively laicized, popularized, and turned toward the importance of authentic subjectivity in the form of belief and "inner asceticism." For simplification down to a single sure key makes the one thing needful to salvation accessible to every believer, whether professional or not. Nonetheless, a Great Tradition type of elites continue in practice to dominate the intellectual and institutional life of the reformed faith, though it may be an elite of a different structure than before, less monkish and sacerdotal, more academic and ministerial.

So it was that Jodo Shinshu, the largest denomination of reformed Pure Land Buddhism, rejected celibacy and priesthood in principle. Its founder, Shinran, like Martin Luther set aside his monastic robe to marry. The sect is technically an association of lay devotees of the Amidist faith, though in practice it has long been controlled by hereditary lineages of priests, most prominently of the Otani house.

Reformed simplification makes spiritual life more congenial to participation in "ordinary" life in a world seen as increasingly secularized. Priesthood, monasticism, and elaborate rites appropriate to specialists are devalued, though institutional and charismatic leadership is not. Yet the very fact that leadership is noncelibate and family-based puts it on a par with leadership in other areas of society, reducing the gulf between sacred and profane worlds. The relation between the reformed, this-worldly, "inner asceticism" style of religion and the rise of modern capitalism, proposed by Max Weber and Richard Henry Tawney, though always controversial, seems not irrelevant to understanding modern Europe and Japan. (Many of the great mercantile, banking, and later industrial families that laid the foundation of Japan's economic achievement are of Pure Land background.) Only when parallels between Islam in the twentieth and twenty-first centuries and the era of the Protestant Reformation in Europe are fully understood will the full significance of Islamic developments that appear alarming to many be grasped and placed in historical contest.

Reformation leads to a process of development in the religion that lasts for half a millennium. Here are a few characteristics of those five hundred or so years.

First, we must make the important observation that reformation usually begins and takes its classic institutional form only in one part of the religion's world. That place will be on its periphery from the perspective of the religion's place of origin and traditional centers of power, a place missionized only fairly late in its expansion, and of a different language and culture from the ancient strongholds: Japan for Buddhism, Bengal for Hinduism, Germanic northern Europe for Christianity, Iran for Islam. Only the Chinese Neo-Confucian reformation, of a somewhat different nature, did not have a clear geographical focus.

The bulk of the religion, outside that place, will be affected only indirectly by reformation, through reaction against it, as in counter-reformation Catholicism, or through a gradual, diffuse influence. But from this point on, the reformation forms of the religion represent its intellectual and historical edge. At the very beginning of the Reformation era, radical reformers may endeavor to establish a sacred utopia. As these efforts inevitably fail, the religion settles into a comfortable relation with society; yet it is still yeasty, capable of novel and energetic ventures both in its reform and counter-reform wings.

In the middle or late Reformation period, the religion will show an upsurge of expansiveness and missionary activity—the potent spread of Neo-Confucianism to Korea and Japan; the evangelism of Pure Land,

Nichiren, and Zen Buddhism in Japan and beyond; in Hinduism, the Bengal-based rise of such movements as the Ramakrishna Mission and the exportation of the faith to the West; in Christianity, the great nineteenth-century missionary and social gospel movements.

Toward the end of the Reformation period, there comes a trend toward theological liberalism. Thinkers carrying the subjectivism characteristic of reformation to new heights interpret the religion in fairly relativistic, naturalistic ways believed to be compatible with the best current secular or scientific world views—the naturalistic Buddhism of Ashikaga and Momoyama Japan (Yoshida Kenkô, the Zen of Higashiyama culture, later Bankei); the ideology of the nineteenth-century "Hindu renaissance" (Roy, Vivekananda, Radhakrishnan); Christian liberalism from Schleiermacher to Tillich. Understandably, liberalism produces conservative reactions, but liberalism—and the strongest of the reactions, such as those of Aurobindo or Barth—represent the last great intellectual effort of the faith.

Finally, we may note that at the close of the Reformation era, its values tend to spread through the whole of the religion, though often in partial and unacknowledged form. (This lays down one sort of foundation, quite unintended, for the next stage, the Folk Religion stage, by diffusing localized, laicized, independent notions of faith.) The Hindu reformism of Gandhi and Bhave diffused such ideals of reformation piety as simple faith and transcendence of caste; Roman Catholicism after Vatican II is certainly more "protestant" than before. It may be pointed out that at the very end of the Reformation period, a sort of resurgence of energy often arises; it may seem a rebirth, but may really be more of an afterglow. It represents the last period when the religion and society, including the intellectual establishment, interact on more or less equal terms. One thinks of religion and the independence movement in Hindu India, or the theological renewal of the first half of the twentieth century in Christianity, and the religion's rapid spread in the "southern" world.

In Buddhism, the Reformation period is basically that inaugurated by the new Kamakura period movements in Japan: Pure Land, Nichiren, and Zen in its Japanese form. These represented a return to simple textual and experiential sources (the Pure Land texts, the Lotus Sutra, direct experience), popularization, and the use of a single simple sure key to salvation accessible to everyone: faith in Amida Buddha, the Nichiren *daimoku* chant, Zen sitting.

The Heian order had broken down partly for economic reasons, in which wealthy, nonproductive monasteries played their part. Military leaders of clans in outlying regions rose up against the court in Kyoto, one house, the Minamoto, becoming supreme and shogunal.

If Heian Japan was dominated by the elegant refined courtier and the esoteric monk, Kamakura was characterized by the simple, direct man of action. Moreover, times were troubled, and pessimism was in the air. People talked of the Buddhist idea of the *mappô*, the last age, when doctrine and morality would deteriorate so much that one could be saved only by faith, if at all. To meet the new age, three new forms of Buddhism arose—Pure Land, Nichiren, and Zen.

We have seen how each offered a single, simple, sure key to salvation, one equally accessible to all, and so effected the simplification, popularization, and laicization of religion. In effect, *mappô* pessimism was turned on its head: if salvation were only by faith, then everyone could be saved, and a new and hopeful age was inaugurated in the world—an idea that appealed especially to the fierce prophetlike Nichiren.

In Chinese religion, the reformation was the emergence of Neo-Confucianism in the relatively secular Song era (960–1279); it became state orthodoxy in the Ming (1368–1644) and thereafter. In interaction with Buddhism and Taoism, but also in response to needs for simplification and inwardness, Neo-Confucianists put emphasis on the inward state of mind of the sage, on settling one's mind and so seeing the *li*, or principles of things.

Partly in response to the issues raised by Taoist and particularly Buddhist thought, Neo-Confucian philosophers greatly enhanced their tradition's metaphysical foundation. It became a comprehensive worldview concerned with the nature of mind and the ultimate origin of things, with simple methods of meditation, as well as a social philosophy—although it never lost the ideal of the philosopher finding joy in the midst of family and social life, not in permanent withdrawal from them. The leading Neo-Confucianists, Zhu Xi (1130–1200) and Wang Yangming (1472–1529) taught that one great ultimate is manifested in the principles *(li)* of the myriad separate things, as the light of the moon is broken onto many rivers and lakes. Through reflection on particulars, especially in human morality, one can know the ultimate.

By means of ideas such as these, the spiritual and intellectual side of Confucianism was given a transcendence that made the practice of Confucian rites and virtues a more deeply religious path than before, even a sort of mysticism in the midst of a life of service. The movement took on popular religious forms in mass meetings offering lectures on self-cultivation. It emphasized the "Three Teachings"—Confucianism, Taoism, and Buddhism—as coequal Chinese traditions and ways of self-realization.

Coming to Japan in the teachings of such persons as Hayashi Razan (1583–1657), Neo-Confucianism emphasized the idea of the good society as the supreme good. To this, Hayashi added Zhu Xi's basic concept of intuiting the *li*, or principles of things, above all, one's own *li* (*ri* in Japanese). This inner essence, different for each person, is inherent, yet it must be cultivated. When that is well done by everyone, then society will create itself properly and harmoniously. A truly good society, then, would be one whose institutions allowed full expression to the true *li* of each person and class, and only to the true expression.

In practice, that idea legitimated class division and social control under the Tokugawa and later regimes in Japan, yet it showed itself a true reformation impulse by also producing, as in China, mass revivalist movements. The popular *shingauku* (heart-learning) movement of Ishida Baigan (1685–1756) made central the cultivation of the heart's original purity, holding that human nature is one with the natural moral order. Ninomiya Sontoku (1787–1856), the "peasant sage," was a vigorous advocate of rural welfare, whose basic philosophical concept was *hotoku*, "returning virtue," a sense of obligation arising out of the individual's dependence on nature and human society. Life, he said in good Confucian manner, is a process of cooperation, of returning good in gratitude for what is received.[2]

Thus, like other reformations, Neo-Confucianism emphasized individual subjectivity—faith and heart-centered morality—yet, at the same time, it allowed one outwardly to accommodate oneself to an established social order. But the long-term social, as well as spiritual, effects were more revolutionary: much of modern Japanese capitalism, and no less Chinese communism, can be seen as Confucianism, deeply dyed by the Neo-Confucian revival, under another name. The same ideas of the pure heart as able to give itself to others through selfless loyalty, founded on *ho-toku* and to desire above all (in the Chinese communist slogan) to serve the people, under the guidance of intellectual elite cadres, says as much.

The Hindu reformation began in Bengal with the Caitanya Krishnaite movement of the sixteenth century, emphasizing pure simple faith and worship toward Krishna, de-emphasizing Brahmanical rites and caste, and making inward fervor compatible with life in the world as a believer. The Hindu reformer Visvanbhara Misra, known in religion as Caitanya (1486–1533), was a contemporary of Martin Luther (1483–1546), though it is exceedingly unlikely they ever heard of each other, or if they had, would have thought they had much in common. Yet both, in a time of social change and alienation, preached faith in a single incarnate divine savior and in a deeply loving inward relation with a personal God.

Caitanya, born in Muslim-ruled Bengal, traveled India promoting devotion to Krishna and chanting the deity's name. He was profoundly moved by the *Srimad Bhagavatam* with its idyllic accounts of the Beloved Lord's childhood and his youthful love for the gopis or cowherd girls who followed him about as he played his flute. Especially did he delight in Radha, the Lord's favorite of all among his lovers. He identified himself so fully with those scenes of transcendent beauty that he was considered himself an incarnation of both Krishna and Radha together. In 1516, Caitanya settled at Puri, in Orissa, where he taught disciples and experienced a rapturous and sometimes tormented spiritual life. In his capacity as Krishna, he knew the joy and love at the heart of the universe; yet as Radha, he was in anguish over the apparent absences of her divine consort though she/he rejoiced in the lover's homecoming.

His fervent inner life was centered entirely on Krishna as the supreme personal God. That deity was not a mere avatar of Vishnu, as in orthodox Vaisnavism; matters were rather the other way around. In Caitanya's school, Vishnu represents only the universal power and presence of the Lord who, as Krishna in his heavenly Vrindavan, is the central consciousness of all that is and the lover of all souls. The message is simple: souls are in bondage to ignorance and rebirth until, accepting the love of Krishna, they awaken to realize their true nature as Krishna's beloved servants and may then inwardly join him, the gopis, and his other lovers in his eternal paradise. The Caitanya tradition insists that this is the true inner message of the Vedas; a restoration of Vedic culture would place Krishna at its heart.

Caitanya's message flourished in Bengal and Orissa, where it deeply affected culture generally. Together with Bengal's role as the main conduit of western influence into India, Caitanya Krishnaism surely had some impact on the ferment that made this state a center of spiritual and political renewal. Like bhakti generally, Bengali Krishnaism tended to downplay caste, to want to reduce Hinduism to a single simple devotional essence, and to exalt the humanizing effect of inner feeling. Some of the same subjective and social themes, though from an Advaita Vedanta rather than bhakti perspective, were revived in the nineteenth-century Hindu modernization movements centering in Bengal: the Brahmo Samaj, the Ramakrishna Mission, and their kin. Rabindranath Tagore, the great Bengali poet of modern Hinduism, was deeply affected by the ecstatic reformer. More recently, Caitanya Krishnaism has come to the west in the form of the "Hare Krishna" movement of A. C. Bhaktivedanta Swami.[3]

As Max Weber pointed out long ago, India did not have a reformation with the same economic consequences as the European, or one might add the Buddhist in Japan. This was largely because India was dominated by alien rulers during most of the reformation era, whether Muslim or British. But it must be recognized that Caitanya's reformation beginning around 1500 led, like the European reformation, from inward faith toward liberalism and social change, while maintaining dialogue but not identity with other major social institutions. Nityananda, a major disciple of Caitanya, was a casteless renunciant deeply concerned with the lower social orders,[4] and at Caitanya's teaching even outcaste Candalas were cleansed. We are also told that kings, including a drunken Yavana (foreigner; probably Muslim) king, were moved by Caitanya's devotion and ordered support be given him. The Yavana is said to have wished he had been born Hindu so that he could be a devotee with that exaltè of Krishna.[5]

The outline of the Protestant Reformation in Christianity is well known. One point that might be noted is the way this reformation, like all such, brought a radical pluralization of the religion's forms of expression and an acceleration of its history. Despite some sectarian movements, for its first 1500 years Christianity, both Eastern and Western, maintained a generally Catholic image, hierarchical and sacramental, which gave it a reasonably consistent identity throughout time and the Christian world. Only a relatively few forms of Christian expression were heavily utilized.

Then suddenly (by historical standards), an astonishing array of new forms of expression appeared, from the ornate shape of baroque Catholicism to Lutheran sermons and Quaker meetings, from Unitarian rationalism to Pentecostal fire. In the same period, both its inward drive and historical circumstances favored the religion's expansion until it became the largest and most diverse the world had ever known.

What this portends for the future remains to be seen. One could argue that, like Buddhism and Chinese religion, Christianity has run through a wide repertoire but one that in the end must be exhausted; that by doing so much in these five centuries, it may have, like a bursting rocket, cast its brilliance and is now falling amid still glowing embers. Or it may be that this remarkable creativity suggests a future capacity to let new occasions teach new forms and duties.

If our hypothesis is correct, the Islamic reformation is just beginning. What is going on in Islam today has been depicted as Islamic revival, reformation, and revolution;[6] and if these are interpreted as endeavors toward living again, forming itself anew, and turning once more (to extract the literal Latin meanings of these words), then they are not inappropriate. All apply to a reformation in our sense as they change, diversify, and update a religion, prolonging its life by five hundred or a thousand years.

Islam in the world around us is in fact displaying many of the initial characteristics of the Reformation period in the history of a world religion. There is a response to secularizing trends, an inward fervor, the early desire to create an ideal society, the emergence of a new kind of elite, a drive to return to the religion's source and simplify Islam to the practice of the Shari'ah, the fundamental law. On the surface, the Islamic reformation often appears to be the rebellion of nonelites, the "masses," against outside influences, especially from the West, and against local leaders who were perceived as too compromised by association with them. This was evident in the Iranian revolution of 1979, the explosive outburst of long-pent-up hostility by ordinary people against the dominant class. Led by fiery Muslim preachers, the dispossessed seized upon pure Islam as the symbol for what they stood for and stood against.

Yet the picture, as always, is not black and white; the leaders of reform are themselves often Western-educated intellectuals who have reacted against what they saw outside the Islamic world. They insisted that Islam, far from being an awkward roadblock to modernization, was as good (indeed better) an ideological framework for building a just social and economic order as Western socialism or capitalism, and at the same time a sure rampart against the corroding influences (chiefly from the West) that traditionalists saw threatening family life and pride in land and culture.

A good example is Sayyid Qutb (1906–1966), a leading ideologist of the Egyptian-based Muslim Brotherhood and reportedly a major intellectual influence on Osama bin Laden and the al-Qaeda movement. As a young man, Qutb had been enamored of the West. He loved English literature and took a position with the Egyptian Ministry of Education. But he reacted against anglophilism in the late 1940s as a result of British domination of Egypt during World War II and the creation of the state of Israel. After the war, he came to the United States to study education, but he was humiliated by what he felt were denigrating American attitudes toward Arabs. He came to feel that young, Westernizing Muslims like himself struggled too hard to fit alien models, that instead they should proudly affirm Arab and Islamic culture, recognizing that rightly applied Islam provided an alternative to both capitalism and communism.[7]

Qutb was arrested for alleged participation in a plot by the Muslim Brotherhood, of which he was a prominent member, to kill Egyptian President Gamal Abdel Nasser in 1954. In 1966 Qutb was again arrested, and this time secretly executed, for his last book, *Maalim Fi al-Tariq* ("Signposts on the Road" or "Milestones"). That dangerous work emphasized Islamic concepts of the lordship of God and the absolute equality of all human beings as the only basis for a society grounded on harmony with nature and human nature. This society can be created by properly interpreting the Qur'an and observing the model set by the Prophet and the rightly guided caliphs. The danger came when the author went on to refer to the present as a *jahiliyya* ("period of ignorance," the term conventionally used for the time before the revelation), even in supposedly Islamic countries. For the Arab upper classes, he contended, are alienated from their Muslim roots, and the West has imposed its boundaries and standards on lands that should be only under the star and crescent.[8]

General principles underlying the initial outburst of the Islam reformation have been summarized by Lawrence Davidson in this way:

- The Muslim world is in a state of decay.
- The decay is the result of Western intrusion, including Muslim adoption of Western models for society and individual behavior.
- To correct this decay, the Islamic world must be re-Islamicized, by reintroducing the Shari'ah and purging it of Western adaptations.
- The only way to re-Islamicize Islam is to repoliticize Islam itself.[9]

The political aspect may seem disproportionate in Islam compared to other reformations, but should not be surprising. First, it is understandable in light of the historical circumstances of emergence from colonialism, and moreover it reminds us that Islam particularly stresses the importance of the faith being not only subjective, but also the model of an ideal society. At the same time, the political side of virtually all reformations must be kept in mind: nationalism and Protestantism, the Ming adoption of Neo-Confucianism as state ideology, the Japanese prophet Nichiren's insistence (unrealized so far as his wing of Buddhist reformation was concerned) that the state must express exclusive allegiance to the Lotus Sutra.

Iran in the early 1980s presented a dramatic example of Islamic resurgence. Iran as the major Shi'ite nation and not a part of the Arab world in which Islam began was like Germany in sixteenth-century Christendom or thirteenth-century Japan to Buddhism, "peripheral" yet important. Moreover, its Shi'a heritage provided several motifs conducive to a reforming, revolutionary mentality. As a minority in the Islamic world and often (though not in Iran) under Sunni rule, Shi'ites are accustomed to thinking of worldly rulers as unjust and usurpers, like the line of caliphs who persecuted Husain and his line of "true" imams. The belief in a lineage of living supreme teachers after the Prophet (even if now in "occultation") rather than in an unchanging law suggests the likelihood of new guidance under charismatic leaders; "ayatollahs" and other prominent *mujtahid* (jurists) are widely regarded as earthly deputies of the hidden imam.[10]

Finally, the point has been made that Iranian Shi'a, rich in esoteric teaching, contains a "gnostic" theme declaring that humans can be perfected in this world, though to do so they must thoroughly embrace Islam and live in an Islamic society. Thus, the Ayatollah[11] Khomeini, spiritual leader of the Iranian revolution, insisted that his creation would be a republic, but an Islamic one—meaning that though the people have a choice of rulers, all candidates must be Muslim and chosen by rules based on Islam. This regime, in turn, would be a universal model for a proper society.[12]

Under the leadership of the Ayatollah Khomeini, the Shah Muhammad Pahlavi was toppled in 1979, and an Islamic republic established. The resplendent monarchy had lost popular support for reasons such as those already suggested. In its place came the classic revolutionary scenario of ecstatic mobs, reprisals, serious economic and social disruption, and the emerging outlines of a state more egalitarian, more isolationist, and more founded on Islamic law than what went before. Although the Islamic republic continued in principle, within twenty years or so, the initial fervor had dwindled and Iran gradually became a "normal" country again.

How is Iran's case like a religious reformation as well as a political revolution? And how are similar, though not totally successful (except, for a time, the Taliban in Afghanistan), movements in other Islamic countries also like a religious reformation and political revolution? As we have seen, these upheavals first represented desire to return to sources thought to contain the original, essential core of the faith, the Qur'an and the Shari'ah.

The reformation mood rejects, above all initially, the liberal approach of Vedanta, Tendai Buddhism, Renaissance Europe, or movements in early twentieth-century Islam, as well as many others past and present. Liberalism basically says that the most authentic expression of a religion for its age is that which most makes it compatible with the age's best consensus scientific, philosophical, and social thought, and therefore aligns it with reform of the sort favored in the most prestigious educational and political circles. But although it may have its ideals in these areas and although it is not necessarily against science, philosophy, or social change in principle, reformation is first and above all determined by inwardness and radical consistency in religion: inner faith consistent with the sources and the essence of the faith, even if that sets it against the world, for its truth is not one with the world in any particular time or place, but is above time and place and judging them all.

That judging principle is far simpler than the complex social and philosophical issues weighed by liberalism, for it is based on a single simple sure key, in this case, faith in the Muslim God and his revelation in the sacred texts. As a kind of symbol and guaranty of that simplicity, the reformed faith espouses relative simplicity of worship and organization, rejecting or minimizing such elaborations as the cult of the saints, and favoring immediate charismatic leadership over complacent religious establishments. However, when possible, the two are brought together, as in Iran and Afghanistan, to make persons of reforming bent leaders in the mosques and clerical schools.

In the Islamic reformation, early attempts to create a holy society based on its principles have drawn antagonism and have created the image of the reformation as it appears to unsympathetic observers, as did efforts in the same direction by radically consistent Protestants of Calvin's Geneva, of Anabaptist Münster, and of Puritans in the English commonwealth and in Massachusetts. As justified as that negative image may be in these cases, it must be realized that there is more to the religion's overall reforming impulse than a totalitarian city on a hill.

The Protestant reformation was often stained with the blood of martyrs on both sides and of innumerable soldiers in the wars of religion; yet, in the end, it did much to wrench Europe into the modern world. Ultimately, reformation leads toward liberalism and democracy as well as toward their opposites.

Reformation is powerful enough to change the direction of a religion, at least in part of its domain, and to energize its life for a half-millennium or so of fighting religious wars, forming denominations, sending out missionaries, building universities, and founding schools of theology. In time, however, even these dynamics weaken. The outer world more and more changes; even the reformation religion in all its varieties does not have a response on equal terms to everything the age presents, though it may well provide adequate refuge for ordinary people from the churning confusion. For it must be realized that it is not always expected or desired that religion should look and sound contemporary; part of its appeal may be as an alternative to the present, as a voice from the past always a little out of synch with the contemporary world and thereby able to judge it by outside standards, and refresh those within it with water from other wells. Ultimately, the Reformation cycle will be exhausted, and it will give way to the Folk Religion stage. The faith will continue but with less and less of an elite institutional and educational superstructure.

Before examining the nature of folk religion in detail, it may suffice to indicate that we mean by it religious attitudes, practices, and institutions preserved in families and local communities, but having little rapport with the major structures of society or the mainstream of its thought and culture. It depends more on traditionalist and charismatic authority than on rational authority; it is cosmic and feeling rather than history and mind oriented; it may involve some recovery of devotionalist and even wisdom-era cosmic religion motifs as reformation simplification loses its sharpness.

When the Reformation era ends, that of Folk Religion begins. The radical change and acceleration suggested by the onset of reformation in interaction with the emergence of a new kind of society is five hundred years in the past. After that upheaval, as new social changes occur, the religion seems slowly to lose touch with the major structures of society—political, economic, educational, cultural. Religion is no longer their equal; rather, it maintains a rich life just below their radar, except, of course, when it offers them markets and votes. But it matches less well than before the subjective fullness of the society and the psyches of individuals therein. Unable to reverse this distancing and having exhausted its intellectual and creative potential, it no longer attracts the sort of leadership that could keep alive its great tradition. It can long continue on the popular level in favorable circumstances, for reasons we shall consider in the next chapter. But it now offers little that is truly new and does not afford the kind of equal leadership it once had. Thus, in its fifth and terminal stage, a Great Religion continues, perhaps for several centuries, as popular or folk religion.

This stage may not, however, be fully understood, for only two examples have arisen so far: Chinese religion, since the beginning of the Jing period (1644); and Buddhism, since around the same point. Since the seventeenth century, both religions have displayed little vigorous intellectual life or cultural creativity, and what was there (Hakuin's Zen or Kang Yuwei's Confucianism) had none of the historical force of, say, Gandhi or Martin Luther King Jr. at the end of the Hindu or Christian reformation periods. Instead, the Chinese and Japanese governments of that period were generally as secular as any premodern regimes, using the institutional religion of their societies as instruments of control. Popular Taoist, Shinto, or bodhisattva cults flourished mightily, with their great pilgrimages and frenzies. But art and literature were increasingly secular, as in the celebrated *ukiyo,* "floating world," prints and stories of Japan. Real intellectual life in both countries and in Korea centered on philology and philosophy in the Confucian tradition but of little real religious content. In the Theravada Buddhist countries of Southeast Asia, Buddhist practice has remained vigorous, but too little innovative Buddhist intellectual or cultural energy has been visible in recent centuries. We will now look at the world of last-stage Folk Religion.

CHAPTER NINE
FOLK RELIGION

What is the last stage of religion really like, the one in which Christianity and Hinduism are presumably now entering? To my mind, a highly appropriate model could begin with Robert Redfield's concept of Great and Little Tradition.[1] The Little Tradition refers to the way of life of ordinary people; the Great Tradition to the ideas, values, and practice of the elite. What we have in the Folk Religion stage, I think, is a religious Little Tradition continuing unabated, though decapitated of a corresponding living Great Tradition.

Let us review the essential features of this picture. Restricting our discussion only to religion, the Great Tradition of a society refers to the dominant religion as it is carried by its highly educated elites, usually priests and monks (and only the cream of these). In traditional societies these persons can wield appreciable political and economic power, and they may well be closely associated with the kings and aristocrats who patronize them and make their courts centers of Great Tradition learning and culture. The Great Tradition's version of the religion is highly literate and engaged in exegetical scriptural study and works of philosophical theology; it is likewise transmitted through education of good quality. It exploits as fully as possible the Great Religions' potential as religions of a remembered historical moment, with scripture, wisdom, and a rich cultural system capable of export throughout the world.

The Great Tradition's institutional structures, needless to say, are highly routinized, but they can produce persons of marked though generally conventional wisdom, as well as placement. Being aware of history because of its closeness to the literary heritage and the centers of power, the Great Tradition takes a long perspective and values institutional stability. It tends in fact to emphasize the historical rather than the cosmic aspects of the religious worldview, to prefer intellectual sophistication to unbridled feeling, to mistrust charismatic personalities, and to value interaction with the society's "mainstream" cultural and social life. It loves excellence in religious art and architecture, and those who patronize such excellence.

The Little Tradition is, in premodern societies, the same religion as it is understood and experienced by peasants, who, being nonliterate, know things only as they are in the present or as secreted in myth. It has small concern with formal philosophy or history; it is oriented to cosmic rather than historical time; it concentrates on worship and experience more than theory; and it is basically transmitted through family, community, and charismatic figures such as shamans, "holy men," and wise women, as well as through the local priestly representatives of the Great Tradition. In the villages, however, the priestly representatives usually find that they do well to tacitly accept as "implicit faith" the Little Tradition's understanding of the sacred.

Little Tradition religion centers on seasonal festivals such as Christmas, on family and community folkways, on things that are *done*—for example, pilgrimage and rite—and on nonrational experiences such as miracle and mysticism. All this, rather than the books and culture of the Great Tradition, constitute religion. Little Tradition people are likely to feel, fundamentally, that they cannot really affect the course of society as a whole or the politics and policies of kings and courts except by provoking a miracle—that is, through a peasants' revolt, a revival, or a crusade, rather than by rational means.

As Redfield emphasizes, the Great and Little Traditions continually interact with each other. The Little Tradition receives its fundamental symbols from the Great, even though it may accommodate them to its ageless patterns, making them cosmic, atemporal, and subjective rather than historical and philosophically rational. Saints become transcendent, semidivine powers rather than historical figures; the cross, a sign of sacred space as much as of an historic event. The folk of the Little Tradition may perceive their coreligionists among the elites of the Great Tradition with a strange ambiguity, at once uncritically adulating them for their learning and hierarchical splendor and hating them for their relative wealth and prestige and for their presumed hypocrisy and self-importance.

For their part, the Great Tradition elite look upon those of the Little Tradition with an ambivalent combination of admiration and bemused contempt. Sometimes, like the Slavophiles of Russia in the nineteenth century, they may pass through phases in which they hold that, for all its seeming naiveté, peasant faith is somehow really deeper and purer than their own. At other times, with Josephite passion, they may attempt, heavy-handedly, to reform it up to their own standards. Sometimes rulers find it to their interest or perhaps material to their own salvation to patronize and take into their confidence an outstanding charismatic figure of impeccable Little Tradition background—a Gyôgi in Nara, Japan; a Rasputin; or a Billy Graham. The Great Tradition ecclesiastical elites, however, are more likely to remain aloof from such a one. On the other hand, there are persons who genuinely and effectively mediate between the two traditions, making the best of each accessible to the other, such as John Wesley and his Japanese counterpart, Ninomiya Sontoku.

As Redfield points out, a Little Tradition can continue with a vigorous life of its own long after the Great Tradition by which it was nurtured has vanished and perhaps been superseded by another. The villages of Mayan Indians in the Yucatan that he studied, though superficially touched by the Catholic Great Tradition, still preserved Little Tradition usages grounded in the long-extinct Great Tradition of the Mayan empire. "The shaman-priests of the villages," he reported, "carried on rituals and recited prayers that would have their full explanation only if we knew what was the ritual and the related body of thought at Chichen Itza or Coba."[2]

For though a Little Tradition no doubt benefits from interaction with a corresponding Great Tradition, and without it is bereft of important potential for sophistication and flexible, creative responses to new situations, it has a capacity to survive indefinitely on its own level, continually renewing its charismatic wells and even surviving persecution. That is what Buddhism and Chinese religion have done for several centuries, and Hinduism and Christianity are about to do. (For while Buddhism and Chinese religions maintained their outward appearances, Great Tradition in the form of prominent monks and mandarins, at least until the twentieth century revolutions in China and elsewhere, those quasi elites had had little real spiritual influence except on the popular or folk level, the connection of religion in the respective countries with forward-looking education, modernization, and great-tradition art having dwindled away since the exhaustion of Reformation impulses.)

Like all Great Religions in civilized society, Christianity has long had both Great and Little Traditions. Its Great Tradition, as both secularization theory and our hypothesis of stages in the life of a Great Tradition have hoped to demonstrate, has about run its course for now. But its Little Tradition, far from quickly following suit and meekly accepting the arrival of successor, and now perhaps secular, Great Traditions as evidence of its disconfirmation, shows every sign of preserving its own Little Tradition level of Christianity, and perchance surviving as long as Mayan religion in the Yucatan. Indeed, this may be Christianity's era of greatest influence so far as worldwide numbers and distribution are concerned, but its forms in the "new Christendom" of the twenty-first century and after—evangelical, pentecostal and other sectarian movements—are Little Tradition in character.

The emergent vitality of evangelical, pentecostal, and conservative Catholic forms of Christianity and the diminishing of liberal Christianity are sure signs of this tradition's passage from Reformation to Folk Religion styles. Liberalism, characteristic especially of late–Reformation period expressions of a religion, works out of the assumption that religion should be articulated in a way convergent with the best science, philosophy, and political ideology of the age. It thereby takes for granted religion's equal intellectual standing and valid social leadership with the elite bearers of the Great Tradition in that society. In such a situation, religious leaders will have come from the same families and gone to the same universities as the major "establishment" figures in politics, the life of the mind, or art; they will adapt the religion's discourse to the way such persons talk and think, in so doing making each side respectable in light of the other. Moreover, insofar as the religious "establishment" or "mainstream" sees itself and is widely seen as the custodian of the fundamental values and spiritual heritage of the society, it needs to sanctify and sanction the world in all its diversity, if only to make what prophetic criticism must be offered all the more valid.

It is fair to say that major leaders and respectable denominations of Christianity in its traditional European and American heartlands were in this position up to the 1960s. Its bishops and principal preachers were (unlike others) quoted without condescension in the respectable news media on issues of the day; its theologians like Paul Tillich and the Niebuhrs labored to reconcile science, society, and faith. Whether or not scientists, statesmen, and secular intellectuals always agreed with them, they seemed to honor them as equals, and the theologians appeared on the covers of news magazines. But that day appears now to be little more than a memory. Religious liberalism has, it is said, become sectarian, and the Great Tradition role has fallen more to Evangelicalism. The tumult of the 1960s stirred up the world and in innumerable ways left it irrevocably changed, not least in our view marking visibly the final exhaustion of Reformation energies in Christianity and the advent of the Folk Religion era.

Evangelical Christianity can never have quite the same place as liberal or "establishment" Christianity. Nor would it presumably want to have that role, at least when it is thinking clearly about its heritage (so different in its dissenter background from that of "state church" Protestantism) and its fundamental conception of religion and society. (It is not thinking clearly when it wants to establish its own de facto state church, as in issues like school prayer.) Evangelicalism says that religion only compromises itself when it adapts, in the liberal manner, its language to that of the "best" science, ideology, philosophy, or art of the era, though it may certainly be in dialogue with them. Rather, it can only speak in its own scriptural language, holding fast to the form of sound words (2 Tim. 1:13) while proclaiming the words of eternal life (John 6:68).

That is because the unique words of scripture are timeless in the sense of being above contemporary society, judging it. Ideally, believers see themselves as contemporary with the Bible, trying to live out the next chapter of the Book of Acts, even as they are among those who see themselves not to be part of any elite or Great Tradition, but who, as the despised of the earth, have to live their spiritual lives in obscurity but with a power known to them alone, in good Little Tradition manner. As the religious liberal Great Tradition fades, the Little Tradition, old and new, is what is left.

The Little Tradition style of religion is what has variously been called "peasant religion" and "folk religion," and within the context of modern society, "popular religion." Peter W. Williams has made quite creative use of the category in a study of popular religion in America. As he accurately points out, the classic peasant or folk Little Tradition is only a "first form of religion we might call authentically popular," in contrast to elite religion or the religion of undifferentiated societies.[3]

Regarding peasant/popular religion, let us turn again to the work of William Christian on medieval and early modern Spanish religion. In his excellent study *Local Religion in Sixteenth-century Spain*, he has like Redfield found two levels of Catholicism: a Great Tradition represented by the intellectual and institutional Church, and another which is local, timeless, legitimated by miracle, giving much place to spiritual cause-and-effect in the form of expecting concrete blessings in response to devotional vows made and kept.[4] This Little Tradition religion was corporate as well as individual, not seldom expressing itself in communal religious acts mounted for such purposes as warding off plague or drought. Christian makes the point, however, that this style of "folk" Catholicism was practiced in the cities as well as in the countryside, and by members of the royal family alongside their patronage of the Great Tradition, as well as by the lowliest peasants.

The clergy often played a strangely ambivalent role between the two levels. They were certainly aware of popular-level religion. Priests were not unknown who promoted its cults enthusiastically or even trespassed the boundaries of orthodoxy altogether by performing magical conjurations to dispel locusts or storm clouds in response to popular need. Most, however, may have held attitudes little different from those Christian reports among priests today regarding the local shrines favored by the laity:

> Even how the fierce pride with which some brotherhoods or town authorities guard the books of miraculous images, even from the priest, leaves no doubt that whatever canon law may say, local religion is theirs. The priests are usually from different villages. They often speak of local devotions with a bemused tolerance, occasionally wondering out loud about "pagan superstition." But when asked about the shrines of their home villages, the same priests speak with tenderness, excitement, and pride. For them the religion learned at home, embedded in the home landscape, transcends the doctrinal attitudes learned in the seminary, which they may apply elsewhere.[5]

This popular religion was chiefly the religion of local chapels and shrines, and it was typically based on apparitions and miracles and their associated devotional vows, festivals, pilgrimages, relics, indulgences, and special acts of penance or honor. This religion, Christian states, was popular in the sense that it was predominantly lay, though clergy participated in it. But it chiefly met the needs of lay life, especially corporate, community life, rather than the needs of the universal Church or the gifts of eternal salvation, which were its prerogative.

It is not the case, however, that popular religion downplays questions of theodicy or salvation, but rather intertwines them deeply with more mundane matters of protection and healing. In another book, *Apparitions in Late Medieval and Renaissance Spain*, William Christian shows that the God behind appearances of the Blessed Virgin or the saints in this setting—as in later apparitions down to La Salette or Fatima—tends to be remote and quick to send punishment, though Our Lady promises to restrain the Lord's hand as long as she can.[6] Yet the offenses are often largely spiritual, such as blasphemy or failure to attend mass, and the boons that nonetheless accompany these hierophanies combine healing for the living with injunctions that prayers and masses be offered for the dead.

Petitions from out of the Great Tradition, such as the Lord's Prayer and Hail Mary, are urged by the heavenly visitors, though in a way that seems to make them principally charms or symbols of implicit faith. On a deep structural level, a situation not entirely different obtains in popular Protestantism as well. Here, too, in such traditions as the Pentecostal, one finds an intricate—though ecstatic—mix of supernatural healing, prophecy, and admonition, of joy in the Spirit, and of concern for divine protection again sinister forces imperiling the faithful. However, in a religious situation far more pluralistic than late medieval Spain, a simple identity of the local community and the faith community can no longer be assumed, as much as many popular religionists might desire it.

Popular religion today represents remnants of past Little Traditions and filtered-down aspects of the Great Tradition, together with popular responses both of rejection and of utilization of the fruits of modernization and secularization. Bearing that in mind, I would nonetheless like to speak of modern religion in the Christian world as folk religion to emphasize the instructive parallels between today's religion and that of classic Little Tradition societies.

The differences between the two are obvious. Strictly speaking, modern religion is only metaphorically folk religion in the peasant sense. Modern popular religionists are not genuinely illiterate and have at their disposal not just the rude tools of a peasantry but all the fabulous devices of a high-tech age for travel, communication, and computing. The fact remains, however, that the Great Tradition's *meaning* of literacy often escapes them, even as does any message contained in the medium of the written and published word. For modern popular Christianity as for folk religion, religious communication from scripture, testimony, or preacher is *essentially* miraculous, experiential, and charismatic. The words of the Bible are miracle-producing charms, not historical texts whose exegesis requires persons of elite education; the revivalist or television preacher is a shaman evoking an Other World of miracle and meaning, not a lecturer whose words require reasoned reflection.

This style of religion may seem at first glance vulnerable to the vicissitudes of history and change. Actually, it is extraordinarily impervious to them, as in the case of the Maya. Let us survey some basic patterns of Little Tradition religion and see how well suited they are to favor the survival of religion on this level for long periods. They are particularly well adapted, in fact, to ensure the long-term survival of the religion in the absence of Great Tradition institutions.

Transmission through Nonliterary Means

In traditional folk religion, this means that the faith is passed on through folklore, community example, or oral and exemplary transmission from parent to child and from specialist (shaman, wise woman, local priest) to disciple. In modern terms, it means transmission by media that are either nonwritten (preaching, radio, television) or outside the literary mainstream (like the Internet), by traditions and group attitudes essentially rooted in the local community, and by specialists who although perhaps seminary-trained are basically oriented toward perpetuating locally grounded traditions rather than interaction with the intellectual elite. This means, in our day, transmission through the electronic media, through books that though widely read are considered to inhabit a religious ghetto and may not appear in book review columns or bestseller lists of national secular media, and through the immediacy of a locally experienced religion in which signs and wonders are not lacking. Its personalities are legitimated more by charisma than by education in divinity. All these marks work for survival, for they leave faith untouched by the vicissitudes of bookish culture.

A Local, Personal, and Experiential Quality

This feature is contained in the previously mentioned extraliterary style of transmission. That kind of religious transmission does not communicate ideas so much as it triggers experiences. The words and gestures of such transmissions are condensed symbols that, in the familiar local cultural context, evoke paradigmatic experiences and images—from childhood, from earlier spiritual stirrings, from the conventional lore of the religion. The phenomenological sociologist Alfred Schutz, following William James, has discussed the various "subuniverses of meaning" that parallel ordinary "working" reality: the worlds of dreams, fantasies, play, and religious reality. Moving from one to another involves a sort of "shock," he tells us, like falling asleep or waking up.[7]

In the case of the religious world, a trigger symbol—a sacred word, sign, or picture—as well or better than rational exposition, can induce the subuniverse in which the religion is true personally and experientially. It can make one know the presence of Jesus walking beside one, or feel the Spirit moving in one's heart. This process is crucial for Little Tradition survival. That religious tradition carries on because of its ability uncritically to accept the reality of its subuniverses in the face of potential disconfirmation by "working" reality, a disconfirmation that, as we shall see, increasingly weighs upon the Great Tradition as it passes through its numbered days.

But the Little Tradition becomes more and more detached from the Great Tradition even as the latter becomes more detached from elite education, politics, economics, and art. The fundamental reasons the Little Tradition possesses that survival ability are, first, its local legitimation, where disconfirmation may not have much conscious strength; second, its regard for words as triggers rather than as rational discourse; third, its willingness to balance the claims of rationality with those of personal life needs; and fourth, its ability to counterattack in the form of "folk" criticism of the rationalism that is, for the Little Tradition, a value based on foreign (that is, nonlocal and nonexperiential) classes, needs, and traditions.[8]

Specialists Who Are Basically Shaman Priests

Like the Mayan, these include those who perform sacerdotal functions in offering routinized prayers and rites, but who also derive their call from subjective experience. In the modern world, many if not most popular religious figures fit this description. The story of the "call" and initiatory experience is usually an important part of their mythos, and it is continually renewed by an appeal based much more on charisma (properly endowed in such an experience) than on overt routinization. This "call" allows for perpetuation of leadership essentially outside the values of Great Tradition educational institutions, though these may be used formally. Leadership is therefore produced by the same kinds of locally legitimated triggers that confirm and perpetuate the faith itself. In the emergent Folk Religion stage of Christianity, this scenario means the evident increasing importance of the revivalist, television evangelist, megachurch pastor, popular Christian writer and novelist (e.g., the "Left Behind" series), and indigenous Third World Christian movements. To indicate the difference in mentality between the 1950s, the last age of the "old order," and now, note that although Billy Graham began his revivalist ministry with a seven-week "crusade" in Los Angeles in 1949, to much attention in the popular media as movie stars accepted Christ, the influential liberal *Christian Century* published no story on him in 1949 or 1950.

Renewal of Charisma in Movements such as Cargo Cults, the Ghost Dance, Revivals, or the Charismatic Movement

The Little Tradition can engender movements that seem to respond to new conditions on its own terms. We cannot here engage in a full discussion of such movements as responses to modernity, a matter over which an immense amount of anthropological ink has been spilled. But we should note that though they may ultimately fail, such movements do "buy time" for conventional Little Tradition religion in hours of crisis; indeed, they may also give it something else to do while the corresponding Great Tradition crumbles before traumatic cultural shocks. In contemporary Christianity, evangelical, pentecostal, antiabortion, antievolution, or "pro-family" campaigns may serve. Such movements can preserve essentials of the Little Tradition, sometimes for as much as several generations, by appearing to meet the enemy with folk religion's own weapons: miracle, charisma, and tenacious belief, as well as whatever political strength the cause can muster. The combat itself reinvigorates the blood of the Little Tradition; it usually bestows enough victories to give it fresh short-term validation; and it suggests that if change is imperative, it can therefore change in its own way under the aegis of signs and visions and anointed leaders—which also means that it remains the same. The survival value of this capacity is obvious.

Permanent, Visible Objects such as Amulets, Holy Pictures, and Scriptural Books, Regarded as Signs and Triggers of Religious Reality

Stress on symbolic "hardware" is one way the Little Tradition eludes confrontation with the Great Tradition's texts and rational thought, and its vulnerable relationship with other major institutions. Instead it concentrates on that which, so long as the religion itself lasts, is holy through its own self-validation.

The Little Tradition ultimately survives because it avoids what the Great Tradition regards as the assurances of religious survival: the great texts, the intellectual tradition, and institutional solidity. The Great Tradition's dependence on word, considered as vehicle for discourse rather than as talisman, is its most fundamental distinction. The scholarly brahmin feels most secure with the Vedas, as does the learned bishop with the Bible, the Creeds, and the Church Fathers. Their textual orientation need not be construed in any narrow, conservative sense; it is the charter of the theological liberal as much as the traditionalist, only the words (or their connotation) being different. The spirit has been well put by David Tracy as he argues that the evolving life of a religion can be understood as ongoing dialogue with its great texts, not just authoritarian submission to them.[9]

Yet the Great Tradition's word orientation contains a fatal Achilles' heel. It directly makes the religion's hierophanies historical and therefore distanced in time. Though the faith may have a Grand Narrative telling how we got from then to now, what happened "then" is nonetheless only a mediated experience. In Paul Ricoeur's phrase, the "immediacy of belief" is "irremediably lost." We half sense that words discolor as well as convey their reference—that is, in the literary sense of words understood not as charms that directly evoke what they bespeak but as symbols to be interpreted and analyzed. In Buddhism, the second and less adequate age of the Dharma, after immediacy had passed, was that of dependence on sutras. As

Ricouer again put it, with the coming of the text, "we can no longer live the great symbolisms of the sacred in accordance with the original belief in them." The "primitive naiveté" is forever lost, and we can at best only "aim at a second naiveté in and through criticism."[10]

Indeed, it may begin to dawn upon savants of the Great Tradition, as it has upon the postmodernists, that words themselves fictionalize. What the historical words of a Grand Narrative create is not the past but a separate reality—one may say a subuniverse—fabricated out of a few shards from the past. It pulls and nags at humans not because it is true, but because it is precisely other than what we know by ordinary experience to be true. This is no doubt especially true of those pasts that validate religions. Their other reality may even offer what the critic George Steiner has called a cultural equivalent of Jacques Cousteau's dizziness of the depths, an intoxicating euphoria more alluring than life on the surface.[11]

But the fact that this allure is constructed of an Indra's net of words will sooner or later also come through to those who approach the tradition mainly in terms of words. The cleavage of words from reality, though a subtle observation, is one eventually made in literate cultures. It is implied in all study of texts as texts, even when most traditionalist. The coming of this observation is the Great Tradition's own foredoomed nemesis; though its dark advent may wait centuries or millennia, it is embedded in the Great Tradition's own operating premises from the beginning, like hidden canker eggs whose spawn will eventually devour their host. A Great Tradition of a Great Religion—born of the discovery of history and living by the instruments of knowing human life as historical existence (narratives and institutions)—likewise dies in historical time and under exposure to historical awareness. In the end, it can avoid a postmodernist critique no more than it can fail to see its history as a triumphalist Grand Narrative in its palmy days.

The fictionalizing quality of words does not mean, in the case of the texts of a great religious tradition, that the original hierophany did not happen, only that it could not have happened for its original experiencers exactly as it is portrayed in words. Something behind the words is unrecoverable, just as "all the words in Shakespeare" cannot fully convey the experience of anyone's average half hour. Yet, as these realizations arise from textual and intellectual labors, a Great Tradition wearies itself in struggles against them; it is as much from the resultant lassitude as from actual disconfirmation that it loses its grip on education, art, and its own institutionalization. Finally, its proud custodianship of the sacred words becomes an incubus it can neither love nor shake off. This tortuous passage amounts to a new Discovery of History: like the other, a compelling loss of "primitive naiveté" for those who understand it; and now a double loss, not only of the original preliterate vision, but also of the believing naiveté with which a Great Tradition views itself and its mission at high noon.

Even in late afternoon, of course, one may faithfully try to recover the sunrise. The reformation was an attempt of a part of the Great Tradition, as well as of popular religion, to get back behind the words again: it works, but only at the cost of laying out new words that in the end become fresh chains of Grand Narratives and doubts. Whether a second reformation is possible is a prospect not yet tested.

The Little Tradition, at least in its pure form, has none of these problems. It depends, in the Zen phrase, on "transmission outside the scriptures" even while making a talisman of scripture. It is thereby spared the verbal Saturn who devours his children, and will live longer, centuries longer, than those who live by words. Although it cannot truly annihilate time and live eternally in the first generation of the faith, much as it may wish to, the Little Tradition is able to produce successions of experiences—miracles, conversions, the presence of charisma—that give the sweet flavor of primitive naiveté. It matters not, in this respect, if the Little Tradition's conceptualization of that first generation deviates wildly from the historical facts. The point is that, for the Little Tradition, sacred power is present now as it was then, as the charismatic movement believes it is confirming daily, doing works as great or even greater than in that time. Before that power, then and now are one.

In conclusion, then, we affirm that secularization theory, to be discussed more fully in the next chapter, is correct in its perception of the drift of things—but only for the Great Tradition. Insofar as secularization theorists have for the most part been chiefly concerned with the Christian world, particularly Europe and North America, they have essentially caught Christianity in its process of transition to the Folk Religion stage—that is, they are witnessing, and describing, the death agonies of its Great Tradition. What they have not fully comprehended, however, is that the religion's Little Tradition can survive such an event, and indeed it can seem little affected by it—as the tremendous vitality of Christianity today in the southern hemisphere and "Third World" so clearly demonstrates. Like Buddhism or Chinese religion, it can linger as folk religion for several centuries, until confronted by situations beyond its intellectually and spiritually enfeebled power to control, like those that led to China's Communist revolution.

The crisis of transition to Folk Religion, like all stages in the life of a Great Religion, has come more profoundly from the working out of processes internal to the religion than from external causes. Yet, obviously, no religion is immune to external history. We shall now consider what factors in the environment of religion in the contemporary world are most likely to affect its future.

Does the present state of religion actually confirm our five-stage hypothesis? To answer this question fully and to then proceed with our argument, we need first to examine in some depth the debate over secularization. Is the alleged decline of religion in the modern world a clear reality, a learned illusion, or might not the facts—whatever they may be—also be amenable to interpretation through a third possibility, such as the working out of the stages in the lives of the great religions that we have proposed?

CHAPTER TEN

THE MODERN WORLD AND SECULARIZATION

Does the hypothesis that the world's largest religion, Christianity, is now entering a Folk Religion stage, even as the next-largest and most vital religion, Islam, is entering its Reformation, help in any way to resolve the secularization conundrum?

To those who believe in secularization, the modern fall of religion from the privileged status it is alleged once to have had is a patent reality, the kind of thing "everyone knows." They often seem to respond to their critics with a hint of irritation that supposedly intelligent people should refuse obstinately to accept such an obvious fact, as though talking to a flat-earther. But, on the other hand, critics of secularization theory point to their own obstinate facts. They note religion's continuing prosperity in much of the modern world; its protean ability to take new forms and seize new opportunities as the world changes; and its ability to exploit the social and technological novelties of the twentieth century rather than retreat before them. Critics may query whether a theory that requires so many qualifications and superimposed epicycles to make it fit the facts as does secularization may not be a sociological equivalent of Ptolemaic astronomy.

Nevertheless, the idea of secularization persists. At least until recently, most significant sociologists and historians of religion have accepted it in some form. Indeed, if we follow Durkheim's reflections at the conclusion of *The Elementary Forms of the Religious Life*,[1] or the later observations of Bryan Wilson,[2] we must concede that secularization theory is built into the very nature of the sociological enterprise. For if, as the latter must assume, religion can be interpreted, in part or in whole, by sociological analysis, then that religion is dethroned as absolute monarch and subjected to a higher law. In Durkheimian parlance, if the real though unacknowledged object of religion is society itself, then religious knowledge can be replaced by sociological knowledge, and must be when the latter arrives on the scene. The sociologist by the very act of sociologizing also secularizes; insofar as his or her work has any impact on the attitudes of society as a whole, secularization is furthered.

The fathers of sociology, from Comte, Durkheim, and Weber on down, assumed in principle the truth of Peter Berger's definition of secularization as "the process by which sectors of society and culture are removed from the domination of religious institutions and symbols," together with its subjective corollary, the "secularization of consciousness."[3] They then proceed to explain how and why this removal has come to pass, and to deal with questions of to what extent religion has a future. Here, differences have arisen.

The role of religion in society has been studied basically from two sociological perspectives. One, stemming from Emile Durkheim, has emphasized its origin in society itself and its role of giving cohesion to society. Religion provides the myths, rituals, values, and sense of identity that bind a community together on the level of symbol and feeling, inducing members to make procommunity choices.

The other, grounded in the work of Max Weber, stresses what may be called the cognitive and operational aspects of religion: its way of providing knowledge of the supernatural and of managing human response to it or manipulation of it. For Weber, this knowledge and power were primarily transmitted to and through individuals—charismatic persons, magicians, priests—rather than residing in a Durkheimian social effervescence. Of course, religion's social impact, as well as its indirect origin in societal problems and needs, is pervasive. The exploration of that interrelationship was Weber's abiding concern.

The Durkheimian and Weberian approaches are not necessarily inconsistent, and most subsequent work in the sociology of religion has drawn from both. But each maintains a different emphasis in the understanding of religion with immense bearing on the problem of secularization. We shall examine each in turn, beginning with the Durkheimian.

If religion rests in the cohesion of society, its health depends on the extent to which society coheres and likewise the extent to which religious symbols and acts reinforce this cohesion without people being aware that it is society, rather than transcendent religious realities, that is the true object of religious feeling. An extreme Durkheimian could argue that if society is the true focus of religion, then religion will persist as long as there is society, since all societies by definition have some kind of unifying symbol and structure. This proposition has led to some rather quixotic theories suggesting that seemingly secular means of social bonding, from Maoism in China (before the reaction against the Great Cultural Revolution) to the spirit of American pragmatism, are "really" religious despite the lack of a supernatural referent.

Although this approach obviously illumines important functional continuities, it makes the definition of religion so elastic as to render the word less useful than it ought to be. In light of religion's historic meanings, those concerned with public awareness of supernatural realities, one would expect to see in something properly called *religion* that awareness conveyed simultaneously through, say, Joachim Wach's three forms of religious expression—the theoretical, practical, and sociological.[4] In this vein, Peter Berger has criticized Thomas Luckmann's interesting argument in *The Invisible Religion*, that religion is any universe of meaning human beings create to manifest their capacity to transcend biological nature.[5] In effect, then, any social phenomenon becomes at least potentially religious. But, Berger contends, when modern science, for instance, becomes a form of religion, as it may under Luckmann's definition, the utility of the word is weakened. Berger prefers to limit religion to the positing of a *sacred cosmos*, an objective moral–spiritual order legitimated by supernatural reality, by the sacred in something like Rudolf Otto's or Mircea Eliade's sense.[6] Under this definition, we can take note of the countless permutations the sacred, in its dialectic with the profane, is able to take; but, at the same time, the possibility of true secularization, the disappearance of the sacred altogether, cannot be excluded.

Peter Berger is Durkheimian insofar as he assumes as his base point the social construction of a sacred reality that unifies cosmos, society, and the individual into a seamless whole. He likewise perceives a progressive disruption of this primordial whole in history. Fragmentation of the unified cosmos begins as far back as the Old Testament, and was advanced by the Reformation, involving a "disenchantment of the world" that makes lines of demarcation between the sacred and the secular. The sacred is more and more pushed to some transcendent point beyond the confines of this world altogether, or it is restricted to "specialized" institutions such as the Christian Church.

This is, clearly, a social process of secularization, the negative of the modernist Grand Narrative, even though as Berger tried to show in *A Rumor of Angels,* the experiential sources of religion have not necessarily dried up.[7] They have, however, become quite personal, privatized, and at best express themselves only in relativistic religious forms within a pluralistic situation; in a disenchanted world, the Transcendent must be found in whatever fragmented bits and pieces it can be. Only the most obdurate will to believe can sustain more than a functionally relativistic belief in the truth of each. The sacred canopy of old is shattered.[8]

Or, perhaps the canopy has rather fragmented into divergent centers of meaning: the more and more estranged Great and Little Traditions, each with its Durkheimian cohesion linking religion to its own kind of science, social science, or political ideology. The scattered fragments may include small communities devoted to "social justice," "biblical" values, or single-issue crusades like those against war or abortion, and for racial reparations or school prayer.

An important aspect of the Durkheimian tradition is the civil religion discussion, associated with Will Herberg and Robert Bellah.[9] Despite the obviously fragmented pluralism of religion in the United States, these writers contend that country has also known a common (if attenuated) religious expression centered on such doctrines as belief in a divine providence guiding the destiny of the nation, together with ceremonies and symbols of the state as a community with sacred meaning. These workings have counterbalanced the rampage of pluralism and saved something of the Durkheimian function. By now, however, the ghost of civil religion has perhaps only contributed to polarization, as each side, the "liberal" remnants of the Great Tradition and the "biblical" Little Tradition, claims to be the true heir of America's common faith.

However one evaluates it, though, civil religion has apparently not proved of adequate mettle to withstand the onslaughts of secularization. Herberg regarded it as little more than a pious façade, of little weight compared to the testimony of the traditional faiths. Bellah, who at first took its significance as an expression of shared values even in a pluralistic situation more seriously, has acknowledged that in recent decades it has become a "broken and empty shell."[10] If values unite all Americans, they are now wholly secular, pragmatic ones, without even such a vestigial sacred canopy legitimating them as civil religion. In true Durkheimian fashion, when the social nature of the sacred is discovered, its days are numbered, and sociological knowledge has replaced religious truth. In other words, although America may be religiously divided more or less evenly between liberal and conservative mentalities, just as it seems to be divided virtually fifty-fifty between the values represented respectively by the blue and red states in the 2000 election, it is still united by purely secular wisdom about how to live in a pluralistic society and maintain reasonable civility in such a situation—and so far this appears to be manageable.

The question of the future of religion in Durkheimian terms is one of whether religion can persist when fragmented into bits—or even into two parts—strewn through a society still reasonably homogeneous in all respects but religion. For despite much talk of general fragmentation, it is clear that stable, advanced nations, such as the United States and those of Europe, are still largely unified in most important areas except religion. Indeed, owing to the effects of mass media and rapid transportation, they may be becoming more so. The government is not about to collapse; a complex and well-meshed economic system sends standard brands out to the remotest hamlet; people laugh and weep at the same television series in Maine and California and Australia; and educational systems are turning out more and more identical products across the world as far as secular skills and attitudes are concerned. Computer programming and marketing are far more identical in Boston and Bombay than are Calvinism and Krishnaism.

Despite its occasional attempts to market comparable standard brands and employ the same mass media, only religion seems incapable of attaining a similar unity. It does not really unite supposedly one-religion countries such as Spain or Sweden anymore, much less (apart from the remnants of civil religion) a country like the United States. Otherwise identical computer scientists may be agnostics or fundamentalists; clean-cut Catholics and Quakers may enjoy the same Disneyland rides or television shows side by side. Perhaps it doesn't matter; on the other hand, it doesn't gel.

It may be, as Peter Berger tells us, "increasingly difficult to maintain the religious traditions as unchanging verity" in this situation.[11] Religious groups can only shore up their own particular subworld and hope that, as far as their universal validity is concerned, the civil religion golden rule of "No offense" is kept and no one will be so uncivil as to point out that, with respect to any reasonable claim to universal validity, with so many emperors trying to share the imperial vestments, each individual sovereign at best dons only a few tatters.

Nonetheless, it is obvious that some powerful force, some slow inertia or nuclear bonding, is keeping religious consciousness awake and religious groups alive despite what in terms of Durkheimian sociology ought to look like a pretty desperate situation. Their social cohesion role dissipating (save as it still serves class or ethnic needs), their claim to ultimate truth called into question by the relativizing fact of pluralism, their inability to move toward the same sort of homogenization as the rest of American and other culture painfully obvious—what sort of hope can religious groups have? Yet they persist and even flourish. Is it in fact as perennially resilient folk religion that they continue? This is a tradition that doesn't really expect to be a dominant culture except in its dreams anyway. Is it only a religious Great Tradition that is under threat of losing its Durkheimian privilege? We shall return to this paradox.

Some Weberians paint a somewhat rosier picture for religion than is common in the contemporary Durkheimian camp, with its elegies for a sacred canopy. Talcott Parsons, for example, contends that religion has in fact adapted itself with some success. He acknowledges that when societies were simple, elements we might call religious and others we might not were fused together in a single web of meaning, as in Berger's sacred canopy. As societies grew more complex, "differentiation" set in, with religious and secular institutions assuming different functions. Indeed, religious and worldly components of the individual psyche came to be differentiated. But this process, which some might call secularization, does not necessarily mean that religion is becoming less significant. In a world of specialists, religious specialists may be as credible as any other. Indeed, the fact that religion is increasingly individualized (and in a pluralistic world, a matter of individual choice) might well serve to make it more important to an individual as such than when it was more or less an automatic part of tribal life. We have noted how this perspective helps explain the vitality of Evangelicalism in the compartmentalized, pluralized modern world. Further, religion's moral influence on seemingly secular institutions such as business and politics in a nation with a religious heritage may be indirect, but it cannot be discounted.[12]

Andrew Greeley, combining both Durkheimian and Weberian approaches, comes to a similar cautiously optimistic view. There will always be religion, he asserts, since society requires it on Durkheimian grounds. Although perhaps a society could theoretically cohere on nonreligious values, no empirical evidence exists for this happening satisfactorily. But Greeley also argues for Parson's differentiation theory and Berger's pluralism, affirming that the Durkheimian role can be played by differentiated, pluralistic religion in a complex society. Under modern conditions, when fragmentation is a "given" of human experience, it does not automatically disqualify religion in the eyes of most; Greeley responds to Berger's ruminations on this matter by pointing to the fact that it is precisely the countries where religion is most pluralistic or even polarized, such as Holland, Ireland, and the United States, that it is apparently healthiest. In the modern world, competition among religions is expected and, far from weakening faith, seems to keep it alive and alert.[13]

Another sociologist who is skeptical of secularization hypotheses, but who is somewhat hard to place theoretically, is David Martin. His basic theory of religion seems to be Weberian in that it is cognitive, having to do with an "orientation towards the world" that includes a "transcendent vision,"[14] which has an operative role parallel to that of science. But of his own theory of secularization, he says that "Durkheim provided the frame."[15]

Fundamentally, though, Martin has conducted a campaign of elegant rear-guard fencing against proponents of general secularization theories. He is not so unwise as to say there is nothing to secularization at all. In an essay on secularization and the arts, he discusses the common observation that the style and content of music and the visual arts have become progressively more secular since the Middle Ages. He contends that this trend is not necessarily a barometer of society generally, but its instances can all be given special explanations. The change and decay that all around he sees in this particular field is, he holds in good High Tory fashion, all to be blamed on the influence of French culture.

So far as secularization as a "unified syndrome of characteristics subject to an irreversible master-trend" is concerned, it is an illusion. He makes the usual arguments that the data are inconsistent and difficult to interpret, that even where religious participation can be shown to be declining, as in his own England, a "subterranean theology" of religious-type attitudes persists and that secularizing sociologists are blinded to these things by their own arbitrary definitions and reductionistic assumptions about religion.[16]

Nonetheless, the man who once said that the word *secularization* "should be erased from the sociological dictionary"[17] later wrote a book titled *A General Theory of Secularization*. Here David Martin argues for a short-term, "highly empirical" use of the concept. Again the French Revolution and its ilk are blamed for what reality there may be to secularizing trends. The latter stems from a vicious cycle set in motion when religion and a substantial part of the population are polarized against each other, as was the Church and its largely reactionary supporters against the working class and liberal opinion in France during the revolutionary era, a gulf that remained a deep and bitter cleavage in French society for well over a century. This disaster is apt to occur when society and religion are first posited in "monopolistic" terms, as was Catholicism in France especially after the revocation of the Edict of Nantes; in countries such as Holland and the United States, where two or more faiths have long shared spiritual sway, the French experience is not likely to occur.[18] However oversimplified this interpretation of religious history (and, of course, I have oversimplified Martin's book-length presentation of it), its kernel of truth serves to reinforce Greeley's contention that secularization is spotty and often illusory and that religious pluralism, far from being the firebrand and terminal symptom of secularization in the modern world, may actually be its antidote.

Martin's cautious and critical use of the secularization concept is continued in his *Dilemmas of Contemporary Religion*,[19] in which, looking to the short-term future of Western religion, he anticipates a weakening of the central core of Euro-American cultural life through liberal pluralism and critical skepticism, but he expects that this decay will be met at the periphery by ethnic and religious resistance.

One sociologist who has few doubts about the reality of the secularization process is Martin's fellow Briton Bryan Wilson.[20] As befits the Weberian tradition, Wilson is inclined to give more significance to changes in the cognitive role than in the social role of religion. Here he sees little ground for hope that religion, in anything like its traditional form, will rise again. The real change the world is undergoing is not in formal religious belief or practice, but in regard for the supernatural—that is, in everyday belief in miracles, witches, and the like. On this front, the real underpinnings of mass religiosity are being cut away. Those "secular" theologians and their sociological allies who attempt to salvage a religion without the old-fashioned supernatural are too sophisticated by half and have little relevance to the true situation.

For Wilson, the sort of theory that says a modern man is "really" religious because he washes his car religiously every Sunday morning or finds his ultimate concern in loving his wife or mistress, or that views the modern miracle-free church as more than the residue of a dying heritage, is simply engaging in definitional sleight of hand. Religion, if it means anything, must mean a downright belief that the supernatural is real and impinges readily and often on ordinary human life. That belief, and behavior associated with it, has been steadily dissipated by science and the march of modernity, even in people who think of themselves as religious. Therefore, religion has declined, and secularization has advanced.

Put this way, I suppose even the most ardent antisecularization theorist, after much hemming and hawing, would have to agree with Wilson, although anyone who has been around evangelical and charismatic circles can affirm that supernatural signs and wonders are still a good way from total decline even in the supposedly most advanced societies. Wilson is clearly speaking of secularization endemic to the elite Great Tradition camp while the folk religion of the Little Tradition continues unabated. The question implicitly posed by Wilson is: How long can the Little Tradition persist without a Great Tradition?

Although we might be more sanguine about the Little Tradition's durability than he, the inevitability of the process is advocated by Wilson in his response to a rambling, learned article by Daniel Bell. Bell argues eloquently, if not with particular originality, that religion does not die but changes.[21] Like others, he grants that a process of secularization occurs as religion retreats from various areas of public life, but insists that it is only pulling back to its invulnerable redoubt in the private sphere. Religion, Bell declares, can operate in the cultural and personal lives of persons without being socially functional or affected by changes in social structure. This is ultimately because it deals with perennial human questions and concerns for meaning, which persist regardless of social change.

Wilson answers that religious attitudes do in fact follow changes in society, though perhaps with a time lag. Any view that culture and belief for the average person can be hermetically sealed off from what is going on in the society of which he or she is a part is hopelessly naïve or elitist. Belief in hell, for example, has notably declined with the modern rise in living standards, as this world has become far less of a vale of tears than it once was for most. In the same way, private religion cannot forever survive a loss of public function or social reason for its worldview. The questions of meaning may, of course, continue to be asked, but this does not mean they need to be put or answered in religious terms, which (as we have seen) would mean for Wilson supernatural terms.[22]

Despite such objections as these, others too have seen a future for religion in the personal arena. Huston Smith has argued that the retreat of an institution from certain public roles to more private ones is not necessarily an unstoppable process that will lead to the institution's demise. He points to the parallel example of the family. Family life also no longer plays as public a role as it once did, nor is it as "extended" as it once was; however, it shows no signs of disappearing. Rather, despite all the strains on the nuclear, personal-life family that remain, people continue to marry and remarry. They move out of the family as autonomous individuals into the workaday world, then at the end of the day withdraw back into it as the venue of personal, private life.

Family and personal life on the one hand, and public and occupational life on the other, are today separable and detached in a way unimaginable even a hundred years ago, when the family farm, the family business, the home above the shop, and family ties helping one get ahead, whether prince or commoner, were the way of the world. Now all these are pale shadows of their former power. Husband and wife are each more likely to be autonomous persons in the business and professional world, as are their children after them; whether one happens to live in family or not in one's off hours means relatively little, professionally speaking.

Yet for all that, the family lives on in the personal sphere. Can this be a message, Smith implies, for the future of religion? Perhaps secularization, like "defamilization," can proceed only so far in the human world as we know it.[23]

The obvious difference, however, is that the family has a base in biological and nurturing imperatives that most people, despite proposed alternatives, seem to find compelling. We have noted certain of them in connection with the emergence of the species; religion itself seems only to afford them sanctions. The sociobiologists notwithstanding, religion apparently has no imperative of itself on quite the same level as that which sets men and women in families; it is either more personal or more social. Its real role, if our approach is correct, is in reifying images connecting subjectively with our universal and infinite environment to make it humanly meaningful. Its ultimate future depends on the continuing need for such images, which can be a bit more subtle than Wilson's old-fashioned supernatural and which can be far less trapped in sociological reductionism than Durkheimian social effervescence. Science and art have thus far not been able to fully duplicate them in the lab or the studio, despite strenuous efforts, less by scientists and artists than by philosophers and popularizers of science and art.

Let us sum up the discussion so far. Virtually all secularizationists would agree that, as far as its visible, moral, and institutional impact is concerned, religion has progressively withdrawn from several major areas of human life in recent centuries, though much difference obtains as to whether this is a general or special phenomenon and whether it is reversible. Richard K. Fenn has offered a detailed model for this process, indicating five major stages by which religion moves from being an undifferentiated cement of society as a whole to the increasingly "privatized" faith of many moderns.[24] We shall glance at Fenn's model with a view to seeing how it may fit in with our model of religious history. His five stages are as follows.

Separation of Distinct Religious Institutions

Although the separation of religion from the rest of society has undoubtedly been on course since the first steps toward division of labor, which may have included the setting apart of shamans as specialists in the sacred, this initial stage in the secularization process can be associated in particular with the appearance of the Great Religions. Despite their important imperial and other alliances, they consummately were religions that saw themselves as having no necessary connection with other institutions, especially in their international and cross-cultural aspects, for their scriptures, hierarchies, and institutions were essentially self-perpetuating, moving from one dynasty or society to another and enduring both persecution and patronage.

Demand for Clarification of the Boundaries between Religious and Secular Issues

The linguistic connotations of the final word of this heading, "issues," must not be overlooked. The point is not to determine in some vague way what is religious and what is secular, but precisely what can be spoken of in religious language, and what must not. What words belong to God and what to Caesar? What to the City of God and what to the City of the World? Answering these types of questions was very much the task of both the medieval (Devotional) and Reformation stages in all religions. In the Middle Ages, it involved residual church-and-state issues left over from the imperial alliance, such as the investiture controversy in Europe and, on a deeper level, the definition of sacred and profane space within the psyche—thus, chivalry and devotionalism's long fascination with the parameters of human and divine love, and medieval mysticism's distinction between inner and outer religion. The latter issue, long coming to a boil in the devotional cauldron, eventuated in the Reformation's characteristic emphasis on inward faith and "disenchantment" of the outer world. The result was increasingly sharp distinctions in practice, and often in theory, between the spheres of church and state, religion and science, or capitalist economics and charity. These "issues," however, left popular religion more and more free to go its own way in devotions and crusades unsponsored by the Great Tradition.

Development of Generalized Beliefs and Values That Transcend the Potential Conflict between the Larger Society and Its Component Parts

The boundary clarification between the sacred and the secular leaves a wound, for society is no longer unified under a single implemented worldview. This calls for the discovery of new worldviews that are nonreligious, or only nominally religious, but that also embrace both now-compartmentalized traditional religion and the separated aspects of state and society. By our schema, they are the products of a rationalist enlightenment that tends to follow, as a sort of reaction, the initial Reformation ferment. In the Christian West it is represented by the democratic, and later socialist and Marxist, ideologies stemming ultimately from the values of that era, and also by civil religion; in the East, by the secularized and politicized Neo-Confucianism that became the official ideology of the Tokugawa regime in Japan and the Manchu dynasty in China, or the rationalized and universalized Hinduism of groups like the Brahmo Samaj and Ramakrishna Mission. Finally, a frankly nonreligious Great Tradition is left, under the aegis of modern communism or capitalism, leaving religion in the private or Little Tradition sphere.

Minority and Idiosyncratic Definitions of the Situation

This step includes the attempt of "withdrawal" sects and cults to return to the undifferentiated situation for themselves at the cost of alienation from the "mainstream" settlement. Sect formation has been a feature of religion at least since the Axial Age, and probably is always in part a compensation for the destructive side of secularization, also an eternal tendency from a very broad perspective. However, sect formation displays special proliferation in the stage just after ideology and civil religion have shown themselves unable to handle the situation with the degree of intensity and transcendent reference some demand. Thus, nineteenth- and twentieth-century Christianity has spawned a vast array of revivalist and perfectionist sects; within Catholicism, it has produced "cults" such as those of the Sacred Heart and apparitions of Our Lady, each producing on a small scale a total, undifferentiated world of meaning based on one-pointed emotional focus and consistent lifestyle. Similar movements in the East, such as bhakti cults and the "new religions" of China and Japan, could be cited, as the line between the continuing and increasingly secular Great Tradition and the surviving folk-religion Little Tradition is clarified.

The Separation of the Individual from Corporate Life

The title suggests that the withdrawal of spiritual life into ideology and sectarianism fails to compensate for the loss of undifferentiated faith. This last stage, if carried by everyone to its logical conclusion, would mean the demise of all corporate religious institutions and public symbols. It clearly has not been arrived at yet by much of the world, and empirical evidence confirming that this is the final stage of the process is at best inconclusive for the present. It may represent the situation in the People's Republic of China for the great majority, as it may for the subjective state of a substantial minority of the rest of the planet, especially such "advanced" societies as Western Europe and Japan. What remains to be seen, however, is whether the low level of religious participation in those places represents secularization as a historical process or is the "ordinary" religious indifference that has always characterized a fair proportion of the human race when pressure to conform is off. On a less acute level, this stage may correspond to our Folk Religion stage, which does not entail the dismantling of religious institutions as such. But it does disestablish and privatize religion to the extent that it makes it essentially local, ethnic, family, or "popular" in its center of gravity, and it keeps it separate from the other major "corporate" institutions of society.

I will now examine the same process in terms of human experience in recent centuries in five areas: economics, politics, education, art and literature, and religious institutions. I think we shall see more clearly how in the Christian West we are moving toward Fenn's last stage and our Folk Religion stage and how this transition has already happened in the folk-religion Buddhist and Chinese religious worlds.

Economics

The great power that the Christian church and similar Buddhist and Hindu religious institutions held in the economic life of the Middle Ages was through its role as landowner and as political, even military, force. It also made economic influence felt through the use of moral influences such as the ban on usury. This power, however, has now become peripheral. Capitalism, as it replaced the feudal order so congenial to ecclesiastical hierarchical parallels, has no direct investment by religion comparable to its economic role in the feudal order, though religion often has a dependency relation to it since its institutions require donations from capitalist sources. One can, of course, further argue with Weber, Parsons, and others that capitalism was fired in no small part by the "inner asceticism" of the reformation outlook and that its values still have a real though unspoken role in modern economic institutions.

But the very fact that these values have come to be largely unspoken in religious terms and have no other relation to religion except religion's dependence on capitalism's profits contrasts markedly with the feudal situation. It would suggest that, in this sphere, secularization is in process, in the sense of a separation of religion from coequal status with the major other institutions of society; in addition, the process seems to have been abetted by the Devotional and especially post-Reformation subjectivization of religion to inward faith and corresponding "disenchantment" of the world. The whole movement is a clear example of Fenn's demand for demarcation between sacred and secular: the economic order is declared secular (save as, of course, for the fact that godly people might be working in it), even as the church ostensibly remained a power in its own inward realm. Thus, in a folk religion situation, religion has little relation to economic power—even the Vatican Bank does not have the world economic impact it once did. So it is today, broadly speaking, in all religions except Islam, with its greater Reformation-era demands for identity with the power-wielding state.

Politics

The intimate (though often uneasy) medieval alliance of church and state has clearly given way to separation for all practical purposes. Even in those nations that still retain a nominal state church, its influence on day-to-day policy making is minimal and not even predictable when issues of great moral or institutional interest to it are at stake, save in the Islamic sphere. As in the economic arena, a dwindling residual influence may remain in the "values" of the state, as articulated by civil religion and the pieties of politicians. In terms of Fenn's steps, countries such as Germany and France, which once had robust state religions, have now virtually reached the fourth stage. They have seen the boundaries of religion "clarified" at the cost of severe national polarization; they have passed through enthusiasms for surrogate national ideologies; and now it may be argued that even the "mainstream" religions of these countries are acquiring sectarian characteristics in their homelands. The situation is not identical everywhere. But whether the situation is one of uneasy alliance, antagonism, or indifference, one can say that hardly anywhere outside the Islamic world do religion and the state meet as natural partners or equal negotiators. Certainly they do not in the Buddhist or Chinese religious lands, where they are peripheral to serious politics, except for religion's ideological use in Japan in the nationalistic era. Religion and the state are, rather, disparate forces, like creatures of land and sea, who would clearly prefer to be left alone to go their own way, but must occasionally meet at water's edge to admire or snap at each other. This is secularization insofar as the two are no longer parallel institutions, but of different orders; they retain, however, the power to affect each other. Agents of governments still arrest and kill troublesome religious figures, and these figures still rally the humble against what they perceive as oppression and injustice.

Education

In a comparable way, education has moved from being, if not quite the ecclesiastical monopoly sometimes supposed, at least subject to weighty religious input on all sensitive matters to generally secular control and content in Europe and America. The rise of classical and scientific studies in the Renaissance, the establishment of public schools, and the end of mandatory conformity to Anglicanism in English universities in the nineteenth century were landmarks of this trend. Although some European school systems retain token religious instruction, most state-sponsored education, including in folk-religion China and Japan, is essentially secular; religious education must be obtained voluntarily in religious institutions—except in the Islamic world, where, as one would expect of our schema, earlier models obtain. For many people, from those who applaud to those who fear secularization, nothing symbolizes and actualizes more effectively than this the peripheral character of religion in the "real" world. For nowhere has the boundary between religion and other issues been more carefully and restrictively drawn; surrogate ideologies more persuasively preached; religion pushed more into sectarian stances; and, indeed, Fenn's last stage of the privatization of religion more nearly approached, than in education.

Art and Literature

Perhaps no process of secularization is more striking or, one might add, more puzzling and deeply ominous for religion than the decline of the sacred in art and letters. Puzzling because what it really means is that, over recent centuries, religion has held less and less interest for the most intelligent and creative members of society; for this phenomenon, no easy explanation presents itself except in arguments that are really circular. Ominous because one wonders with what sort of vigor religion can survive without the support of such persons. The pattern is clear: several centuries ago, the bulk of great music, sculpture, painting, and writing in Europe was permeated with religious themes, as it was earlier in Asia. Today, although plenty of third-rate and derivative religious art is produced and although such artists as the early twentieth-century symbolists have drawn from alternative esoteric strands of spirituality, art based on the dominant religious traditions that could be called original and distinguished is minuscule. The European decline of the sacred in art has been irregular. The nineteenth century brought forth little that was not highly imitative in religious music, painting, and architecture—with its various "revivals" of Gothic, Byzantine, and comparable themes (though some of it required technical skill); in letters, however, it gave us fresh religious visions as rich as those of Blake, Dostoevsky, and Hopkins. But in the twentieth century, the harvest has been skimpier yet. With the exception of a few self-conscious traditionalists such as T. S. Eliot, the most powerful spiritual passions in the arts have been from women and men who seem more precursors of an age of privatized faith than church-oriented. One could mention such persons of uncovenanted grace as Scriabin, Camus, and Le Corbusier.

Nor does there seem to be any significant innovative Buddhist, Confucian, or Taoist art or literature in its Folk Religion era. The situation is less clear in Islam because of the peripheral role of art in that spiritual culture.

Religious Institutions

Finally, we come to the decline of religious institutions, which have attempted to parallel the other major institutions of society we have cited. We mean, of course, the great national denominations and universal churches that in the nineteenth and twentieth centuries in particular established public identities, bureaucracies, and local branches comparable to those of a state, a major corporation, or a school system. Much evidence lately suggests that this pattern is slowly breaking down. In the United States (the supreme "denominational society") and elsewhere, budgets for national church offices have declined; tension and even schism are on the increase between local churches and the national organizations; and denominational loyalty is clearly less important to large numbers of people than in the past. Cross-denominational alternative structures—both local and national, including youth organizations and electronic media ministries—often compete successfully with denominational churches, suggesting a move into Fenn's penultimate step involving minority and idiosyncratic definitions of the spiritual situation.

The growing frequency of church switching suggests that denominational identity is fading as an important value. William R. Swatos has suggested that religion is reverting to its natural base, localism, as it seeks to preserve its identity against adverse trends in the general culture, trends against which denominations—precisely because they parallel the structures of that same general culture, with its national and international political, corporational, and educational entities—are ill prepared to defend themselves.[25] But such a trend, if large-scale and irreversible, would be no mere blip on the charts. It would signal a turning of the tide of major religious–historical importance, for it really suggests nothing less than a reversal of the dominant trend of Great Religions during their first two thousand years of history—a trend toward finding national and even international bases of power to which the local is distinctly subordinate, toward defining their spiritual culture preeminently in relation to the major elite culture rather than the local, and toward making the local outposts franchises for the dissemination of a great tradition, rather than primarily places for the definition of local culture. Making localism central could only mean that a Great Tradition was becoming a folk religion.

To this litany could be added more subjective aspects of the decline of conventional religion: Bryan Wilson's decline of general belief in the supernatural; the decline of religion as important influence on mainstream intellectual life. With regard to the second, here let us only allude to the prospect that although *religion* remains vital in many places, *theology* seems to be taken less seriously than it once was by intellectuals generally, and even by the churches. Only a generation ago, theologians of the highest caliber—for example, Karl Barth, Paul Tillich, the Niebuhrs—were known to the thinking public; appeared on the cover of *Time* magazine; and were regarded as at least significant, even by those of the intellectual mainstream who may not have agreed with them. Now, though theologians of the merit of Hans Kung or David Tracy have been at work and recognized in our day, one is hard put to think of any who have had quite the public or intellectual impact of those departed giants. Though they may equal them in mental power, the times have changed and the public reception of theologians is not what it was. Similarly, churches both liberal and conservative appear willing to proclaim their doctrines without the benefit of much rigorous theological work; one increasingly senses a populist mood in religion that tacitly rejects the benefit of such labors to authentic faith.

In short, we have a situation in which religion as an institutional force is losing power to affect economic and educational life on a large scale, and political life as well in most of the Christian world, save in a narrow range of issues. Religion as a cultural force is losing power to influence the course of music, literature, art, and intellectual life. Furthermore, what many would see as the real foundation of religion, belief in the supernatural and its intervention in human affairs, has faded until few people in modernized society actively believe in it, except for the special cases required by their own orthodoxy or unless validated by science as parapsychological phenomena. But any need for such validation gives the show away as far as the continuing authority of religion is concerned.

Qualifications must be made, of course, but they do not seem to vitiate the overall picture. In the late twentieth century, much was made of the political effectiveness of the "religious right" in the United States. In the Third World, the set of attitudes and activisms associated with "liberation theology" were also notable. But both must be distinguished from the political role of *institutional* religion; religious rightism and liberationism sometimes can be seen instead as another version of the localist, popular folk religion that may be the gravedigger and successor to traditional institutional religion. This is a form of folk religion very different, needless to say, from the faith-healing and holy-wells varieties; but its presence should not be completely startling when we consider the sporadic but longstanding association of popular religion with radical, even millenarian, movements expressing the protest of oppressed classes—from the early Quakers to the White Lotus rebellions of China—movements that frequently had definite political agendas.

But it might be observed that, if the American religious right, and left, and "Third World" liberation theology, fade in importance—as may already be happening—that would be because they are in fact not truly folk-religious, but shaped by Great Tradition ideologies, whether conservative or Marxist, and transmitted by theologians who themselves have "establishment" training and connections. They may therefore be unable to compete with a force like the worldwide expansion of truly popular, Little Tradition Pentecostalism and the more pragmatic sort of politics it seems to engender, especially in the southern hemisphere.

Religion is clearly more powerful in politics, economics, and education in the Islamic world than elsewhere. I would argue that this is the case because Islam, as a younger faith than Christianity, is now at a stage of development similar to that of Christianity in the age of the Reformation.

But looked at in terms of centuries, the secularization pattern seems undeniable in Europe and in the Great Tradition classes in America from the perspective of what has traditionally been the form and role of religion. Claims that religion can survive in a chastened and personalized but nonetheless subjectively authentic state may be true in some individual cases, but they do little to reassure one concerning the prospects of a society that religion once legitimated and in which it once flourished institutionally. We cannot forget that, although both Durkheim and Weber accepted the fact of secularization and regarded it as progress insofar as it brought a truer understanding of the reality of things, both were fearful of its human consequences if the transition from religious to scientific knowledge were not skillfully made. Durkheim feared social chaos without the bond of faith, and Weber the excessive bureaucratization of life as the social order was "rationalized" and charisma pushed along with the sacred to the periphery.

And yet . . . and yet . . . doubts nag at the bold assertion that religion as we know it is on the way out. It has too often been declared on its deathbed before, and there are those American statistics that seem to fly in the face of secularization. Up to 40 percent of the U.S. population still participates in a religious activity weekly. People are converted, transformed, and reborn; they pray and give and enjoy the fellowship of spiritual assemblies as though faith were still in its prime. They experience gifts of the Spirit and anticipate apocalypses while the "outside" world goes on in its secularizing way. In 1998, 95 percent of Americans prayed, and 60 percent said religion was "very important" to them. And in 1996, one out of three reported having had a religious or mystical experience.[26]

True, survey evidence does show some trends unfavorable to traditional religion in the United States. Robert Wuthnow cites evidence indicating that, at least in certain geographic areas, belief in a conventional theistic concept of God and in life after death has declined 20 percent between the 1940s or 1950s and the 1970s. In place of it, he sees an upsurge of ideas of a "mystical" sort, which he interprets as claiming that "the very definition of reality itself is subject to human control," a perception that would make such mysticism highly compatible with Fenn's last individualizing step in secularization. Wuthnow is appropriately cautious in the use of such data, pointing to the complexity of "trends" in a country such as the United States, but also suggests that diversity can only increase in the foreseeable future.[27]

We have, then, a world of mysticism and salvation that shows no obvious sign of rapidly passing away. But this religious world is increasingly a *separate* world. It is sealed off by more and more profound barriers of language, interests, attitudes, and institutional style from the other worlds we live in that are shaped by science, technology, secular education, and "rationalized" government, politics, and economics. The world of faith subsists without much creative interaction with "high" culture, though it has no small rapport with popular culture, at least in the United States.

But even though this separate religious sphere is experiencing the decay of those institutional structures that most parallel the rationalized bureaucratic state or corporation, we would be mistaken to imply it is merely slipping into infinite fragmentation. The new religious world does have its structures and institutions. Although somewhat weakened, denominations survive, and their politics can generate quite a bit of heat. Cross-denominational and local organizations thrive, along with structures of leadership that, whether in person or in the form of the television shaman, contain large charismatic elements and give much place to voluntary labor for the Lord.

Precisely because of features such as these, the structures and institutions of American religion are becoming, in Weberian language, "less rationalized and more charismatic," with such elements of rationalization that remain devoted not to the routinization of charisma so much as to its perpetuation as charismatic experience on the periphery of an increasingly rationalized world. Thus, in American religion, the most obviously successful organizations—and these are in fact notoriously rationalized and bureaucratic on the operative level—have recently been those dedicated to evangelistic crusades and television preachers of great charismatic appeal.

This spiritual world, transmitted increasingly through the continual renewal of charisma rather than through routinized structures of education and institutionalization, has decreasing interaction with the "outside" intellectual and cultural domain. Its values, no doubt rightly, are felt to be unsympathetic, as thought and structure yield pride of place to faith and charisma. Religious institutions abide, but their value is felt more as visible assurances of the mythos' validating present charisma and experience, as perpetuations of an Eliadean *illud tempus* when faith was bright and fresh, than as major channels of the transmission of faith today. The transmission role instead comes to be dominated by popular books, magazines, the electronic media, and the family and social milieu. Formal religious institutions of the denominational type have less and less control of the form in which faith is transmitted in the face of such local or charismatic media.

The survival, and indeed the flourishing, of American religion in a pluralistic, spiritually inconsistent, sacred canopyless era is simply a sign of Christianity's passage into the Folk Religion stage. Unlike Reformation divines or their liberal epigoni, folk religionists are little concerned about rational consistency, legitimation in relation to a Great Tradition, or even denominationalism, no more so than the postmodernists with whom they oddly and unwillingly coexist. The vibrant folk religion world is far more one of faith, feeling, miracle, and crusade—and that is the postmodern, postdenominational world in which American religion now dwells.

We shall next see what this state means for the present and future of religion in the world as a whole.

CHAPTER ELEVEN
RELIGION AND THE CLASH OF FAITH-CIVILIZATIONS

Despite all the talk of secularization, religion in the early twenty-first century occupies a surprisingly prominent place in world affairs. Divisions that boil down to Christian versus Muslim, Jew versus Muslim, Hindu versus Muslim, or between different sects of each, appear to be those most volatile on the international scene.

Efforts are made, and rightly so, to show that other factors than the purely religious are involved and that all of a religion cannot be stigmatized for the excesses of some. Yet, clearly, it is not without significance that religious flags are often flown by the combatants in today's and tomorrow's headlines. Not since the Protestant Reformation—and, indeed, perhaps not even since the Crusades—has religion seemed so powerful a mobilizer in the international world, even though it had only recently been thought to be retreating irreversibly into the "private sphere." But with the collapse of the communist world and the end of the Cold War in 1989, three things have happened in terms of the deep structures of world history.

First came the end of Marxism as a modern "Grand Narrative," or ideology, indeed, as the supreme and most extreme example of "emancipation through progress" and the "unification of knowledge" around a single unifying principle. That axiom was the "dialectical materialism" of the Marxist view of history, and that ideology's demise as a world-historical force did more than merely abolish one grand narrative. The fall of the Berlin Wall seems to have symbolically left dubious all such monolithic, wall-like interpretations of the past and extrapolations into the future—except, perhaps, for the religious interpretation. For spiritual understandings of history are based on such different, and admittedly "unscientific," foundations, ones that seem to be hardly in the same game. Communism was therefore rightly called pseudoreligious. Both the level of commitment it evoked and its eschatology seemed a secular knockoff of the Judeo-Christian apocalypse and millennium—not to mention its ability to establish itself as the one true church, quite capable of persecuting, torturing, and killing heretics and nonconformists.

Second, with this end came the end of world division in "secular" terms: capitalism versus communism, freedom versus authoritarianism. The Enlightenment view that the real issues of past and present history are best understood in the form of worldly abstractions like these, rather than in the form of concrete cultural or religious language (France versus Germany, Christianity versus Islam), is difficult to apply in the current situation. All four of these categories—capitalism, communism, freedom, authoritarianism—seem to be able to coexist in a country like China (though not in equal degree), and the picture is rather mixed everywhere.

Third has come the end of the idea of revolution as a secular apocalypse capable of purifying a nation through violent upheaval and then bringing in a secular millennium—another covertly religious motif in secular guise. For if apocalyptic is seen, as it usually is by nonbelievers, as the ultimate in religious fantasy, then the age of reason and progress has also been a sublime age of apocalyptic fantasies of the spirit—so long as they are to be acted out as the shaking of the foundations here below, rather than as war in heaven. Over exactly two centuries, from the French revolution of 1789 to the collapse of Communism with its revolutionary idealism in 1989, this doctrine was the stuff of dreams and of not a few attempts at enactment. The fundamental theme may have been as old as European peasant revolts and White Lotus societies in China, but over those two hundred years, revolution also seemed compatible with the most advanced and secular modernism.

For a modern revolution is simply an apocalyptic speeding up of the idea of progress, an endeavor to realize all the promises of modernism *now*, even as traditional apocalyptic is a speeding up of what might otherwise be gradual eschatology; the apocalyptist is willing to suffer the horrific "apocalyptic woes" of the end times, the last release of Satan whose wrath is all the greater because he knows his time is short, for the sake of an imminent breakthrough of joy beyond hope just when all seemed darkest, as the new heaven and earth arise.

So also the joy of the secular apocalyptist of political revolution. The revolutionary mystique appealed to moderns who were characteristically impatient and, especially in the days of the world wars and the Cold War, understandably prone toward polarized, dualistic models of reality, those that pit the children of light against the children of darkness, that legitimate revolution. Revolution as righteous gesture also answered to the modern ideal of social justice, to be wrought out of such an apocalyptic struggle, and it answered as well to the role of elites, idealized in the revolutionary activist vanguard.

But after 1989, the revolutionary ideal seemed to lose its frisson. Too many revolutions had by then gone sour, turning into reigns of terror or corrupt despotisms of the left or right. Fundamental contradictions in revolutionary ideology, and between it and the realities of human nature, became apparent.

In Marxism's and revolution's place has arisen what might be considered a pragmatic application of something like Edmund Burke's political philosophy (originally articulated, of course, in opposition to the revolution in France), applied not always so much on behalf of conservatism (as it sometimes is) as for the sake of gradualist, unideological reform that gives due place to the importance of continuities in human society, of which religion is among the most significant.

Burke believed in the wisdom of tradition and in the importance of the "covenant" across generational lines in society. Even if they contain some evil, traditional institutions embody that link with the past and are not to be lightly discarded. To search for too great a purity in the political and social word, such as that dreamed of by revolutionaries, is to invite fresh corruption.

The world and humanity are imperfect, and the quest for perfection in the social order spurious. The political obligation is to correct finite, present ills and preserve established liberties, not to risk destroying all for the sake of perfecting all overnight. Thus, as is well known, Burke favored the Irish and American rebellions, believing they were intended to preserve concrete liberties and bring about incremental change within the structures of established institutions; however, he opposed the French Revolution because it was supposed to produce a wholly new society based on rationalism. Undoubtedly, what most deeply offended the Whig thinker was the French republic's novel philosophical base: first, it was founded on abstract and hypothetical belief in "atomistic" human liberty and equality; second, its belief that a wholly new and irreversible human order could be commenced in historical time.

In my view, Burkeanism is where we are now. In most places in the world, from the United States to the former Communist nations, from Europe to China and Japan, there is a sense that politics or social philosophy based on abstractions, ideologies, or dreams of perfection is exhausted. It has been shown not to work, but nothing has been shown *to* work, even by statesmen with the best intentions, except a Burkean process of incremental change in the context of continuing institutions. Substantial, not to mention revolutionary, change in the polity of any major nation seems at present only a remote possibility, though incremental changes to meet new economic, demographic, and ecological realities continue, as it were just beneath the surface. I myself consider such American political changes as those of Roosevelt's New Deal, Truman's Fair Deal, and the Civil Rights legislation of the 1960s to be entirely the sort of reform Burke envisioned—needed change pragmatically conceptualized, and carried out within the structures of continuing social and political institutions.

Some half of the European Union countries retain traditional monarchies, even though the Union seems to be gradually diminishing the sovereignty of each into what eventually may be more like a single nation. In addition, the United States retains its sometimes creaky eighteenth-century constitution, including even the absurdity of the electoral college, into the twenty-first century, though pursuing space-age policies on many other levels. Obviously, the covenant with the past is important to legitimacy and a people's spiritual well-being, and nothing better seems workable or even imaginable in a time like this. Whether or not the name is invoked, we are in a Burkean age.

Such an age might also seem to be an age without absolutes, and so it is: revolutionary fires are now being banked—with one exception. Religion. Religion is admitted into the Burkean age by virtue of its being part of the covenant with the past, but religion is not always just a compliant church teaching gentlemanly virtues which that eighteenth-century philosopher–statesman knew. Religion can also be a wedge that, once admitted, brings absolutes back into an age without absolutes and passion into a politics of pragmatism. So it seems to be with religion in the political world today.

Indeed, most importantly for our study, the world religions—essentially those we have considered in this study plus Judaism—are what, after all the debacles, is left standing as centers of transcendent meaning, and so of absolute, not pragmatic or incrementally realized, national cohesion and personal identity. They are, therefore, what alone remains as conscious, intentional forces for historical change. Change there will be, of course, as changing technologies make for changing economic configurations; particularly charismatic political figures come and go as well. But for a thorough-going worldview capable of evoking change in terms of one's deepest sense of personal and cultural/national identity, only religion remains, for better or worse.

That is why Samuel Huntington, in *The Clash of Civilizations*,[1] views the present world situation in terms of cultural blocs, or "civilizations" that, like tectonic plates, rub up against each other to create upheaval. Most of these "plates" are identified with a religious outlook. They are the Western (western Europe and Anglophone/Francophone North America, plus such outposts as Australia, New Zealand, and even the significantly once intercivilizationally embattled Falkland Islands), Latin American, African, Islamic, Sinic (Chinese), Hindu, (Eastern Christian) Orthodox, Buddhist, and Japanese. The Sinic, Hindu, and Japanese are based essentially in one nation, though with wider cultural influence; the rest are multinational, but in Huntington's contemporary world, that counts for far less than their role as one of nine civilizations in conflict. In the new world so defined, historically important confrontations will no longer occur within these blocs but on the "fault-lines" between them.

There are, of course, a few anomalies: the Philippines, the Pacific and Caribbean island nations, and Israel. The last, like the twelfth-century crusader state whose territory it essentially governs, is certainly an anomaly to the vast Islamic civilization world around it, but neither is it an unambiguous outpost of the Western camp from which the majority of its original founders (though not all its present settlers) immigrated. While this is not the place to sort out all the issues involved in conflict between Israel and its neighbors, one point—surprisingly not emphasized by Huntington—is appropriate in our context: the unique religious basis of Israel.

Its anomalous position cannot be viewed apart from its status as the only Jewish state in the world; it cannot be viewed religiously as one with the Islamic civilization around it, nor with the basically Christian "West" from which its original settlers and institutions derived. Of course, Christianity and Islam, as "Abrahamic" faiths, share and stem from Judaism's spiritual heritage. But this relationship has scarcely diminished the frequent antagonism between them. Indeed, it may sadly be the case that, just as hatreds sometimes are bitterer within families than between mere co-inhabitants of the same town, so religions which have lived together too long, and which know and understand—or misunderstand—each other too well, may be more vitriolic in their mutual dislike than they are toward rivals on the other side of the globe.

The unique case of Judaism forces reevaluation of categories many might like to keep undisturbed. Judaism is neither a "great" religion (in our geographic and demographic sense, not in terms of intrinsic worth) nor a minor one (in light of its immense historical importance), in practice neither completely of one "civilization" bloc or another. But it is always salutary to reexamine categories. For although every religion is unique in its own way, none is as distinctive or has had as remarkable a history as the Jews. Judaism always seems to be the exception to every rule of history, just as Jewish thought or even the mere presence of the Jewish community has so often pointed up the limitations of whatever "universal" truth and practice someone else has tried to lay out. Toward the ancient empires and polytheisms, toward Eastern mysticism and Christian salvationism, toward modern nationalism, dictatorship, Communism, mass culture, and disbelief, Judaism—or at least some segment of Judaism—has always said "Yes, but. . . ."

It has not opposed all of these things: Judaism has had mystical systems worthy to compare with those of India, and it also has its share of skeptics; and it has been and is today expressed in nationhood. But it has always been wary of making an "ism" out of them and then saying that mysticism, or skepticism, or nationalism is the end of meaning and truth. Jews had had a tendency to say, "Yes, but perhaps there's another side. If the majority worldview leaves us out, it's not the complete and final truth."

So no doubt with our schema of world religious history, and so also with the clash of civilizations modeled as final and complete truth. If Israel tells us anything—if there is meaning to its challenging placement at the cynosure of world conflict, on the civilizational frontier of West versus Islam—the Jewish state tells us two things. First, the anomaly of Israel forces us to rethink not only secularization but also simplistic and idealized views of religion's role in world affairs. Second, that anomaly compels us to think of world conflict as truly religious conflict in its ultimate nature, and not merely as civilizational. For insofar as religion, in a broad cultural sense that even nonreligious Israelis might acknowledge (as well as most Muslims and many Christians), is the profoundest remaining locus of personal and group identity in today's world, it will be the most problematic as well.

It would be false reductionism to "explain" the Middle East conflict in a way that said religious confrontation is only a front for economic and geopolitical struggle. A truer "reductionism" would be to acknowledge that on the deepest level the battle *is* religious, in the sense that down there it is about personal and group identity, about symbols of who one *is* in relation to the world and the cosmos and their modes of expression, and to this the other factors are epiphenomenal. It is not really about making a little more money that crusades and civilizational wars are fought, though it may be about whose image and superscription is on the money.

Of course, some will point to secular sources of conflict behind religious wars. The Crusades were fought not only for the Cross and the Holy Places, but also because of population growth in Europe. The wars of the Reformation were not only over justification by faith, but also changing economic patterns and the increasing assertiveness of northern Europe. No doubt there is a level of truth in these contentions. Yet surely what people *thought* they were fighting for is also important. The religious dimension not only affects the symbols and subjective temper of the struggle; it also places it within the world history of religion and the specific history of each faith.

The last indicates, as we would expect, why the religions do not appear to be equal. They are unequal not only in numbers but, far more important, in relative vitality as the driving force behind civilizations and the "clash of civilizations." In this respect, Huntington's book seems already to be dated. Not all of his lines are along significant religious lines.The "West," Latin America, and increasingly sub-Saharan Africa are Christian; and both China and Japan share a Confucian/Buddhist spiritual heritage. However, severe as economic strains may be between "North" and "South," or China and Japan, flashpoints leading to possible war on a large scale are not increasing between these entities, but along the fault lines between major world religions, including here Judaism.

Of course, one thinks immediately of Islam and its frontiers with Judaism, Christianity, and Hinduism. Huntington makes a great deal out of Islam's "bloody borders," suggesting that religion possesses a peculiarly warlike nature. Without downplaying at all contemporary terrorism committed in the name of Islam, it seems to me that one making such a judgment categorically has not read the Bible or studied Christian history lately, or for that matter reflected on the wars and atrocities of Hindu, Buddhist,[2] or Confucian kings in the heyday of those faiths as "civilizations." From the point of view of our schema, it is not so much the intrinsic nature of a religion, whether "peaceful" or "bellicose," that is at issue, but the place at which it is at in its own religious development. Religions sometimes seek to expand or consolidate their state-supported gains by force in the Imperial period; they preserve their hegemony the same way in the Devotional stage; and they may be especially determined to let right prevail by might in the Reformation stage, both externally and internally.

If Islam is presently beginning its Reformation period, that would help explain its bloody borders, but one would be hard put to find anything in Islam today worse than the terror that not seldom accompanied the "conversion" of the New World more or less simultaneously with Christianity's early Reformation period, or the Catholic and Protestant martyrdoms of Europe, or the horrors of the Thirty Years War. Reformation is, on the one hand, a process of simplification of faith; on the other, it is a response to deep inner anxieties about its continuing validity in a changing world. Both make for the kind of slogans and temperament easily expressed through the sword or by suicide bombing.

Toward the end of the Reformation period, however, when the era's theological impulse is likely to show liberal as well as integrative tendencies, religions may look back on those times with distaste and pride themselves instead on a capacity for tolerance or even pacifism. So it was with nineteenth- and twentieth-century liberal Christianity, with Hinduism in the days of Vivekananda and Gandhi, and so perhaps it will be with Islam several centuries from now. On the other hand, the onset of folk religion may impel a recrudescence of militancy, as the populist spirit lying behind peasant crusades and folk messianic movements reasserts itself; in addition, the Great Tradition, likely to be liberal or at least judicious, has weakened to the point that it is ineffective in countering such impulses. Folk religion is also quite amenable, under the right circumstances, to cooption by the state in support of patriotic military ventures: the emotional zeal is there, ready to be tapped. And again, the religious elite of the Great Tradition, which in their days of coequal authority with the state might have been prepared to face down politicians and populist warriors, are relatively defanged.

All these considerations ought to indicate why the religions of today's world are unequal in role, vitality, and geopolitical influence. Let us look at the specifics. First the most important: half the world's population (six billion at the beginning of the twenty-first century) belongs, at least in broad cultural terms, to two of the world faiths. Christianity claims two billion souls, and Islam one or a little more. These, together with Judaism with its influence far out of proportion to its numbers, constitute the three Abrahamic faiths and are at the center of today's religious/political ferment.

The Christian third of the world is in a remarkable position at present. Its numbers have more than doubled in only half a century, partly due to natural population increase and partly to rapid evangelization, especially in Africa and parts of Asia. Both forms of growth have, in a real sense, occurred in traditionally Catholic Latin America. There rapid population growth, together with changing religious patterns induced by urbanization and an upsurge of Pentecostal and other Protestant movements, have brought revitalization to both wings of Christianity. The region now has fresh importance to the Christian world overall. What all this means is that the Christian "center of gravity" is moving to the southern hemisphere, to what is sometimes called the "Third World."[3]

That move is only abetted by the relative decline of its onetime heartland, not to mention the power-center of its elite Great Tradition, Europe. Today the great churches and cathedrals of Europe are largely empty even as the population of Europe itself is declining, while Christian numbers are growing, sometimes explosively, elsewhere in the world: To see thronged places of worship and vital Christian faith, one must now go to Nairobi, Seoul, or São Paulo, rather than London, Paris, or Rome. Nor does the latest theological vogue out of Oxford or Switzerland transfix the intellectual believing world as it once did.

The numbers of active Christians in the United States remain impressive, at some 225 million in 2000; however, they represent only a little over 10 percent of world Christianity, and that percentage will decline as the twenty-first century advances. Worldwide, by 2025, half the world's Christians will live in Africa and Latin America; by 2050, only about one-fifth of the world's three billion Christians will be non-Hispanic whites, whether in Europe, North America, or anywhere else.[4] That augury may be startling to conventional images of Christianity as a "white man's religion," and it may also be startling in the face of declamations like Hilaire Belloc's resounding "Europe is the Faith," to which that trenchant Catholic writer appended, "The Church is Europe; and Europe is the Church." But Philip Jenkins, in noting the religious-demographic projections, comments that "soon, the phrase 'a White Christian' may sound like a curious oxymoron, as mildly surprising as 'a Swedish Buddhist.' Such people can exist, but a slight eccentricity is implied."[5]

How does this pattern fit in with our model, which suggests that as Christianity is moving south, it is also moving into its Folk Religion stage? It fits in very well, I believe. The large and growing numbers do not belie this assessment; in fact, all religions are probably largest and most widely distributed as folk religion because they are heirs of centuries of expansion and as the result of natural population increase. But—and this must be said without any hint of condescension—the style of much southern Christianity best matches the characteristics of folk religion presented in chapter 9. Theologically conservative, it generally lacks the sort of elite Great Tradition that is concerned with how the faith shows congruence with the "best" of science or philosophy or with comparable great traditions in art, literature, education.

Whether Pentecostal, independent "new" Christian movements, Catholic, or derived from "mainline" Anglicanism or Protestantism,[6] this Christianity is more preoccupied with subjective spiritual feeling, personal rectitude, and such practices as spiritual healing and expelling demons. Its moral values are likely to stress the kind of sobriety and work ethic that help its members keep their bearing in a society changing from peasant to urban, and otherwise to reflect the traditional values of the society. This latter point has led to tension between "First World" and "Third World" branches of major denominations like the Anglican on such issues as the ordination of women and homosexuals (about which the First World is likely to be more liberal), as well as the toleration of polygamy (of which the Third World may be more accepting).

Nonetheless, Christianity, as the twenty-first century opens, is in an anxious and even dangerous phase as it slides from one way of being in the world to another. Christians are prone to be jealous of what cultural and geopolitical influence they retain, as they sense that on some deep level that kind of influence is slipping away—unless on the level of popular crusades hard for leadership to control.

Islam, on the other hand, is shaped today by the outward confidence and deeper level anxiety of the Reformation stage. A confrontation of two such spiritual adversaries is tricky: each must show confidence even as the world and its roles in it change, while at the same time, each has reasons for inner doubts as that world becomes more and more obviously not the one in which their faith first resonated.

The role of Christianity is confused by the new "split-level" presence the faith has in the world as the nominal religion of the majority of the planet's "advanced" societies, where it is mixed with post-Christian culture. Those ready to proclaim a new Christian holy war against Islamic or other perceived enemies find themselves first in dialectic against coreligionists more informed by the religion's own peacemaker tradition and then against more pragmatic secularized neighbors. At the same time, the geopolitical role of the "New Christendom" to the south is as yet far from clear. Perhaps it could be aroused to a crusade. For the present, it seems content to meet the religious and social needs of individuals and families, often with a directness and intimacy that the previous religions, as larger-scale institutions dominated by elites, had not in popular eyes. (It is thus actually the folk-religion character of the New Christendom that sustains its appeal.)

According to our schema, Hinduism is the other religion that, like Christianity, is moving from the end of a Reformation phase to folk religion and is finding itself deep-level in a comparable situation. It does not have the worldwide spread of the New or even the Old Christendom, although its direct and indirect influence worldwide—through Vedanta philosophy, yoga classes, and the importance of Gandhi in inspiring nonviolent action by others like Martin Luther King Jr.—is not to be discounted. As India, 75 percent Hindu, becomes the most populous nation in the world during the twenty-first century (as is expected), Hinduism will certainly remain a major "civilization" and world religion.

Its outward conservative confidence and flourishing folk religion–type institutions, combined with some alienation from intellectual elites and perhaps some inner questioning, is not dissimilar from the Christian picture. Hinduism now seems to be more represented by conservative and confrontational voices (like those of the Bharat Janata Party, in power as of this writing) than by the liberalism of late–Reformation era persons such as Swami Vivekananda, Mohandas K. Gandhi (who claimed to be as inspired by Ruskin, Tolstoy, and the Sermon on the Mount as by Hinduism), or India's philosopher–president Sarvepelli Radhakrishnan, even as the liberal Christianity of the late nineteenth and early twentieth centuries seems to be likewise in decline as the religion's most conspicuous face to the world. Both are religions with greater numbers than ever before, yet they are also religions sensing themselves in a precarious transitional position, if not under siege.

What about Buddhism and the Chinese religions? Because of their great effective losses in China as a result of the Communist revolution, neither has the numbers on paper they had before 1949. The relative ease with which they succumbed to the alien ideology or sheer secularism or (to a remarkable extent in Korea and even China) Christianity suggests that even their Folk Religion stage was virtually exhausted, at least in the Chinese heartland. But Buddhism retains some strength in Japan and in the Southeast Asian Theravada Buddhist countries, as well as in the West, where a number of spiritual seekers have discovered the Dharma.

The fourteenth Dalai Lama of Tibet (b. 1935), perhaps the second most prominent world spiritual leader (after the Pope), has brought the religion wide visibility and respect. But despite his role as spokesperson for the oppressed Tibetan people, one cannot say that Buddhism has the geopolitical significance of Christianity, Islam, or Hinduism. It remains to be seen whether that ancient pathway to Nirvana will continue to diminish as an institutional religion—though, of course, its historical and intellectual legacy should linger long regardless of such a structural decrease. It also remains to be seen whether—for nothing is deterministic—it finds a way to keep alive its temples, monasteries, and lineages despite the "decline of the Dharma" over some three millennia that the Buddha himself had predicted. Or will it revitalize itself, even undergoing a new reformation reshaping it for a new kind of world? (Perhaps that reformation would be centered in the West, where, according even to many Asian Buddhists, the religion has more spiritual power, and more creative and adaptive energies, than in its ancient strongholds.)

Less sanguine hopes can be raised for the Chinese religions, Confucianism and Taoism. A few Confucian temples and rites are nostalgically maintained in Korea and Taiwan, and Taoism is widespread—it is very difficult to say how much—in Taiwan, the Chinese diaspora, and in the People's Republic of China, very much as folk religion. There seems little hope, though, for effective institutional revitalization. What is of greater interest is the continuing *noninstitutional* influence of these traditions. Confucian values regarding family, work, the individual (in relation to the social order), and the state continually and fundamentally shape culture alike in China, Korea, and Japan, whether under Communist, corporate, or even Christian guise. One could almost say that Chinese communism is Confucianism under another name, with its mottos like "Serve the people," the ancient sage's virtues of beneficence and mutuality, and the Party cadres like the elite mandarins of old. Japan's hierarchical society and paternalistic corporations have presented almost a capitalist version of the same.

As for Taoism, it too seems to be perpetuated mainly in the form of attitudes perhaps not even consciously attributed to the religion. One could make a case, in fact, that Taoism has really had more influence in America than any other Eastern religion! Consider how many more martial arts studios there are than explicitly Buddhist or Hindu temples (not to mention Taoist); how many surfers wear the yin/yang symbol; how much people talk about the "Tao" of this or that, or about "going with the flow"; and how much cultural influence the *Star Wars* movies have had, their concept of the "Force" clearly based on the *chi* or *ki* of the martial arts. And despite Buddhist and Confucian influence, the martial arts are fundamentally in the Taoist tradition. Perhaps this is the fate of religions after the Folk Religion stage: to become ongoing sources of ethical and cultural values, independent of any institutional structure at all, like classical religion in the Renaissance.

CHAPTER TWELVE

SUMMATION AND A LOOK AHEAD

We have outlined a possible model for the histories of large world religions. They are five in number: Buddhism, Chinese religion, Hinduism, Christianity, and Islam. They began some twenty-five hundred years ago, in the wake of the invention of writing and the "discovery of history." These are religions that clearly originated in historical time and have distinctive histories, being responses to issues of understanding and, as it were, "fighting back" against time and its attendant suffering in the context of the realization that we humans live under conditions of irreversible history.

They are no less religions of fresh understanding of humans as separate and unique individuals, living under individual responsibility for moral and spiritual choices, for liberation or salvation, or bondage to the wheel of *samsara,* or damnation. These characteristics are focused in the special characteristic of the religions from out of this era: their exaltation of a particular "founder"—or, in the case of Hinduism, an Ishvara (saving) deity or avatar like Krishna—who manifests crucial divine activity in the midst of history. That paradigmatic person reveals the full potential of the individual as sage, enlightened being, savior, or envoy of God. The life, teaching, and ancillary wisdom of this person and the nascent movement are presented with the help of the latest communications technology, writing. Of itself, that tool puts them well ahead of older religions with roots in the preliterate past of bard and myth.

Set on a historical course at a particular point in history time, at least by their own self-understanding (except for Hinduism), these faiths then have all one way or another followed the five-part series of stages of development outlined in this book: Apostolic, Imperial/Wisdom, Medieval/Devotional, Reformation, Folk Religion. By the beginning of the twenty-first century, the religious impulse set in motion by the discovery of history and the new individualism of literate antiquity was within sight of running its course: two of the five were completing the Folk Religion stage; two were entering it; and one was entering its Reformation stage.

And where does religion go from here? Will religion disappear from human life altogether when its discovery-of-history cycle has run out? Will it take new forms—forms unrecognizable to us as religion and almost unimaginable to us now? Will those forms perhaps be related to new forms of consciousness transcending the present human, the spiritual component of possible but over-the-horizon developments like virtual immortality, implanted biocomputers linked to the brain, or a true global consciousness created technologically by implanted "radio-telepathy" devices enabling all minds to work as one? (What would be the religion of a global brain made up of all the individual minds of all persons in the cosmos, enhanced by downloads from supercomputer databanks accessing countless googolplex bits of information from out of the depths of space and time? Possibly by the end of the millennium now beginning. . . .)

On a more modest timescale, will the present religions, or at least the most vital of them, manage to "reinvent" themselves and perpetuate their lives centuries or millennia longer? Or will new religions arise to start the cycle over again? On the other hand, might the future bring, as some idealists hope, a universal syncretistic religion, perhaps "mystical" in tone, made up of the "best" of all present faiths?

This is not a book of prophecy, and we will not pursue these prospects extensively, beyond pointing out that history very often does the unexpected. As Philip Jenkins rightly points out in *The New Christendom*, the rapid growth of Christianity in the postcolonial southern world was not at all what many anticipated. There were those who thought that, because missionary Christianity was, in their eyes, so closely linked to European soldiers and governors that, when the latter departed, so would their faith. Yet Christianity has grown *more* rapidly in postcolonial Asia and Africa than ever it did under European flags, though by and large its churches then began. Apparently, dark-skinned peoples were able to discern more clearly the difference between the religion of Jesus and its often-nominal European/American cohorts than some gave them credit for.

Could a new religion under a new founder suddenly mushroom with the same unanticipated success, sweeping across nations and continents in the wake of imminent social, communications, and consciousness changes? Could it be as far-reaching and as threatening to many as were the communications and discover-of-history changes around the earlier set of founders? Could the Axial Age be reenacted with one or several new religious founders? Certainly, there is no lack of candidates for that awesome role. Over the last century or so, many thousands of prospective founders have started as many new religions. Some of them have drawn adherents in the millions. Yet, thus far, none of those claiming to be entirely new religions rather than novel movements within older faiths has shown real promise of becoming a dominant religion in one or more important culture areas, much less playing the role of the Axial Age Great Religions.

Serious barriers stand in the way of such large-scale religious innovation today. First, the very spiritual individualism brought by the first wave of Great Religions, now interpreted widely as individual freedom of religion apart from state compulsion, stands in the way of the Imperial stage that makes a new religion world-class. Under present-day political conditions, the religion of the king is not necessarily the religion of the people, and the most advanced societies are also likely to be the most pluralistic in faith. A new religion may, of course, have such an appeal as the key to contemporary spiritual conundrums as to sweep much before it, but it is hard to imagine it sweeping all, unless consciousness changes so much that we don't even recognize it as religion in the traditional sense of the word.

Moreover, one fears that the sort of exposure afforded public figures today by the mass media would make the charisma of a new founder and the world viability of his or her movement harder to establish now than it was two thousand years ago. The mystery, the glamour of a personality seen only by some and reported in writing only years after his or her departure, in an age when myth as a vehicle for meaning readily intertwined with literal truth—this scenario is no longer accessible to us. Imagine a Jesus, a Muhammad, or a Buddha in modern dress, featured regularly on the evening news and subject to the labors of investigative reporters. Perhaps they would remain intact as great and good persons, as have a few contemporary heroes of the spirit. But whether they would in our kind of world retain that numinous aureole that makes them the subjects of theologies and the central symbols of Great Religions that swept the earth is, to my mind, more doubtful. I am not sure our age could, or perhaps should, receive such a founder as did the Axial Age. Its lines for the communication of information are not right for the handling of new kerygma and saving persons; depending on how one looks at it, they are too dense or too thin for such a burden. The best they can do is keep the word flowing about those already established.

The nature of those religions stands in the way of a similar new religion displacing them. What they displaced was basically local, preliterate, charismatic folk religion; what they replaced that with was religion of a new type: historical, universal in claim, articulately philosophical or theological, elaborately ethical, highly institutionalized. That kind of religion resists replacement in kind in all sorts of ways by making the salvation stakes high and by the force of an institutional structure in place. The new religion would probably have to be as much a new *kind* of religion as the Axial Age religions were to their predecessors. So far, this sort of competitor has not appeared.

The dream of a few idealists of a world religion made up of some sort of combination of the present world religions is extremely unlikely, at least as a conscious construction. The actual dynamics of religious history strongly militate against this sort of syncretism. The religions, as we have seen, are at different stages of historical development and are not wholly compatible in cultural roles. Moreover, we find that historically when current religion fails to meet current needs, the upshot is frequently new revelation and new intensive religious movements, most often within an existing faith, not contrived syncretism. As often as not, perceived failure in current religion calls for conservative, integralist solutions rather than ultraliberal ones.

In the same way, the "universal mysticism" for which some have yearned—a faith centered on the teachings of the great mystics of all heritages, which they see as the true heartland of the spirit—is, for better or worse, not likely to become the tangible religion of the future for more than a few pure spirits. Mystical experience in itself is a profound and liberating thing, but it is individualistic. To have historical meaning, it must in some way be embodied in a social movement, which in turn will be governed by all the norms that rule the history of religion. If the mystical movement is syncretistic, it will suffer opposition from traditionalists. If it is essentially within a Great Religion, it will finally share its fate, though it may be the spark of a revitalization, even a new reformation. It may, on the other hand, be afflicted by the tacit—and ultimately futile—social conservatism implicit in some mystical quests. Those that do not align themselves to sects or movements with a strong social critique illumined by the beams of eternity, but are more eager to transcend than transform the world, in effect uphold the status quo.

To be sure, the twenty-first century future seems uncertain because so many ominous and unpredictable developments are looming over the edge of history. In this century, the "status quo" may change virtually every year. Climate change, probably incited by global warming, perhaps accompanied by significant rises in sea level, could create economic devastation and even mass population shifts on a scale that induces major religious changes as well. Epidemics comparable to AIDS, possibly even more general, are not impossible; no one expected AIDS before it happened either. Tensions, most likely along one of the globe's religious frontiers, could escalate into world war, bringing all the unpredictable historical changes usually let in by war. If one or another of the Great Religions is blamed for the war by world opinion, that could seriously affect its fortunes.

On the other hand, humanity may find a way around the worst consequences of its ecological and militaristic follies, and religions have a good deal of resilience even in the face of bad news. It may be that the world in the twenty-first century will continue as it started out: a mix of both good and bad indicators, lurching from one crisis to another, but without any one apocalyptic event. Even so, the religious landscape will be far from the same in 2100 as it was in 2000, as it was breathtakingly different, globally, from 1900. In the latter year, the world was dominated and largely ruled by persons of white European descent in Europe and North America, mostly Christian. That hegemony was supported by the fact that they represented a third of the world's total population, as well as most of its economic might. By 2000, that ruling race, though still clinging to economic preeminence, was down to a sixth of the world's total people, and by 2050, it will be no more than a tenth. Europe will probably actually shrink in population over the twenty-first century.

The United States—not "white" but by the middle of the twenty-first century a nation with a "brown" majority, and so, in a sense, really part of the "South"—will grow but only slowly. Well over half the world's people will live in south and east Asia by 2050. By that year, when India is the world's most populous country and China is second, the United States will remain third, and Russia will be fourteenth. No other European country except Germany at twenty-third even appears in the top twenty-five, and Germany, at an estimated eighty million (about the same as today), will be smaller in numbers than such nations as the Philippines, Vietnam, Sudan, and even Saudi Arabia.

Despite India's first place and China's second, the majority of nations that will make up the top twenty-five (populationwise) in 2050 are, as of today, predominantly Christian or Islamic. The overall balance between those two largest religions will remain much as it is now, though with Islam growing closer to parity with the other faith because of even higher rates of population growth in its part of the world. Attention must also be given to the nominal character of much of Christianity in its traditional heartland, Europe, in some of whose cities more worshipers can be found in mosques than in the great historic cathedrals. Statistically, in 2050, Christians should number 3,051,564,000; Muslims, 2,229,282,000; Hindus, 1,175,298,000; and all other faiths—together with the officially nonreligious—less than a billion each out of a world population of nearly nine billion, of which the "big three" make up over six billion.[1]

But consider the difference in the coming demographic pattern from the present, especially for Christianity. As we have observed, following Jesus will go from being predominantly a "white," European and North American faith to one dominated by, and so inevitably increasingly defined by, nonwhites in what the former were once pleased to designate the "Third World." What changes in Christianity's image and role this shift will entail I would not now presume to say, but it seems beyond doubt they will be overall compatible with our definitions of folk religion.

In conclusion, let us note again that patterns of religious history, though suggestive of probabilities, are not deterministic. Just as any one person can at any time decide to defy the statistical probabilities and join a religion highly anomalous to his or her social setting—and this happens all the time—so whole populations could unexpectedly do the same all together. And they have. Needless to say, the larger the numbers of people involved, the less the probability they will all move in the same direction at once—that is, until group dynamics come into play. When sufficient energy is built up for a change, that in itself can bring in laggards and enhance movement.

One cannot then rule out massive religious change, or a new Reformation in Christianity, or another religion. But if things remain as they are, one can expect patterns of reformation, folk religion, and terminal decline to keep on the course they are now tracing, until perhaps technologically induced changes in consciousness have so modified the human race that Axial Age understandings of religion are entirely obsolete. Then, in their place may arise radically new and to us incomprehensible modes of relating to the cosmos and its ultimate mysteries of space, time, and mind.

NOTES

Preface

1. Robert Ellwood, *The History and Future of Faith* (New York: Crossroad, 1988).

2. William Nicholls, ed., *Modernity and Religion*. SR Supplements 19, Canadian Corporation for Studies in Religion (Waterloo, Ont.: Wilfred Laurier University Press), 19–44.

3. Alan Paton, "A Literary Remembrance," *Time* 131, no. 17 (April 25, 1988).

Chapter One

1. Bruce Lincoln, *Holy Terror* (Chicago: University of Chicago Press, 2003).

2. Benjamin Franklin, letter to Eliza Stiles, president of Yale College, circa March 1, 1790, cited in Ralph L. Ketcham, *Benjamin Franklin* (New York: Washington Square Press, 1966), 177.

3. Emmanuel Le Roy Ladurie, *Montaillou: The Promised Land of Error* (New York: Braziller, 1978), 305.

4. Cited in John Gillingham, *Richard the Lionheart* (New York: Times Books, 1978), 36.

5. Le Roy Ladurie, *Montaillou,* 320.

6. Keith Thomas, *Religion and the Decline of Magic* (London: Weidenfeld and Nicolson, 1971), p. 173. See also Peter E. Glasner, "'Idealization' and the Social Myth of Secularization," in *A Sociological Yearbook of Religion in Britain 8*, ed. Michael Hill (London: SCM Press, 1975), 7–14.

7. Martin E. Marty, "The Revival of Evangelicalism in Southern Religion," in *Varieties of Southern Evangelicalism* ed. David E. Harrell Jr. (Macon, Ga.: Mercer University Press, 1981), 9, 11–21.

Chapter Two

1. Henry David Thoreau, *Walden* (New York: New American Library, 1942), 198–99.

2. Henry David Thoreau, *Journal* (New York: Dover, 1962), 8:134.

3. Jean-Francois Lyotard, *The Postmodern Condition: A Report on Knowledge*, trans. Geoff Bennington and Brian Massumi (Minneapolis: University of Minnesota Press, 1984), ix.

4. Lyotard, *The Postmodern Condition*, xiii.

5. Lyotard, *The Postmodern Condition,* iv.

6. Jürgen Habermas, "Neoconservative Culture Criticism," in *Habermas and Modernity*, ed. Richard J. Bernstein (Cambridge, Mass.: MIT Press, 1985), 90.

7. William LaFleur, review of Herman Ooms, *Tokugawa Ideology*, in *Japanese Journal of Religious Studies* 13, no. 1 (March 1986): 107–15. I am grateful to this reviewer for helpful insights into the postmodern debate.

8. Wilhelm Dilthey, *Meaning in History,* trans. and ed. H. P. Rickman (New York: Harper, 1961/1962), 130–31. See also Herbert A. Hodges, *Wilhelm Dilthey: An Introduction* (London: Oxford University Press, 1944), and *The Philosophy of Wilhelm Dilthey* (London: Routledge & Paul, 1952).

9. Hodges, *Wilhelm Dilthey,* 32–33.

10. John Henry Newman, *An Essay on the Development of Christian Doctrine,* ed. J. M. Cameron (1845; Harmondsworth, U.K.: Penguin Books, 1973), 90.

11. Newman, *Development of Christian Doctrine,* 367.

12. "Orangutan Traits Seen as Cultural," *Los Angeles Times,* January 4, 2003, A12.

13. William Cantwell Smith, *The Meaning and End of Religion* (New York: New American Library, 1964).

14. Owen Barfield, *Poetic Diction*, 3rd ed. (Middleton, Conn.: Wesleyan University Press, 1973), 63.

15. Peter L. Berger, *The Sacred Canopy* (Garden City, N.Y.: Doubleday, 1969), 28.

16. Donald Johnson and Maitland Edey, *Lucy: The Beginnings of Humankind* (New York: Simon & Schuster, 1981).

17. Cited in Johnson and Edey, *Lucy*, 331–40. See also C. O. Lovejoy, "Hominid Origins: The Role of Bipedalism," *American Journal of Physical Anthropology* 17 (1974): 147–61.

18. Edward O. Wilson, *On Human Nature* (Cambridge, Mass.: Harvard University Press, 1978), esp. chap. 8, "Religion."

19. Johannes Maringer, *The Gods of Prehistoric Man* (New York: Knopf, 1960), 17–22.

20. John E. Pfeiffer, *The Creative Explosion: An Inquiry into the Origins of Art and Religion* (New York: Harper and Row, 1982), 210–25.

21. Mircea Eliade, *Shamanism: Archaic Techniques of Ecstasy*, trans. Willard R. Trask (New York: Pantheon, 1964).

22. Claude Levi-Strauss, *Structural Anthropology* (Garden City, N.Y.: Doubleday, 1967), 181–201.

23. David Lewis-Williams, *The Mind in the Cave* (London: Thames and Hudson, 2002).

24. Gerald M. Edelman, *Bright Air, Brilliant Fire: On the Matter of the Mind* (Harmondsworth, U.K.: Penguin, 1994), 112–32, cited in Lewis-Williams, *The Mind in the Cave*, 187–88.

25. Lewis-Williams, *The Mind in the Cave*, 80.

Chapter Three

1. See Karl Jaspers, *The Origin and Goal of History*, trans. Michael Bullock (London: Routledge & Kegan Paul, 1953).

2. Karl Jaspers, *Philosophy*, trans. E. B. Ashton (Chicago: University of Chicago Press, 1970), 2:104.

3. The best introduction is Robert Avens, *Imagination Is Reality: Western Nirvana in Jung, Hillman, Barfield and Cassirer* (Dallas: Spring Publications, 1980).

4. Owen Barfield, *The Rediscovery of Meaning and Other Essays* (Middleton, Conn.: Wesleyan University Press, 1977), p. 75, cited in Avens, *Imagination Is Reality*, 26.

5. Barfield, *Rediscovery of Meaning*, pp. 60–61, cited in Avens, *Imagination Is Reality*, 23.

6. The lessening of female power was not always the case in the first generation of a Great Religion, no doubt because at that stage it appealed to many, including women, outside the society's power structure and gave them place. Elisabeth Schussler Fiorenza, *In Memory of Her* (New York: Crossroad, 1983), provocatively reconstructs the leadership role of women in first-generation Christianity. The Koran defined some previously ambiguous rights of women. In these religions, the spiritual significance of the feminine, whether in goddess or priestly roles, was countered on the symbolic level, and soon enough on the practical, by patriarchy.

Chapter Four

1. Alexander F. Chamberlain, "'New Religions' among the North American Indians," *Journal of Religious Psychology* 6, no. 1 (January 1913): 1–49.

2. Ralph Linton, "Nativist Movements," *American Anthropologist* 45 (1943): 230–40.

3. Anthony F. C. Wallace, "Revitalization Movements," *American Anthropologist* 58 (1956): 264–81.

4. Neil J. Smelser, *Theory of Collective Behavior* (New York: Free Press, 1962), 313.

5. Bryan Wilson, *Magic and the Millennium* (New York: Free Press, 1962), 313.

6. H. Byron Earhart, "The Interpretation of the 'New Religions' of Japan as New Religious Movements," in *Religious Ferment in Asia*, ed. Robert J. Miller (Lawrence: University Press of Kansas, 1974), 170–88. I have found both the basic idea and the bibliographical references of this article of great value in preparing this discussion.

7. See Peter Brown, *The Cult of the Saints: Its Rise and Function in Latin Christianity* (Chicago: University of Chicago Press, 1981).

8. James Hillman, "Psychology: Monotheistic or Polytheistic," in David L. Miller, *The New Polytheism: Rebirth of the Gods and Goddesses* (Dallas: Spring Publications, 1981), 120.

9. Brown, *Cult of the Saints.*

10. Eamon Duffy, *The Stripping of the Altars: Traditional Religion in England 1400–1580* (New Haven, Conn.: Yale University Press, 1992).

Chapter Five

1. Elizabeth J. Harris, "The Female in Buddhism," in *Buddhist Women Across Culture,* ed. Karma Lekshe Tsomo Bhiksuni (Albany, N.Y.: SUNY Press, 1999), 59, 61, cited from Pali Text Society translations.

2. See Helmut Gätje, *The Qur'an and Its Exegesis* (Berkeley: University of California Press, 1976), 25.

3. Cited in Cyril Glassé, *The New Encyclopedia of Islam* (Walnut Creek, Calif.: AltaMira Press, 2001), 267. See also A. J. Arberry, *The Holy Koran* (New York: Macmillan, 1953), 18.

4. For a radical but provocative presentation of this thesis, see Alvar Ellegård, *Jesus One Hundred Years before Christ* (Woodstock, N.Y.: Overlook Press, 1999).

Chapter Six

1. Ernst Troeltsch, *The Social Teaching of the Christian Churches* (original German ed., 1911; New York: Harper Torchbooks, 1960), see vol. 2, 993.

Troeltsch made a careful distinction between "church" and "sect." The church is the dominant, established religion of a society, to which the great majority at least nominally belong; it also comprises all those who have not made a deliberate decision to "withdraw" into a sectarian minority. The church therefore contains persons on all levels of spiritual development, but at the same time, it is the custodian of the society's great tradition of belief and values. As well as being a major patron of its art, architecture, and education, the church is also able to offer spirituality to the masses in a way they can accept. "It is," this authority said, "able to receive the masses, and to adjust itself to the world, because, to a certain extent, it can afford to ignore the need for subjective holiness for the sake of the objective treasures of grace and of redemption." In contrast to the church is the sect—small, marginal, and in tension with culture, making high demands on its members to exemplify the life of pure and radical faith: "a voluntary society, composed of strict and definite . . . believers bound to each other," who share a common powerful spiritual experience and "live apart from the world," as it were for the sake of a supernatural realm instead.

2. Cited in Kenneth Saunders, *A Pageant of Asia* (London: Oxford University Press, 1934), 105.

3. Colm Luibheid, trans., *Psuedo-Dionysius: The Complete Works* (New York: Paulist Press, 1987), 52.

Chapter Seven

1. Aldous Huxley, *The Doors of Perception and Heaven and Hell* (New York: Harper Colophon Books, 1963), 171.

2. Huxley, *The Doors of Perception and Heaven and Hell*, 114ff. Huxley assimilates the "yearning" for color he finds in the premodern world with the "antipodes of the mind," also expressed in traditional images of heaven or paradise, usually depicted as brilliantly colored and filled with gleaming, many-colored jewels—like the Heavenly Jerusalem of the Book of Revelation, or the Buddhist Pure Land.

3. Henry Adams, *Novels, Mont Saint Michel and Chartres, The Education of Henry Adams* (New York: The Library of America, 1983), 438.

4. Eamon Duffy, *The Stripping of the Altars: Traditional Religion in England c. 1400 – 1580* (New Haven, Conn.: Yale University Press, 1992), 91.

5. Duffy, *The Stripping of the Altars*, 117.

6. The story is one that seems more like some bleak northern myth than those of sunny India. After Krishna had matured and become a king, one day his chief men fell into a drunken brawl and soon had his whole capital city in a tumult. Krishna's brother, chief son, and best friends were all slain in the rioting. Unable to stop this degeneration into chaos, Krishna left to wander dejectedly alone in the woods. There a hunter accidentally killed him as he sat meditating. Like Achilles, he had only one vulnerable spot, his heel, and there an arrow struck. The god then returned to his eternal spiritual world.

7. From Milton Singer, "The Great Tradition of Hinduism in the City of Madras," in *Anthropology of Folk Religion,* ed. Charles Leslie (New York: Vintage Books, 1960).

8. Swami Prabhavananda, transl., *Srimad Bhagavatam: The Wisdom of God* (New York: G. P. Putnam's Sons, 1943), 256–57.

9. John B. Carman, *The Theology of Ramanuja* (New Haven, Conn.: Yale University Press, 1974), 187, 191, 192.

10. Marin Palmer and Jay Ramsey, with Man-Ho Kwok, *Kuan Yin: Myths and Revelations of the Chinese Goddess of Compassion* (San Francisco: HarperCollins, 1995), 8.

11. Palmer and Ramsey, *Kuan Yin,* 15–16.

12. Palmer and Ramsey, *Kuan Yin,* 28–29.

Chapter Eight

1. Said Amir Arjomand, "Unity and Diversity in Islamic Fundamentalism," in *Fundamentalisms Comprehended,* ed. Martin E. Marty and R. Scott Appleby (Chicago: University of Chicago Press, 1995), 185.

2. See Robert N. Bellah, *Tokugawa Religion* (Glencoe, Ill.: Free Press, 1957); and Warren W. Smith, *Confucianism in Modern Japan* (Tokyo: Hokuseido, 1973).

3. See A. C. Bhaktivedanta Swami Prabhupada, *Teachings of Lord Caitanya* (Los Angeles: Bhaktivedanta Book Trust, 1988).

4. Edward C. Dimock Jr., *Caitanya Caritamrta of Krsnadasa Kaviraja: A Translation and Commentary* (Cambridge, Mass.: Harvard University Press, 1999), 24.

5. Dimock Jr., *Caitanya Caritamrta of Krsnadasa Kaviraja,* 574–75.

6. John L. Esposito, *The Islamic Threat: Myth or Reality?* (New York: Oxford University Press, 1992).

7. Yvonne Y. Haddad, "Sayyid Qutb: Ideologue of Islamic Revival," in *Voices of Resurgent Islam,* ed. John L. Esposito (New York: Oxford University Press, 1983), 67–98.

8. Lawrence Davidson, *Islamic Fundamentalism* (Westport, Conn.: Greenwood Press, 1998), 100.

9. Davidson, *Islamic Fundamentalism,* 12–13.

10. Abdulaziz A. Sachidena, "Activist Shi'ism in Iran, Iraq, and Lebanon," in *Fundamentalisms Observed,* ed. Martin E. Marty and R. Scott Appleby (Chicago: University of Chicago Press, 1991), 345–402.

11. Arabic: "Sign of God"; in Iranian Shi'a, a high-ranking religious authority believed capable of making autonomous religious decisions under the guidance of the Hidden Imam.

12. Farhang Rajee, "Iranian Ideology and Worldview: The Cultural Export of Revolution," in *The Iranian Revolution,* John C. Esposito (Miami: Florida International University Press, 1990), 65–66.

Chapter Nine

1. Robert Redfield, *Peasant Society and Culture* (1956; reprint, Chicago: University of Chicago Press, 1973), 41ff. The distinction is not new, of course; see Max Weber, *The Sociology of Religion*, trans. Ephraim Fishoff (Boston: Beacon Press, 1963), chap. 7, "Castes, Estates, Classes, and Religion."

2. Redfield, *Peasant Society and Culture*, 46.

3. Peter W. Williams, *Popular Religion in America* (Englewood Cliffs, N.J.: Prentice Hall, 1980), 10.

4. William A. Christian Jr., *Local Religion in Sixteenth-Century Spain* (Princeton, N.J.: Princeton University Press), 1981.

5. Christian Jr., *Local Religion,* 20.

6. William A. Christian Jr., *Apparitions in Late Medieval and Renaissance Spain* (Princeton, N.J.: Princeton University Press, 1981). See also, for material on La Salette and other more recent French apparitions, Thomas A. Kselman, *Miracles and Prophecies in Nineteenth-Century France* (New Brunswick, N.J.: Rutgers University Press, 1983).

7. Alfred Schutz, *Collected Papers*, ed. and intro. Maurice Natanson (The Hague: Martinus Nijhoff, 1973), 1:207–59. See also William James, *The Principles of Psychology* (New York: H. Holt, 1890), vol. 2, ch. 21.

8. See the discussion of religious "triggers" and "condensed symbols" in Robert Ellwood, *Alternative Altars* (Chicago: University of Chicago Press, 1979), 47–49.

9. David Tracy, *The Analogical Imagination: Christian Theology and the Culture of Pluralism* (New York: Crossroad, 1981).

10. Paul Ricouer, "The Symbol Gives Rise to Thought," in *Literature and Religion*, ed. Giles B. Gunn (New York: Harper and Row, 1971), 214.

11. Interview of George Steiner by Bill Moyers in broadcast of "Bill Moyer's Journal," June 1981. I am indebted to Professor George Tanabe Jr. for this reference.

Chapter Ten

1. Emile Durkheim, *The Elementary Forms of the Religious Life*, trans. Joseph Ward Swain (original French ed., 1912; New York: Collier Books, 1961).

2. Bryan Wilson, "The Return of the Sacred," *Journal for the Scientific Study of Religion* 18, no. 3 (September 1979): 258–80.

3. Peter L. Berger, *The Sacred Canopy* (Garden City, N.Y.: Doubleday, 1969), 107.

4. Joachim Wach, *The Sociology of Religion* (Chicago: University of Chicago Press, 1944), 17–34.

5. Thomas Luckmann, *The Invisible Religion* (New York: Macmillan, 1967).

6. Berger, *Sacred Canopy*, 175–77.

7. Peter L. Berger, *A Rumor of Angels* (Garden City, N.Y.: Doubleday, 1970).

8. Berger, *Sacred Canopy*, 145ff.

9. Will Herberg, *Protestant, Catholic, Jew* (Garden City, N.Y.: Doubleday, 1955).

10. Robert N. Bellah, *The Broken Covenant* (New York: Seabury Press, 1975), 142.

11. Berger, *Sacred Canopy*, 145.

12. Talcott Parsons, "Christianity in Modern Industrial Society," in *Sociological Theories, Values, and Socio-Cultural Change*, ed. Edward A. Tiryakin (New York: Free Press, 1963).

13. Andrew Greeley, *Religion in the Year 2000* (New York: Sheed & Ward, 1969), 97ff.

14. David Martin, *The Religious and the Secular* (New York: Schocken, 1969), 5. Cf. Max Weber, *The Sociology of Religion*, trans. Ephraim Fishoff (original German source, 1922; Boston: Beacon Press, 1963), see the introduction by Talcott Parsons and ch. 1 especially.

15. David Martin, *A General Theory of Secularization* (New York: Harper and Row, 1978), 13.

16. Martin, *Religious and the Secular*, ch. 7, "Secularization and the Arts: The Case of Music," and ch. 9, "The Secularization Pattern in England."

17. Martin, *Religious and the Secular,* 22.

18. Martin, *A General Theory of Secularization.*

19. David Martin, *Dilemmas of Contemporary Religion* (New York: St. Martin's Press, 1978).

20. See, especially, Bryan Wilson, *Contemporary Transformations of Religion* (London: Oxford University Press, 1976).

21. Daniel Bell, "The Return of the Sacred?" *British Journal of Sociology* 28, no. 4 (December 1977): 419–49.

22. Bryan Wilson, "The Return of the Sacred," *Journal for the Scientific Study of Religion* 18, no. 3 (September 1979): 268–80.

23. Huston Smith, "Secularization and the Sacred: The Contemporary Scene," in *The Religious Situation* 1968, ed. Donald R. Cutler (Boston: Beacon Press, 1968).

24. Richard K. Fenn, *Toward a Theory of Secularization,* Monograph Series no. 1 (Storrs, Conn.: Society for the Scientific Study of Religion, 1978), 32–39.

25. William W. Swatos Jr., "Beyond Denominationalism?" *Journal for the Scientific Study of Religion* 20, no. 3 (September 1981): 217–27.

26. George Gallup Jr. and D. Michael Lindsay, *Surveying the Religious Landscape: Trends in U.S. Beliefs* (Harrisburg, Pa.: Morehouse Publishing, 1999), 10, 46.

27. Robert Wuthnow, *The Consciousness Reformation* (Berkeley: University of California Press, 1976).

Chapter Eleven

1. Samuel P. Huntington, *The Clash of Civilizations and the Remaking of World Order* (New York: Simon & Schuster, 1996).

2. Many in the West think of Buddhism as a particularly peace-loving religion, and perhaps it is. But historically one must also consider the bloody campaigns of medieval Burmese, Thai, and Cambodian kings; the soldier-monks of Tibet and Japan; the relation of Zen to the Samurai ethic; and even the general support of the imperial war effort in Japan during World War II by the Buddhist establishment. Regarding the last, see Brian Victoria, *Zen at War* (New York: Weatherhill, 1997).

3. For an excellent survey of this development, see Philip Jenkins, *The Next Christendom: The Coming of Global Christianity* (New York: Oxford University Press, 2002).

4. Jenkins, *The Next Christendom,* 3.

5. Jenkins, *The Next Christendom,* 3.

6. See David B. Barrett, George T. Kurian, and Todd M. Johnson, eds., *World Christian Encyclopedia,* 2d ed. (New York: Oxford University Press, 2001), 4; John Gordon Melton and Martin Baumann, eds., *Religions of the World: A Comprehensive Encyclopedia of Beliefs and Practices,* 4 vols. (Santa Barbara, Calif.: ABC Clio, 2002), vol. 1: xxix, 12–17.

In 2000, the world Christianity population of 2,105,000,000 broke down to 1,057 million Roman Catholics, 386 million "Independents," 342 million Protestants, 215 million Orthodox, 79 million Anglicans, and 26 million "Marginal Christians." While these figures are far from precise, they give a rough idea of comparable numerical strengths. Very significant is the position of "Independents" in second place after Roman Catholics. According to the definitions in the *World Christian Encyclopedia* and *Religions of the World: A Comprehensive Encyclopedia of Beliefs and Practices,* these include "churches and networks that regard themselves as post denominationalist and neo-apostolic and thus are independent of and uninterested in historic, organized, institutionalized, denominationalist Christianity" (*Religions of the World*, vol. 1, xxix). Examples would be "African Initiated Churches," which typically are groups centering on African prophets, demonstrate charismatic and healing gifts, have impressive baptismal rites, and employ African cultural features such as traditional dance and music, distinctive robes, and attention to ancestors. The also impressive figure for "Marginal Christians," though to me the term does not seem entirely a happy choice, includes such groups as "Mormons, Jehovah's Witnesses, Christian Science, Religious Science, et al." (*Religions of the World*, vol. 1, xxix).

Chapter Twelve

1. John Gordon Melton and Martin Baumann, eds., *Religions of the World: A Comprehensive Encyclopedia of Beliefs and Practices*, 4 vols. (Santa Barbara, Calif.: ABC Clio, 2002), vol. 1: xxx.

INDEX

ABOUT THE AUTHOR

Robert Ellwood is Distinguished Emeritus Professor of Religion at the University of Southern California. He is the author of numerous books on the history of religion, including *Alternative Altars*, *Mysticism and Religion* and *The Politics of Myth*. He lives in Ojai, California.